CONTENTS

For the Maxes
Charlie, Foddy, Een and Edt
(not forgetting the Maxines)

A camel is stronger than a man; an elephant is larger; a lion has greater valour; cattle can eat more than a man; birds are more virile. Man was made for the purpose of learning.

(El-Ghazali: *Book of Knowledge*)

When we first filmed the live tiger I was concerned about the safety of the crew and asked the handler how we should behave. He said we should all keep close together and not straggle. I asked what would happen if the tiger went for one of us. He said the tiger would probably knock us down and lie on us. The danger was that usually the tiger becomes possessive at that stage and thinks that another animal might steal his meat – one of us. I asked him what one should do in the circumstances. He answered that one should hit the tiger across the nose, hard. Asked what this would do, the handler replied, 'make his eyes water'.

You live and learn in the tiger business.

(*'Esso' Magazine*)

PREAMBLE

This is a book about learning: it is about how people come to do more, to know more, and to be more than they were. It is about what learning is, what kinds of things people learn, how they learn them, what makes it easier or harder for them to learn them. It looks at what things people are good and bad at learning, and how they might help themselves, or be helped, to learn better. Perhaps most importantly, it is about the manifold ways in which people get in the way of their own learning – how they constantly ignore the obvious, trip themselves up, and generally undermine and subvert the natural learning ability they possess.

Note that it is about ordinary men, women, and children, unlike many other books on learning. It is not about the tree-shrew, the white rat, or the baboon. It is not – or not much – about special, different, kinds of people, like spina bifida babies, stroke victims or people who make money by multiplying long numbers together in their heads. It is about us.

Also, unlike most other books on learning, it is not a Cook's tour of what some famous psychologists (plus one advertising executive and one insurance claims investigator) thought learning was thirty or seventy years ago. The hallowed works of Watson, Hull, Skinner, Bruner and Piaget are given rather short shrift. Instead I am going to try to take a fresh look at the domain of learning, in a common sense sort of way, with as few theoretical preconceptions as possible, and see what kind of general framework emerges. It will turn out that although the Great Names have often been seen as theorizing in opposition to each other – Skinner *or* Rogers, Bruner *or* Piaget – in fact they are usually talking about different kinds or areas of learning, and thus their ideas are not contradictory but complementary. So what I shall be doing, as I tell my tale, is not to recount their ideas yet again, but to show how and where they fit in to an overall account of the Human Being as Learner, and to provide a kind of high-level psychological Esperanto into which their sometimes jarringly different languages can be translated, and their conjectures understood side by side. Psychology has been much concerned with gathering pearls of varying degrees of wisdom. This book is an attempt to take a handful from the box labelled 'Learning' and *string* them. As we go along I shall indicate through reference notes what theories or findings I am drawing on. For those readers who are not worried about sources or technicalities, and who (like me) find reference notes annoying, they can quite happily be skipped, or referred to only to discover 'further reading'.

In order to make the necklace, I have had to be selective. While some of the pearls complement each other nicely, others clash terribly and cannot be put together. Inevitably, therefore, I have achieved a degree of coherence at the expense of being partial. As we shall see, the philosophical string itself, on which my psychology is threaded, is by no means universally approved of. I think my story works rather well and makes a lot of sense, though many of the details will be wrong or over-simplified. But there are other narratives that look quite different. Let me say this loud and clear, once and for all: I have written forcefully, in the main, as if *my* view were unequivocally *the* view. This is not so, and (as Chapter 1 shows) I do not believe it to be so. But the continual havering of 'In my opinion . . .', or 'It seems to me . . .' is boring, and I have left it out.

Traditionally human learning has been divided into three bits, and around each has grown up a separate culture, language, and literature. These three domains are *action* – man-as-doer; *thought* – man-as-deliberator; and *feeling* – what I shall call, for reasons which will become clear, man-as-defender. While the structure of this book starts from these divisions, my main concern is to show that they are *not* separable, but each has to be understood in relation to the others. It is the interconnections between thought and action, action and feeling, and feeling and thought that are the most interesting and least studied questions in the area of people's growth and development. How does what I think the world to be constrain what I do to it? How do my abilities come to be represented in my conceptualization of myself? How does my feeling about myself influence what I can and do dare to learn? And so on. Particularly we shall see that people's defensive attitude towards their own feelings is born out of an apparent (but not actual) conflict between the doer and the deliberator, and that once this conflict is seen into and exposed as exhausting and misguided shadow-boxing, then learning in all its aspects blossoms. Turn on the light of understanding and the shadow just disappears.

In order to say something about the style of the book, I need to say something about my own personal philosophy of education. The motive behind all teaching (and writing books is certainly teaching) is to convince *you* that what *I* know or believe is valuable and/or right. 'Be reasonable – see it *my* way', as the graffiti-artist put it. Even an apparently dispassionate presentation of other people's views represents a value judgement (whether conscious or not) about what other people and which of their views are worth presenting. Now there are a variety of different ways in which I can try to convince you about X. I can try to do it by logic, by reason: if you agree that these premises are true, and that my reasoning is valid, then you *must* agree that the conclusion, X, is also true. If the parents' separating upsets children, and if emotional upsets cause delinquency, then broken homes produce delinquents. Right? Second, I can try to convince you through experiment: by collecting evidence, directly, of a correlation between parental separation and the antisocial acts of their offspring. Both these methods are currently respectable, and both are pretty ineffective when it comes to changing people's point of view. The failure of anti-smoking campaigns, on the one hand, and the protracted battles within psychology between researchers brandishing 'convincing proof', both logical and empirical that the other's position is 'untenable', on the other hand, show how easy it is not to be convinced if you don't want to be. You may *see* what he's talking about but you don't *accept* it. The mind is very tricky at not accepting what it doesn't want to. Your knowledge may be augmented but your beliefs are not changed.

One of the problems with today's education at all levels is that it does not see that people are usually not changed but *laminated* by the giving of information and argument. Their points of view are very often not developed and expanded but merely overlaid by new knowledge, so that what one believes, or the way one looks at things is not altered but remains buried under a pile of 'facts' – even contradictory facts. In everyday life people are just not that rational. It is now well established, for example, that people possess a well-developed, though intuitive, 'science' that may be quite different from the official science they were taught in school (we discuss this in Chapter 1).

For someone to be changed by something they must in some deeper sense be touched by it. They must feel the relevance of this new point of view to their own experience, beliefs, and concerns. And for this, other methods of trying to convince become useful – through anecdote or poetry, or through demonstrations that the new idea is useful. Take it on trust and see where it gets you. To me such rhetorical devices have their dangers but they are legitimate – as legitimate as the more 'objective' ones – and I shall use them all without apology. So, to return to the style of this book, I intend to use metaphors, examples, poems, jokes, appeals to you to 'wait and see how it turns out', as well as argument and experimental results: anything to get you to be reasonable and see it my way. It will become apparent fairly quickly that the style of argument depends a lot on the topic, so the reader would do well to be prepared for shifts in the former as well as the latter. When we talk about the understanding of language in Chapter 4, for example, I shall rely quite heavily on experimental research. People have very little intuitive knowledge about their own linguistic processes to which one can appeal. In Chapter 6, on the other hand, when we are discussing the beliefs that people hold about themselves, and the effect these beliefs have on learning, there is little empirical research, but a deep fund of personal experience which everybody has, which they can draw on to illustrate and evaluate what I have to say; and it is therefore to this fund that I shall point, as we go along, for corroboration.

Were I a Blake, I might well have written a prophetic and impassioned book, not a reasonable one at all. But though I share his View, I have neither the tools of his imagination nor the current of his anger with which to turn from the View such bright and well-wrought works of art. So I must appeal to the same intuition through the cooler, narrower, channels of comprehension and assent. I suspect, however, that the smell of chalk is less evocative than that of fire and brimstone, so I shall give a little whiff of Will Blake to start off each chapter. (While we are on style, I should point out that I have tackled the he/she problem by using both, rather than by trying not to use them at all.)

I shall be fairly eclectic in where I draw my ideas and example from. Behavioural, cognitive, and humanistic psychology have all gone into the melting pot. Skinner, Kelly, Bruner, and Rogers are here, though they emerge intact only occasionally. And so are Aldous Huxley, Hermann Hesse, Lao Tsu, Werner Erhard, and Neils Bohr. We shall talk about conditioning and personality: we shall also talk about playing darts and cricket, quantum field theory and meditation. I have a D.Phil in cognitive psychology from Oxford; I play darts for the Queen's Elm pub in Chelsea; I am writing this in an ashram in Poona, and I am deeply in love. All these 'me's' are going to have a chance to speak. But I am also a lecturer in the psychology of education, and it is right that this voice will be the dominant and recurrent one – the Chorus. It will also supply many of the examples, for one of my main target audiences is teachers and teachers-in-training. It is my personal opinion that they have often been sold a simplistic, out-of-date, arid, and unuseful psychology of learning and I hope that this book will be an improvement. It should, at the very least, be more fun to read!

It is, in a way, a sequel to my earlier book *Wholly Human: Western and Eastern Visions of the Self and Its Perfection*, which is a somewhat more earnest attempt to push our understanding of people along a bit by combining Western psychology with the wisdom of the East – of Taoism, Buddhism, Sufism, and Zen. This wisdom is not philosophical but absolutely psychological, full of practical, sharp insights that make our twentieth century psychologies look very limited and academic by comparison. All the working-out that went on in *Wholly Human* is presupposed here, though it is possible to read this, for the most part, without realizing just how radically different these presuppositions are from our unexamined common sense. This book *assumes* a view of what people are, and investigates how change and transformation happen to them.

Because I have done my best to integrate a lot of different theories, differently expressed, into a smooth and readable story, my intellectual debts will not be as obvious as they might have been. I would like to expose and acknowledge the most important ones now. Within the 'straight' psychological literature I have learnt most from George Kelly, Carl Rogers and B. F. Skinner, I think. Their thoughts have all significantly altered my own point of view, and their concern to communicate clearly has inspired me to risk being mundane and avoid retreating into technicality. From those who write and talk psychology without being psychologists, Alan Watts helps me to get clear, again and again, about the confusion between map and territory around which Chapter 1 revolves. And Werner Erhard has put into the *est* training some very elegant insights and formulations that I have borrowed, especially in Chapters 6 and 7.

It is always nice to do the personal acknowledgements, and here they are. The first and greatest thank you is to the generations of students – about eight of them now – at the Institute of Education and the Chelsea College Centre for Science and Mathematics Education, who sat for the most part quietly through the lectures from which this book has emerged, listening to me arguing with myself in public and getting far too little opportunity to shoot back. They helped me see that even when I was trying to be logical it sometimes didn't work. They helped me see, by their questions, the many gaps I hadn't closed, or even thought about, and the many possibilities for misunderstanding I had left open. But best of all were the few who really *got* what I was talking about; those who suddenly realized that I was talking about them, and that the saga of human learning is not an academic one, but is full of tragedy and comedy. Occasionally they cried. Sometimes they laughed. These few students who were changed by my words have made it all worthwhile. I hope this book may touch some others, though it is even harder for the written than the spoken word to achieve that. I remember especially Mike Hickie and Dave Ashcroft.

My colleagues at both places have been very good to me, principally by *not* insisting, as they reasonably might, that I be less opinionated and give greater air-time to Gagné, Ausubel, and (of course) Bruner. They include Terry Davis and Normal Worrall at the Institute, and John Head and Brian Davies at Chelsea. My professors – Bill Wall and Paul Black – have been ideal bosses: high on support and low on direction. And my workmates Chris Watkins and Judith Ryder were a real treat to have around.

Some of this book was written at the Shree Rajneesh Ashram in Poona, India, and my presence there for the Spring Term, 1981, was due to three sources: the Rajneesh International Meditation University who invited me; Paul Black, who strongly supported my application for leave, although it made life difficult for him by creating a temporary staff shortage; and the Central Research Fund of the University of London, who paid my air fare. The rest of the book was written in a range of hideaways courtesy of George and Jan Chamier, Polly Lansdowne and, most frequently, Sam Westmacott. Big thanks to all, as well as to Naomi Roth, my editor at Harper & Row, and Mark Brown for support and advice, and to Alison Reeves for typing so fast, so well, and so much.

And finally to Gail, who provoked and supported my own learning more than anyone since my Mum.

Guy Claxton

1984

Personal Theories

If the doors of perception were cleansed everything would appear to man as it is, infinite.

For man has closed himself up, till he sees all things thro' narrow chinks of his cavern.

'The fool separates his object from all surrounding ones; all abstraction is temporary folly.'

Uneasy, because I once thought otherwise but now I know it is true.

This life's dim Windows of the Soul
Distorts the Heavens from Pole to Pole
And leads you to Believe a Lie
When you see with, not thro', the Eye

Everything possible to be believ'd is an image of truth.

CHAPTER 1

PERSONAL THEORIES

It is venturesome to think that a co-ordination of words (philosophies are nothing more than that) can resemble the universe very much. It is also venturesome to think that of all these illustrious co-ordinations, one of them – at least in an infinitesimal way – does not resemble the universe a bit more than the others.

(Jorge Luis Borges[1])

1.1 Constructive Alternativism

Every psychology has a philosophy behind it. The philosophy behind this book is not at all new. It lies at the root of Buddhism and Hinduism, and has been propagated in Western psychology most forcefully by George Kelly.[2] He calls it 'constructive alternativism' and these strutting polysyllables refer to the idea that man (or any animal) does not and cannot know Reality directly. All he has is a *theory* about it. This theory is his only basis for operation, and, because his survival ultimately depends upon it, it is his job to see that his theory about The Way Things Are actually matches The Way Things Are as accurately as possible. The process of testing and improving the personal theory that guides us through life is what we call *learning*.

The metaphor for man that emerges from constructive alternativism is thus that of a scientist. Scientists do two things: they dream up theories about things, and then push the things around a bit to see if they behave in the way the theory says they should. If they do, the scientist thinks up another experiment; if they don't, he thinks up another theory. Most of the rest of this book is about how people (even scientists) spend their lives experimenting, usually unintentionally and unconsciously, with their personal theories. But first it will help to see a bit more clearly what a theory is, what it does, and what its relation to Reality is. We need to do a bit of theorizing about theories.

(From a philosophical point of view[3] this discussion is going to look pretty sloppy – but it is not my purpose to go on sharpening my axe till it is fine enough to split hairs. A common or garden chopper will do at the moment. For example, 'Pawn to queen four' for a philosopher will be 'If all you can know is a theory about Reality, how do you know there is any Reality there to have a theory about? Maybe you dreamed the whole thing.' To which I reply 'Absolutely. "Reality" is itself only an idea within our theory. We don't know if it exists. But for most people who live their lives as if there were a world out there full of teachers and buses and pints of bitter, the assumption turns out to be a workable and a useful one. And that's the only criterion there is in constructive alternativism: not Is it *true*? but Does it *work*?' This, of course, will not shut a philosopher up, but it might just work for an audience of psychologists, who are more concerned with chopping wood than with the sharpness of the blade.)

1.2 **What is a Theory?**

(a) *A theory is a description*   It is a way of representing something in terms of something else so as to render it less complex, and therefore more predictable. A theory can be a picture or a model or a metaphor or a string of abstract symbols or, perhaps more commonly, a *language*. The double helix is a picture-theory of DNA which enables us to understand it and predict its behaviour. The miniature solar system theory for atomic structure was a useful metaphor. Schrödinger's wave equation is a mathematical formula that does a more precise job of explaining how the hydrogen atom behaves. The simplest theories are pictures and metaphors. Does it help us to treat X as if it were like Y?, we can ask. Is the atom like a currant bun? Is memory organized like a library? Does the heart work like a pump?

It usually turns out in science that such analogies are very productive up to a point, but eventually have to be replaced with a more abstract symbolic theory – a mathematical or technical language has to be created. This is one of the problems that sub-atomic physics faces. The currant bun and the solar system failed to predict accurately enough, but with them one had a good 'feel' for what the atom might be like. There was no problem about what they *meant*. Today's theories – quantum electrodynamics, S-matrix theory, and the like – are mathematical systems that predict quite well but one is left wondering what they mean. What do the abstract symbols correspond to in Reality? In 1927 Neils Bohr proposed one solution – the so-called Copenhagen Interpretation – that asserted that this was ultimately a silly question. But the matter is far from settled, and may never be. There probably is no picture, no tangible metaphor, that will enable us to comprehend the strange sub-atomic world in terms of our everyday experience.[4]

The most obvious examples of everyday theories are natural languages, the ones that people converse in. (They are called 'natural' because there are now 'unnatural' ones, like computer languages, that have been deliberately created for technical purposes.) Every language provides a system of categories and rules for breaking undifferentiated Reality up into chunks and talking about them. We tend to assume that the chunks actually exist, that Nature comes ready perforated, like a toilet-roll, and all we have to do is tug gently and it falls apart into natural categories. For each of us it looks as if our language is *the* natural one, and the divisions it contains not invented but discovered. 'The French call it l'eau; the Italians aqua; the Germans Wasser; whereas we English just call it exactly what it is . . . water.'

But this can't be so because different natural languages carve the same Reality up in different ways: and we can't all be right. English focuses on nouns (objects) and describes their relationships. 'My grandfather's house had a tree beside it.' In the American Indian language Hopi this would be rendered in terms of *events*. 'When it was grandfathering and it was housing, it was treeing, too.' Even put this way in English it looks as if there is some thing – 'it' – doing it all. But the 'it' exists only in the language, the theory, not in Reality, just as it does when we say 'It is raining.' There isn't any 'it' that is 'doing' the raining. There is simply 'raining'. Or take another example. In the samurai culture of Japan great emphasis was placed on 'bushido' – the way of the warrior. This single ideal lumped together such 'manly' qualities as courage, skill in fighting, ruthlessness and cruelty, with what our culture has considered more 'feminine' attributes, like deep appreciation of nature and the reading and writing of poetry. It is very difficult for us to see all these as forming a single, natural package or concept. For a samurai their juxtaposition was as fitting as leaves on a tree. Thus the theory is always different from the data, from the area of experience it is about, in just the way a map is different from the terrain it maps.[5]

(b) *Theories contain conventions*   Like maps, all theories actually contain ideas, divisions, notations that are not present at all in the terrain – like the 'it' in 'It is raining'. A map may contain contour lines and numbers; it may mark motorways in yellow and countries in different colours. Yet though these conventions have no counterpart in Reality, they are very useful. They help us, provided that we understand them rightly, to *use* the map to get around or to see political boundaries. A real railway has two lines, but on a map it has only one. There is no need for us to worry about the safety of the train on this account. We do not expect the countryside to turn from pink to blue as we go through customs, nor do we have to beware of tripping over the contour lines as we climb the mountain. When we find a ruined church that is not marked on the map, we do not have to deny its existence: we simply mark it in. But as we shall see when we come to people's personal theories, sometimes we are not nearly so clear about the nature and function of conventions, and get ourselves in a muddle.

(c) *The best theory depends on what you want to do*   There is no 'best' theory about anything, just as there is no 'best' map of a particular area. All theories are devised for a purpose, and the best one is the one that helps you achieve that purpose most speedily, most effectively, or with least effort. Many different maps can be made of the same terrain, and each will be differentially good for different jobs. An A–Z Street Plan of London is no more or less 'right' than the *Motorist's Road Map of Great Britain*. Both of them show London, but they pick out and highlight different things about it; they have different scales and conventions. One is good for people who want to get *to* and *through* London; the other is best for people who are travelling *within* London between places that are not on the major through-routes. We cannot judge the 'goodness' of a map by how much it 'looks like' the territory, either. The map of the London Underground train networks looks nothing like London, nor indeed does it bear a very accurate relationship to the train routes themselves. All the twists and turns are ignored and distances grossly distorted. Yet it is a very successful map, because it picks out and represents very clearly just what the tube traveller needs to know.

Thus an important thing to remember about theories is that they may show different aspects of the same Reality. Because there is no one 'best' theory, we may need several rather different-looking theories about the same phenomenon in order to account for it. This may sound obvious in the world of maps, but in science it has been a hard lesson to learn. Physics had to struggle with the question 'Is the electron *really* a wave or a particle?' before realizing that it isn't either. Each is a metaphor, an 'as if' picture, that can contain some but not all of the behaviour of electrons under different conditions. A single metaphor that did the whole job would be more elegant, of course, but there is nothing wrong, nothing illogical or contradictory about looking at the electron through two different, even incompatible, metaphors. Neils Bohr, the source of this insight in physics, which he called 'The Principle of Complementarity', was knighted by the Danish king for his services to science, and chose as his motto the phrase *'Contraria sunt complementa'*.[6] Many scientists – psychologists included – still do not appreciate that theories are metaphors or descriptions created by human beings about some area of their experience for a particular purpose. Theories are manufactured and consumed; they are commodities, not Truth. This becomes *very* important when we turn to people's everyday, personal theories.

(d) *The best theory depends on what you are looking at*   Theories have a history. They grow. And how they grow depends on where they were first planted. The 'character' of a theory is fixed in its infancy quite as much as the character of a child. All theories are heavily influenced not only by the job they are designed to do, but the phenomena they were originally designed to explain. This original area of concern George Kelly called the 'focus of convenience' of a theory, and every theory has one. If I start my map-making in the middle of the North Atlantic, I shall end up with a very different product from the one I get when I start at Hyde Park Corner. Different scale, different conventions, different priorities.

(e) *Theories outgrow their strength*   Having invented a theory of one sort to look at one kind of thing for one purpose, it is natural to see what else you can do with it. To change the analogy for the moment, a theory is like a set of tools that you have assembled to do a particular job: to maintain your bicycle, let us say. Now you begin to wonder what little jobs around the house you can do as well, or whether your tool-kit will be of any use to you in helping your girl-friend strip the engine of her motor-bike. It makes good sense to get as much mileage out of your theory as you can. Do you need to buy an 'A–Z' or will your *Motorist's Handbook* be good enough? Gradually you discover the range of experiences and purposes for which your theory works: George Kelly calls this the 'range of convenience' of the theory. Outside this range it begins to get tongue-tied: its images and pronouncements become clumsy and confusing, rather than helpful, and eventually it falls silent. This is what happened with waves and particles. Each was a metaphor with a long history of being helpful. But each, when applied to the behaviour of electrons, began to fall short. For each there were some phenomena that it could not contain. Electrons fall on the borders of the range of convenience of both the wave and the corpuscular metaphors. And new concepts, like that of a 'wave packet' had to be invented that preserved their advantages while transcending their limitations. As I move from my trusty push-bike to a moped to a small car to a sports car to a private jet, so my tool-kit has to expand at the same time.

(f) *Theories aren't falsifiable*   If theories are never absolutely right, it follows that they can't be proved 'wrong' either. The Popperian[7] image of theories being falsified is a bit too simple, if we see them as points of view, metaphors, or languages. No one would want to argue that English is 'wrong' or Japanese is 'wrong' in putting or not putting cruelty and the poetic muse in the same concept. The concepts and relations that a language uses cannot be right or wrong because there are no concepts and relations in Nature for them to correspond to. Rather they are judged as a rule by their ability to generate plausible explanations and to make accurate and useful predictions. These *statements* that the language generates may be used appropriately or inappropriately: they may be true or false in the sense that they do or do not correspond to What's So. 'It is raining.' Well, is it? 'Hydrated copper sulphate is blue.' Well, is it? In both cases we can go and check. But the language, the set of presuppositions, assumptions, concepts, and rules that lie behind these statements, cannot be true or false, right or wrong. Theories are discarded or altered if they frequently generate inappropriate statements, or if they fail to come up with anything satisfactory at all: in other words if they fail to work.

(g) *Theories direct and restrict attention*   Just as maps emphasize some features of the world and ignore others, so once you've got a theory it directs your attention towards some things and away from others. A physical map automatically interests me in heights above sea-level: a political map in the boundaries between countries. And the particular conventions of the map determine what questions I can ask about the terrain, and how those questions can be framed. Every theory imposes on the theorist, or at least suggests to him, a way of looking at the world that it becomes quite difficult to stand outside. This is why progress in what Thomas Kuhn[8] called 'normal science' is slow, and why 'paradigm shifts' – radical changes in the way we see things – occur only rarely. Once a scientific theory is established it imposes on the scientist, often unconsciously, a basic set of attitudes about which phenomena are worth investigating, how his research questions are to be formulated, and what methods are legitimate for trying to answer them. As Werner Heisenberg once remarked, 'Science does not tell us about Nature: it gives us answers to our *questions* about Nature. What we observe is not Nature itself, but Nature exposed to our method of questioning.' (This realization itself caused a paradigm shift in physics. Previously it had been assumed that the act of observing or measuring something did not affect the thing observed. But Heisenberg's famous 'Uncertainty Principle' made it clear that this just was not so. To observe something is necessarily to interact with it, so the observing instruments, which include the experimenter himself, are not recording an experiment: they are essential participants in it. Doing science is like shining a flash-light on nocturnal creatures. You can see them, certainly: but they do not behave the same way as they do in the dark.)

(h) *Theories are always incomplete*   It is in the very nature of a theory to be incomplete, and therefore fallible and limited – for two very good reasons. First, if a theory is to pick out and accentuate some features of Reality, for a particular purpose, it follows that it cannot pick out and accentuate the whole of that Reality. To be useful a theory has to make simplifications, and that means ignoring some of the detail. It could not be otherwise. We might wish for a perfect map, but a moment's reflection reveals that a perfect map of London, let us say, would be an exact replica of London, of exactly the same size, with all the shops, people, traffic just as it is in the original. And even if one were strong enough to carry it, such a life-size model would be no use at all for finding your way about. In fact it would be no use for anything at all. So for a theory even to be a theory it has to be partial – and it is a natural consequence of this that it must from time to time let you down. Because what is left out represents a judgement, ahead of time, about what is significant and what is not, and such judgements are always turning out to be wrong. Science often progresses through someone taking seriously small details or deviations from what had been expected, that the generally accepted theory had discounted as trivial.

The second reason why theories are always inadequate is that the world is always changing. Even if you have a pretty good idea of what's going on at one time, if you checked it later, unforeseen events will force you to revise it. An earthquake in Tokyo, the explosion of a star in an undiscovered galaxy, the failure of the crops for the second year running, a strike of lightning or a lightning strike – all force you to stop and think again, to incorporate the new information and change your plans. Thus the business of improving theories is unending. The process of submitting your theory to the test of experience is called in science experimenting and in life at large *learning*.

1.3 Learning Theories

Science is the activity of creating communicable theories about physical reality. Psychology creates communicable theories about people's theories about reality – both physical and social. And the psychology of learning creates theories about how people's theories change and develop. It is theorizing about how people develop their personal maps, about how they come to know things, and to see and do things differently. All the comments we have made about theories apply to learning theories, but a couple of points are worth drawing special attention to. First, the domain of learning is so big that there are not just different theories around, but different *kinds* of theories. They differ not just in their basic model or language but in their scale, scope, purpose, and focus of convenience. We might identify four traditions that arose from very different beginnings.[9] There are *cognitive* learning theories, which grew out of experimental interest in the way adults remembered things – usually lists of unrelated words or 'nonsense syllables' or numbers. This tradition was born with Ebbinghaus in the last century and held sway until the late 1960s, when the range of convenience of its 'associative' and 'information processing' models was expanded to cover more complicated kinds of learning like solving problems and understanding language. The 1970s produced a lot of research that mapped the bounds beyond which such simple theories began to falter and fail to be useful or productive.

Then there are *behavioural* learning theories, that began with the attempt to predict and explain the behaviour of animals in simple situations, like learning to press a lever to get food, or to recognize and respond to a new signal for food. Gradually these 'conditioning' models were extended to more general concerns, like the development of physical skills and the role of reward and punishment in the education of children. A third tradition, that of *social and personality* development, started in the 1940s with an interest in how attitudes are formed and changed, and, even earlier, with the desire to account for the differences between individuals in the ways they learn, relate to and make sense of their world. Subsequent decades saw the growth of a wider study of the role of society in the formation of personality, the nature of our sense of 'self', and other more general and profound issues linking the individual to his social world. Finally, again in the 1940s and '50s, *humanistic* learning theories were born from the attempt to explain how people's feelings and their capacity to feel were changed by various sorts of group or one-to-one counselling experiences. Here too the scope grew broader and broader as the concern with 'personal growth' threw up basic questions about the limits of human development and the importance of such slippery concepts as love, vulnerability, acceptance, and the like.

These four approaches to learning were bound, given their initial observations and aims, to go shooting off in different directions. Cognitive theories took over the domain of words, logic, language, reasoning, and knowledge. They become preeminent in the field of education, seeing the role of the teacher as that of instructor and communicator of facts and arguments. They became theories about the *head*, we might say. Behavioural theories, in contrast, paid little if any attention to the intellect, and preoccupied themselves with changes in physical competence that happened outside conscious thought. The important thing was practice and the teacher, if one existed, was seen as a trainer and orchestrator of rewards and punishments. These theories we might symbolize as being to do with the *hands*. Social and personality theories are concerned with matters of the *heart* in the sense that they focus on people's beliefs, opinions, attitudes, judgements about themselves and others. The teacher is often seen here as a model or example or 'exuder' of a certain personal style that is not directly taught but which may nonetheless be picked up by his students. Such theories fall between the two poles of pure reason and raw emotion, the latter being the central preserve of the humanistic theories. It is only within this last tradition that the role of awareness in learning has been studied, and the nature of conscious and unconscious experience, especially of feelings, has emerged as the main concern. Such 'gut' reactions are the medium with which humanistic theories work and, if we scratch around a little for a fourth 'H', we can typify them as being interested in the *hara* – the Japanese word for the pit of the stomach, and familiar to Westerners in the expression 'hara-kiri'. In humanistic learning, the focus is on the teacher as facilitator: he does not model or teach or train, but provides a safe partner to a learner in his self-directed researches into whatever affects him. Slowly these originally disparate traditions are coming back together, and this book is another step towards intermingling. But in the main they are still quite separate.

One problem in psychology has been the attitude of theorists to their theoretical progeny. Failing to keep sight of the fact that theories have foci and ranges of convenience, they have sometimes assumed that their particular brain-child must be applicable to the whole field of learning. Instead of investigating its limits they assert its limitlessness. And this breeds trouble. Thus conflicts between different approaches – that between Skinner and Rogers is a classic one[10] – have often been spurious. The electron, though one, sometimes looks like a particle and sometimes like a wave. The human being, though an integrated whole, sometimes appears as an actor, sometimes a thinker, sometimes a believer, sometimes a confused and agitated seeker of emotional aid. The kind of learning on which each tradition focuses is neither the only nor the 'best' kind of learning there is, and it is by no means certain that an elegant and successful model of a rat learning to run through a maze will be much good at explaining how children learn language. It may be worth trying it out (as Skinner has done)[11] but there is no reason why the exercise has to succeed, and we need not protest too much if it fails.

The story of the blind men and the elephant is well known. Each grabbed hold of a different bit and asserted that elephants were like hose-pipes, or walls, or tree-trunks, or bits of rope. Each produces a metaphor for the elephant's trunk, flank, leg, or tail that is hopelessly inadequate for the elephant as a whole. Not so well known is the occasion on which a primary-school teacher decided to discuss this cautionary tale with her class, but without telling them that the men were blind. Afterwards she asked the children, 'What kind of people do you think they were?' One child replied tentatively 'Please, Miss . . . experts?' Learning is a large, strange, many-faceted elephant, and we will do well to remember these stories as we proceed.

1.4 We Are all Theorists

This preamble is important for the way we as psychologists approach learning. But it also applies directly to the learner himself. We are all theory makers, theory dwellers and theory testers. We live on the basis of a personal theory – a personal map – of what things are like, and we could not live without it. All our knowledge, beliefs, attitudes, expectations, values, opinions, and prejudices are part of this giant theory. All our thoughts, actions, feelings, and sensations are produced by it.[12] It is the vital and unavoidable go-between that mediates all our dealings with the outside world. Nothing has significance in that world; it only has significance *for* somebody. And unless I make a guess about what is significant, what matters, I have no basis on which to act. I cannot achieve anything that is desirable, not avoid anything that is harmful until I interpret whatever-it-is as desirable or harmful. Without my theory, my distillation of what matters out of the raw material of my past experience, I could not even get to the bathroom, let alone order a meal or make friends. Learning happens when I make mistakes, but without the map I would have no idea of what the right road looks like, nor how to find my way back to it.

So it is not hard to see that what we *do* to the world depends on what we consider that world to be: what it contains and which bits are significant. It is a little more tricky to appreciate that all our perceptions are products of the theory, too. Common sense says we see things the way they are, then we make decisions about what's important, and finally we select actions that will get us what we want and avoid what we don't. Common sense is wrong.[13] What we see is an output of our personal theory, not an input to it. The Gestalt psychologist Koffka summed it up when he said 'We see things not as they are but as *we* are.' Max Clowes, of the University of Sussex, puts it another way: 'There is no seeing,' he said, 'only seeing *as*.' Look at Figure 1.1: what do you see? A cube, you reply. But in fact there is no cube there, only a two-dimensional pattern of lines that you see *as* a cube. Your theory jumps straight in and tells you, on the basis of past experience with similar patterns of light and shade, that you will probably get by best if you treat it *as* a two-dimensional representation of a cube. And that hypothesis is presented to you not as a rational conclusion but as the very perception itself. Now take a slightly more complicated example: look at Figure 1.2a. It represents two blocks, one (A) on top of the other (B). What kind of blocks are they? Cubes again. Are you sure? Yes. OK, now look at Figure 1.2b. What shape are the blocks now? Wedges. Both of them? Er . . . (beginning to be a bit suspicious) . . . Yes. But the information you've got about block B is exactly the same in Figures 1.2a and 1.2b. Only block A has been changed. So how come you see B *as* a cube in 1.2a and *as* a wedge in 1.2b? You do not see what is actually presented to you about B at all. You see B in the context of A, and changing A leads you, quite unconsciously, to change

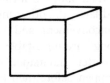

Figure 1.1

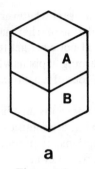

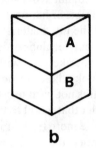

a

b

Figure 1.2a   **Figure 1.2b**

your hypothesis about B. This is not just a party trick provided by the psychology of perception. *All* our perception is interpretive, constructive, hypothetical. Thus how we respond depends not on the way things are, but on the way we see them to be. If I see a coil of rope on a country lane as a snake, I really run away, and have a real heart attack as a result of my panic, even though the snake wasn't 'really' there at all. If I see you as friendly and sexy, I will respond to you one way: if I see you as a headmistress, I will respond quite differently – even though it is the same you.

Even the most fundamental features of the physical world are projections of the human mind. We seem to live in a three-dimensional space through which separate objects move in unidirectional time, and in which events are solidly linked together by a rigid network of cause and effect. This is so basic, so 'obvious' that surely the world must actually be like that. Not so. Twentieth century physics has systematically dismantled this illusion piece by piece, showing us that space, time, substance and cause are all notions imposed by us on reality. Riemann's geometry, by its very existence as a viable alternative to Euclid's, shows the latter to be a way of representing space rather than the 'truth' about it. Schrödinger comments: 'We are absolutely free to believe any geometry we like to be true. We choose the one that is most convenient to us – that is to say the geometry according to which the laws of nature appear in their simplest forms. . . . It may be that one geometry entails complicated laws, the other much simpler ones. In that case the former geometry is inconvenient, and the latter is convenient, but the words "right" and "wrong" are unsuitable.'[14]

Certain experiments are better understood if we allow time to flow backwards, and effects to happen before their causes. Mach showed that mass is not a property of individual chunks of matter, as Newtonian common sense would have it, but can more fruitfully be seen as a resultant of the interactions and interdependency between all the matter in the universe. Mass is a relationship. Einstein boggled the mind even further by denying the separability of space and time on the one hand, and geometry and matter on the other. He assumed, for example, that the geometry of space is in a reflection of the mutual interaction of all the matter in it. So if you shift the furniture about, the shape of the room changes. And physics has had to accept, too, David Hume's view of causality. 'Neither the connection between a single cause and its effect, nor the universality of this connection throughout Nature is in itself manifest, or forms a necessary element of our thought . . . (it is) a convenient habit.'[15] Thus to acknowledge that we live and see through a fallible theory of our own devising is a serious matter, however innocuous the idea may seem to start with. It means giving up the belief that we can ever know anything for sure: the best we can do is act 'as if' and hope it works. When we come to look at the theories people hold about themselves and about each other we shall see just how serious this abandoning of hope can be.

1.5 What is Our Personal Theory About?

Our personal theory has to cover everything that matters – all our significant experience. We can divide this total domain into three parts: theories about the *physical world*, theories about the *social world*, and theories about *ourselves* in relation to these.

The theories about the physical world constitute our intuitive 'natural science' – our personal, largely unconscious physics, chemistry, botany, zoology, and so on. We develop, through our dealings with the world, a practical understanding of weight, heat, light, electricity, gravity, force, of the behaviour of substances when heated or mixed (in cooking, for example), of the habits of cats, dogs, budgies, and so on. We can anticipate how much effort it will take to lift a suitcase, what happens when a match is put to a fire, when an egg is boiled, when the cat's tail is tweaked. And beside this workaday science most of us have, too, a formal science that we learnt at school or college. These two sciences can coexist quite peacefully for the most part, even when they give different answers to the same question. A child may have been taught something about heat conduction, yet insist that a block of ice-cream will stay frozen longer wrapped in silver paper than in a blanket, 'because the blanket keeps things warm'. Another may know about relative velocities, and still fail to appreciate that dropping a stone off a bridge into the path of an express train will have the same effect as hurling the stone at 100 mph at a stationary train – and cause the same damage.[16]

Allied to our intuitive science we have an intuitive mathematics that tells us how to combine and manipulate quantities and measurements. Again, this may or may not correspond to the formal mathematics taught at school. Consider this example.[17] Imagine that the earth were a smooth sphere, and that a loop of string were fitted snugly round the equator. This loop is then cut, six more feet are added, and the new, bigger loop spaced out so that the gap created is equal all the way round. The question is: How big is this gap? Could you push a penny under the string? An apple? Could you crawl under it? Invariably people's strong intuition is that the gap is very small – less than an inch, and often very much less. In fact, much to everyone's surprise, the gap is nearly a foot. You could crawl under the string quite easily. Here is the formal proof, for those who need convincing.

Let the radius of the earth be r, and let the gap created be δr. The new radius, after inserting the extra piece of string is thus $(r + \delta r)$.

Now the difference between the new circumference, C_2 and the original one, C_1 is 6 feet.

So $C_2 - C_1 = 6$

But $C_2 = 2\pi(r + \delta r)$

And $C_1 = 2\pi r$

Thus $2\pi(r + \delta r) - 2\pi r = 6$

So $2\pi pdr = 6$

Or $\delta r = {}^6/_{2\pi}$ = just less than a foot

The proof demonstrates what is in fact the case: that the size of the gap is independent of the size of the original sphere. You get the same gap if you do the experiment with an orange as you get when you do it with the earth. Yet our intuitive maths is firmly of the opinion that this is *not* so. The larger the sphere, the smaller the gap. And until this moment, when the two mathematical systems were confronted with the contradiction, they have existed side-by-side quite happily for years.

About the social world each person has an intuitive sociology, economics, politics, ethics, and social psychology, whether or not he has an explicit knowledge of these subjects. He has a working knowledge of power relationships, of organizations, of class differences, of group dynamics. Everyone has his own somewhat idiosyncratic set of *constructs*, as George Kelly calls them, for describing and relating to other people. For one person a dominant question is: Is she *pretty*? For another: Is he *intelligent*? For another: is he *defensive*? And for a fourth: Is he *possessive*? We all view each other through the spectacles of such judgements and categorizations, and interact accordingly. Note that, as with the snake and the piece of rope, how I approach you depends on the fact that I have construed you as 'possessive', and this may correspond to who you are, and then again it may not.

Finally, everyone has some set of beliefs and information about himself – his personal, largely inarticulated philosophy, psychology, and physiology. This part of the theory is to do with how I see myself, my aspirations and goals in life, my rights and obligations, and with how my body works: what makes me sick and where my heart is.

1.6 What is the Theory For?

If all theories are designed for a purpose, to do a particular job or meet a particular need, what is the purpose of our personal theory? There are, of course, many goals and needs that we want to achieve or assuage, but one underlies all the others: *survival*. The most characteristic feature of living things is that they tend to resist their own demise. Life exists and persists only in opposition to death. This is as true of people as it is of animals, though the existence of such (uniquely?) human acts as suicide or martyrdom makes the story slightly more complicated, as we shall see. This tendency to go on living is an integral part of being alive: it is the central feature of our design specification that we should avoid threats and seek satisfaction of our needs. And in the normal run of events – leaving aside hara-kiri and hunger fasts for the moment – this is not something we have to think about, nor is it even something we can do anything about. The tendency to persist is wired into a living being at a very deep level, way below conscious designs and schemes. When my motor-bike skids, my body manoeuvres itself to avoid falling off without the help of consciousness, and before any deliberation has taken place at all. It is more accurate to say that survival is not something that people *do* so much as something that they *are*.

With animals the picture is clear. It is quite obvious that the dominant theme of their life is their own survival. (They are also programmed to be concerned about the survival of the species; but I shall not say anything more about that here.) They forage for food, scuttle away from a moving shadow, dig burrows to keep them warm and protect them from predators, and so on. But with human beings we have to look rather more closely at the question: survival *of what?* Mostly the answer is the same as it is for the animals: survival of the organism, the physical body. However, sometimes people put their bodies at risk in a way animals do not. They rush into burning buildings to rescue their art collection, they fight duels, they make attempts on the land speed record, they lay down their lives for Queen and country, they jump off buildings, starve themselves to death, offer themselves as human sacrifices and blow the tops of their heads off with a shot-gun. Human beings are capable of rating the survival of something else – their wealth, their possessions, their honour, their principles – higher than their own physical survival, and acting accordingly.

It is not enough to be wealthy, proud, or principled in order to risk your life. Some special relationship has to exist between the person and his possessions, say, before he will sacrifice his physical survival for their survival, and that relationship is *identification*. In some deep sense a person has to consider himself to be his paintings, his honour, his loved ones, so that when he is sacrificing his life he is not at the same time sacrificing *himself*, because his self is identified with something different from or greater than physical survival. For human beings the bottom line of their existence is survival of the self, therefore, and that means the body and/or a variety of other things with which the person is identified. We shall be much concerned with this slippery concept 'self', especially in Chapter 6. Suffice it for the moment to summarize where we have got to: *the function of a personal theory is to prolong and if possible ensure the survival of the person and/or anything the person considers himself to be.*[18]

1.7 How Does the Theory Work?

In order to maximize satisfaction, minimize pain and avoid threats, we have to outwit the world. Our theory provides us with the ability to predict the flow of events, to anticipate its course and thus to intervene and divert the stream in ways that are to our own advantage. We can beat Reality to the draw, fix the machine so we get the jackpot, if we can understand how it works – what follows what, what affects what, whether the strength of my pull or of my prayers to Heaven influence the spin of those little wheels. Life poses an endless series of questions about what I can do. What can I do to impress the examiners, control the class, placate my husband, get to the shops before closing time. Our theory is what enables us to fit our actions to our wishes and desires. It is, in short, a Mechanism for Integrating Needs and Deeds, a description which has been replaced over the centuries by the acronym MIND. Mind is another name for the totality of our personal theory about Reality.

Mind develops out of recorded observations about what's so. I observe the world this time partly so I will know what to do next time. But if all I did were to keep a scrap-book, I would not get very far. We have to boil down our past experience and extract generalizations, categories, and rules from it. If I did not, I could never tell whether this time the same *kind* of thing is happening as happened last time, and would not be able to know whether it was or was not appropriate, a good bet, to act in the same kind of way. 'Ah Ha!' the mind is constantly saying (under its breath), 'this looks like another one of those . . . so if I treat it *as if* it were one of those, then I can guess the outcome of doing various things to it. I can fry it, poach it, scramble it, incubate it or throw it – depending on what I want to achieve.' We have to break the world up into recurring and recognizable chunks: concepts, constructs, categories. Only if my category system allows me to create an analogy between now and then can I bring to bear my knowledge of what I did then and how it turned out. If each experience were a unique, unanalysed Gestalt, nothing would be *like* anything else.

Thus even a simple statement like 'That's a chair', or 'He's maladjusted' represents a theoretical statement. It is not at root an observation about how the world is so much as a set of predictions about how it or he will behave, and especially about how the 'chair' or the 'maladjusted adolescent' will behave *in response to me*. What it means to call something a chair is 'I predict that if I sit on it it will hold me up, support my back, and give me rest; or if I hold it between me and the lion it will afford me some measure of protection.' Or 'A maladjusted child will be emotionally immature, will resist doing what I tell him, will do less well in school than his IQ would indicate, and have a troubled home-life.' All these assumptions and predictions mediate my transactions with him.

This brings us to a very important pair of principles. *What I do depends on what my theory tells me about the world, not on how the world really is*. The snake may really be rope, but I run. The chair may really be a hologram, but I sit on it. The traffic cop may really just want to know the test score, but I still feel shaky in my stomach as he approaches. The class may really be upset about Diana's mother going into hospital, but I react in the belief that they dislike me and are bored with the Vikings. However: *What happens next depends on how the world really is, not on how I believe it to be*. If I make the reverse mistake and believe the snake to be a harmless old bit of rope, that will not stop it biting me. If I stand in the middle of the road and believe there is no bus coming, it will still knock me over.

The interesting thing about *human* interaction, is that these two principles get confused, and knots of belief and counter-belief are developed that may lead the participants to act in appropriate and effective ways, but often do not. Acting on my belief or hope that the policeman is a cricket fan, I say: 'Boycott's having a good knock, Officer, though Marshall seems to be pinning him down a bit.' The policeman, who actually *is* keen on cricket, promptly forgets about the ticket he was about to give me for speeding. *Or*: he hates cricket, and especially jovial cricket-loving jerks in tweed jackets, and decides to give me a ticket rather than letting me off with a warning. What happens next in this case depends on my actions, which stemmed from a belief about him, which creates a belief about me in him. Whether the beliefs, the hypotheses, are *accurate* or not is still not important. This line of thought gets very tangled – as R. D. Laing showed in *Knots*,[19] for example.

1.8 The Theory Makes Mistakes

Any theory is bound to be incomplete, and therefore is bound to let you down. This is because (i) to be a theory it has to simplify and ignore parts of Reality that may turn out later to be important; and (ii) Reality is always changing, over time, in ways we couldn't predict. Mind is a theory, so it too will make mistakes. Some of these errors are due to false expectations; the mind makes an inappropriate analogy between the present situation and past experience, and leads me to act in a way that is out of step with the world. Only if my understanding is accurate do the gears mesh and the cogs of my interactions with the world turn smoothly and deliver the goods. I construe the weather man as reliable and the picnic is a wash-out. I construed you as interested in football last night, and wonder why your flat-mate says you don't want to talk to me today. I underestimate the sophistication of my fourth-year boys, and feel hurt and puzzled when they poke fun at my visual aids. Whenever such a *disappointment* occurs, I can learn, I can improve my theory, by refining my expectations and being more attentive. Next time I will be more sceptical of the weather report, of the apparent interest of a potential girl-friend, of what my tutor told me about fourteen-year-olds.

Alternatively the mind lets us down by 'leaving undone those things it ought to have done'. It fails to anticipate something significant that upsets the plans. How could I have anticipated that Bologna station would be blown up and my business partner killed; that the buses would be on strike; that the birth control pills would be faulty; that I would lose my keys; that horrible 4D would buy me flowers on my birthday? Whenever such a *surprise* occurs I learn by extending my catalogue of significant circumstances.

Most learning happens when mind makes mistakes, just as the development of a scientific theory occurs when a prediction fails to be borne out by experiment. On the basis of its store of expectations, mind selects an action that is likely to result in a desired consequence. When the actual consequence differs significantly from this anticipated consequence, there is an opportunity to learn. Alternatively, mind may fail to come up with an analogy for the present situation – you are flummoxed – in which case a real behavioural experiment is required. You have to take a shot in the dark. Chapter 3 explores these kinds of learning in greater depth.

1.9 We Confuse the Map and the Territory

People cannot bear very much Reality because the complexity, slipperiness, and inscrutability of Reality constantly remind us how inadequate our theories about it are. Mind does not make mistakes every so often: if we are alert we will see that it is doing so all the time. Thus learning and the allied insecurity and incompetence is something that is required of us constantly, from birth to death. At least it is required as long as we remain receptive to our mistakes and alive to our circumstances. But human beings do not like to be wrong too often and they have discovered a way of avoiding being wrong, of having to grow, change, experiment, and learn. They *substitute* their theory for Reality. Instead of the map being a guide to the countryside, it is sometimes assumed to be right, simply because it says so, and if there is any discrepancy between it and the lie of the land, the latter is just ignored or explained away. 'Do not adjust your concepts: there is a fault in Reality.'

When people lose sight of the nature and function of their personal theory, they begin to confuse it with the world of which it is a distorted representation, and this breeds a lot of trouble. If I insist that the way I see things is the way they really are, then my perception becomes (by definition) 'right' and I cannot allow the possibility of my own subjectivity. I have to deny the real castle over there; I refuse to look at it, or call it a hallucination, in order to defend the map on which it doesn't happen to be marked. As we shall see, people do lead their lives to a greater or lesser extent as if the contour lines were really there, stepping over these imaginary trip-wires after every fifty metres of ascent, and as if the castle really weren't there, and missing much of the view. And they get themselves into a frightful mess trying to blame Reality for the failure of their theory because it (Reality) turned out to be different from the way their theory said it *ought* to be. It was nothing to do with me that the outing was miserable: it was the kids, the Deputy Head/the weather/the Government. . . .

This tendency to live in the map, rather than live in the world and *use* the map to get about, is the single most important key to understanding the way people do and do not learn. We shall pull it apart in some detail in Chapter 6. For the moment I shall just cement the idea in your minds with an interesting pair of quotations. The first is from an address that Albert Einstein delivered to the Physical Society of Berlin in 1918. He said:

> Man tries to make for himself in the fashion that suits him best a simplified and intelligible picture of the world: he then tries to some extent to substitute this cosmos of his for the world of experience, and thus to overcome it. This is what the painter, the poet, the speculative philosopher and the natural scientist do, each in his own fashion. Each makes this cosmos and its construction the pivot of his emotional life, in order to find in this way the peace and security which he cannot find in the narrow whirlpool of personal experience.[20]

The second, from Einstein's compatriot, Hermann Hesse, and recorded in an essay called *Mysteries*, is astonishingly similar, even though Hesse uses more dramatic and stirring images than Einstein's 'narrow whirlpool'.

> . . . each of us paints and misrepresents every day and every hour the jungle of mysteries, transforming into a pretty garden or a flat, neatly drawn map, the moralist with the help of his maxims, the man of religion with the help of his faith, the engineer with the help of his slide-rule, the painter with the help of his palette, and the poet with the help of his examples and ideals. And each one of us lives completely content and assured in his pseudo-world and on his map, just so long as he does not feel, through some breach in the dam or some frightful flash of lightning, reality, the monster, the terrifying beauty, the appalling horror, falling upon him, inescapably embracing him and lethally taking him prisoner.[21]

1.10 Man is Not Exactly Like a Scientist

Man-as-Scientist is a useful metaphor for beginning to look at learning, but it has its limitations, its own range of convenience, as all metaphors do. So far it has worked quite well. A *Scientist* has a *Theory* that he tests against his *Data* by generating *Hypotheses*, performing *Experiments* and recording the *Results*. Likewise a *Learner* has a *Mind* that he tests against his *Experience* by generating *Expectations*, performing *Actions* and recording the *Consequences*. In general the correspondence is valid. But the scientist and the learner differ somewhat in their primary goal and in their *modus operandi*. The research scientist's main concern about his theory is: Is it true? His job is to seek out or construct any situation, however artificial or bizarre, that will reveal the limits or the flaws of his theory. The learner's primary concern, on the other hand, is very much with the *utility* of his theory: Does it work? Does it do the job it is supposed to do under the conditions in which it was designed to do it? In this respect he is closer to Research and Development, and Technology, than to pure Science. It follows that the learner has to be concerned with the technical details of his theory. If the ultimate instructions to the muscles are not clear and precise, your actions will be clumsy and hesitant, and you may miss the bus. There is scope for the research scientist to concern himself exclusively with grand issues and 'the ontological status of quantum field theory' if he feels so inclined, and leave it to some other chap to fill in the fine print. The learner has to do it all himself.

Scientists' experiments are sporadic, whereas those of the human learner are occurring all the time. They keep cropping up just in the process of life itself. Thus while the scientist goes out of his way to seek and create critical tests, the learner's task is to be receptive to those data and disappointments that are borne to him on the endless stream of his own consciousness. Specifically he must be alive to those occasions when the theory leads him to make a mistake, or fails to deliver the goods at all. What is crucial in these instances is the mismatch between the predictions and the results: unless that comparison is made, learning will not occur. Here we might say the same thing of the research scientist. It does not matter how neat his experiment or how clean his results if he does not record them, analyse them, interpret them and compare them with his prediction. A scientist who was to ignore all the data that could embarrass his theory – literally, or by 'explaining them away' or calling them artefacts – preserves his theory intact, but at the cost of either leaving it pickled in an immature form, or of decoupling it from Reality so that it continues to grow but only in a way that is grotesque and maladjusted.[22]

CHAPTER 2

NEEDS AND MOTIVES

AH! SUN-FLOWER
Ah! Sun-flower, weary of time,
Who countest the steps of the Sun,
Seeking after that sweet golden clime
Where the traveller's journey is done:

Where the Youth pined away with desire,
And the pale Virgin shrouded in snow
Arise from their graves, and aspire
Where my Sun-flower wishes to go.

Then she bore Pale Desire, father of Curiosity, a Virgin ever young. And after, Leaden Sloth, from whom came Ignorance, who brought forth Wonder. These are the Gods which came from fear, for Gods like these nor male nor female are, but single Pregnate, or, if they list, together mingling bring forth might pow'rs.

To the eyes of a Miser a Guinea is more beautiful than the Sun.

The root function of the mind is survival: survival of my body, my possessions, my power, my security, my self-image, my point of view. The mind is there to help me select or construct the best thing to do in any situation, and 'best' is defined in terms of my current needs, wishes, goals, and desires.

The study of motivation, which is what this chapter is about, is the study of what these best things are, and how they come to be selected. It is only armed with some ideas about this that we can usefully go on to look at how I come to do the best thing better and better – that is, at learning itself. People's needs and wants can be approached in two ways. We can catalogue them, which is what we shall do first. Or we can look at them as *those internal considerations that specify what will count as a desirable consequence of action*. A need is not a need unless there is some state of affairs that will satisfy it: a glass of water, a first-class degree, a Lamborghini, a rich and satisfying relationship. Our variable repertoire of needs defines a variable repertoire of states of affairs that we are motivated to bring about. If the first major presupposition of my approach to learning is that we live and act through a map of reality, the second is that our business in life, what provides our direction and purpose, is the discrepancy between where we are on the map, and where our biology or our upbringing suggests it would be better to be.

2.1 Catalogue of Needs

One well-known catalogue or classification of human needs was produced by Abraham Maslow.[1] He identifies five levels of need. The most basic or primitive or universal he calls *physiological*: the needs for food, water, and so on. The second is also clearly to do with physical survival: he calls it *safety* needs. While physiological needs refer to threats to physical survival from within the body, safety needs are concerned with those from without – predators, forest fires, oncoming buses and the like. At the next level we find the need for *love*: that is, for other people to accept and support us in our journey through life. Though another's love may help to protect us physically, it has more to do with the most soft, delicate, psychological aspects of ourselves. To be loved is to feel a deep emotional security, and ultimately an invulnerability to threats to oneself. The fourth level Maslow calls the needs for *self-esteem* and the *esteem of others*. We all have a self-image which consists of me-as-I-see-myself and me-as-I-would-like-or-ought-to-be. If the disparity between my actual and ideal pictures is great, then I am falling short, in my own eyes, and my esteem of myself is low. There is a basic need, says Maslow, to be not just accepted (loved), but approved of by myself and by that circle of others whose judgements I care about – what I have heard sociologists call my 'esteem-arena'. Finally, there is the need for *self-actualization*: to grow, investigate oneself, transcend one's limitations, fulfil one's potentialities, and to seek for a spiritual peace and wholeness. Maslow's additional claim is that these different needs are organized hierarchically, so that higher-level needs cannot be attended to unless all the lower-level needs are satisfied. You don't worry what people think about you (esteem), if you are hungry or tired enough (physiological).

Murray[2] gives us a rather more detailed, and more useful, breakdown of human needs which he groups under two main headings. First are the *viscerogenic* needs that correspond pretty well to Maslow's first two levels. They are the ones that secure life itself. Murray lists the needs for air, food, water, warmth, sex, urination, defecation, avoidance of harmful stimuli, touch, sleep, and rest. We might add the needs for movement and sensory stimulation. If any one of these (with the arguable exception of sex) is prevented, and its satisfaction inhibited, the human frame cannot continue to function healthily, and eventually it disintegrates.

The second category are *psychogenic* needs, whose frustration leads to psychological rather than physical disturbance – though the two cannot be fully separated, as we shall see when we discuss psychosomatic disorders in Chapter 7. According to Murray we need *prestige* and *status*: we need to achieve and defend a certain level of social standing and approbation. We have a need for *power*: there is an urge to dominate others and to avoid domination by them. We need *affection*: we wish to be likeable to others, to have their friendship and sympathy. We also have a need for *things*: for acquiring and hanging on to material possessions. And finally we need *thought*: we require the freedom to question, to reason, to explore and doubt, to exercise our judgement and our intellect.

2.2 Needs and Desires

It is useful to distinguish needs – those biological conditions that are truly necessary for our survival – from desires – those conditions we have learnt or been taught to want, even to the extent of their absence *feeling* like a threat to survival, but which are not in fact necessary.[3] Most of Murray's psychogenic 'needs' fall into this category. It is arguable, for example, whether prestige and possessions are basic motivators for an Eskimo woman in the same way, or to anything like the same extent, as they are for an American businessman. Needs arise from the present. A person feels hungry, seeks for and ingests food, and the need disappears. Such needs are *variable*, they come and go, and they are *satiable*; one is not impelled to be constantly on the lookout for food or a place to shelter. Desires, on the other hand, are rather more tricky. They tend to form constant themes or biases to our life and perception, so that we are set to seek their satisfaction whatever the transient state of the internal or external worlds happens to be. We think that one more degree, one more promotion, one more million, one more lover is what we need. Yet when we get it, the satisfaction may evaporate almost as quickly as it came. Somehow it is not quite enough. Like the horizon, a desire recedes from you as you approach it, always confronting you with the fact that there is another record to be broken, another branch to be opened, another sacrifice to be made. So desires are in fact insatiable.

Some of our desires are insatiable for another reason. It is not that we achieve what we were after and then find it empty, but that we actually prevent ourselves from achieving the desired goal at all. Perhaps sex is the best contemporary example of this. The potent mixture of licence and taboo that surrounds us encourages adolescents (of all ages) to want more and more sex, to feel frustrated and inadequate if they are not getting it, and at the same time to build insuperable barriers of guilt and reserve. Thus the natural host of developing sexuality is invaded by these conditionings and pressures and becomes an ugly and obsessive craving. Hence the man whose head is full of sex, but when confronted with a real and attractive woman blushes and stammers, and cannot manage even social, let alone sexual, intercourse. In just the same way we desire security and stability in our lives, yet resent it and resist it when it happens. We desire intimacy and love but find ourselves unable to open when they knock on the door.

2.3 Mind Integrates the Desirable with the Possible

The fact that desires provide us with a repertoire of things that we are permanently on the look-out for can make us less intelligent in our dealings with the world than we might be. For, as Hermann Hesse says, in the same collection of essays from which I quoted earlier,[4] 'the eye of desire dirties and distorts. . . . The man whom I look at with dread or hope, with greed, designs, or demands, is not a man but a cloudy mirror of my own desire. Whether I am aware of it or not, I regard him in the light of questions that limit and falsify.' In other words if my head is full of sex, sex, sex, and I see all women through this haze, I will miss the opportunity to see potential friends, collaborators, business partners or chess opponents. If she is not a potential lover, she is nothing.

Thus for the mind to work best it must not be blinded by needs and desires to what is actually so out there. It is indeed a Mechanism for Integrating Needs and Deeds – but in order to be successful, it has to be just as concerned with possibilities, the range of possibilities, that exist for me here now. If I am smart, I will see that this woman is not interested in my body, but she might give me a good game of chess, or be prepared to lend me a mosquito net. The mind must face inward and outward simultaneously if it is to perform its function of producing not just action born of need, but action that is appropriate to its context. Its job, we might say, is to compute, moment-to-moment an optimal solution to the existential equation whose major variables are 'the desirable' and 'the possible'.

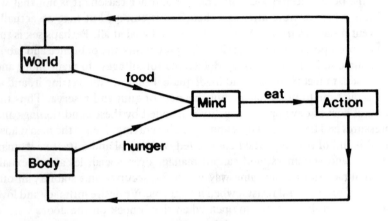

Figure 2.1

Though the divisions become untenable if pushed very far, we might imagine the mind's role in the scheme of things as shown in Figure 2.1. In the simplest possible example, it hears the body shout 'I'm hungry', the world shout 'Here's food', and it computes the solution 'Eat'. And it keeps on saying 'Eat' until the conditions change (see Section 2.5). And when we stop eating, both world and body are saying something else, and the equation has to be solved again . . . and again and again. Every output of the mind, even if only an internal one like a thought or an image, changes its inputs, so it functions, in effect, as a perpetual motion machine.

2.4 Why are People Active?

This is not such a silly question as it looks, and it will help if we spend a little time with it now. A common definition of the field of motivation has been the study of what *initiates*, *sustains*, and *directs* activity. I want to show that the first two-thirds of this apparently reasonable question are based on a misconception about what human beings – and living organisms in general – are, and that the attempt to answer them creates rather than dispels confusion. The dubious assumption we need to winkle out is this: that it is possible for people to be *in*active. To ask the question what causes action, and what sustains it, presupposes that there is an alternative to action; that people are capable of being inert. More than this, it has often been assumed that this state of inertia is in some way an ideal one, and one to which the organism strives to return and out of which it does its best not to be prodded. Man is seen as fundamentally 'homo comatose' and his prototype is Andy Capp. Given this starting point, it is obviously the next step to enquire how activity comes about. If man is a car, what is the petrol? If he is a balloon, what inflates him and causes him to go whizzing about till all his puff is exhausted? Clearly we need some energizing substance, be it 'drive', 'libido' or *élan vital*. Being basically happy where he is, man needs some get-up-and-go for him to get up and go anywhere. Once we start by assuming that complete rest is possible, then activity, its very existence, let alone its direction, purpose or intensity, becomes a problem to be explained, just as the motion of physical bodies was a central problem for pre-Newtonian mechanics.

But is this picture of human beings accurate? Is the nirvana of inertia ever achieved? Both everyday experience and experimental results should make us very wary indeed of this starting point. What do people do when they have 'nothing much' to do, and 'time on their hands'? They play Scrabble, do crossword puzzles, read books, have arguments, pop down to the shed to get on with their fretwork pipe-rack, go for walks, and watch TV. Even Andy Capp watches TV and nips down the pub for a pint and a chat with the lads. Watch the expressions of your fellow-passengers on an intercontinental flight and you will be surprised how little they seem to be revelling in their flying Garden of Eden. You can feel the tension rise more when the head-sets go on the blink than when the wheels go down for landing.

More formal investigations of the same phenomenon have been undertaken, principally in Canada.[5] Students were offered a generous daily wage for staying in a small room in which all their bodily needs (sex being excluded from the viscerogenic category on this occasion) were met, and in which there was nothing for them to do or see. They hated it, and escaped within a matter of hours, often, or one or two days at most. The brave few who stuck it out longer began to generate their own excitement internally: that is, they started hallucinating. If solitary confinement were not anathema to us, it would not be so widely used as a method of punishment and torture. The 'drive'-theorist's ideal state turns out to be intolerable.[6]

The most likely candidate for the state to which we return when there's nothing else to do is sleep. Certainly a look around the cabin of the 747 would suggest so. But research has now shown that though the body is relatively still in sleep, the organism as a whole is far from inactive. Sleep is not a lack of activity but a different activity. It is common knowledge now that the pattern of neural activity in the brain is very similar in the deepest stage of sleep to that when awake. And though in other stages the pattern of firing looks different, it is not quantitatively *less*.[7]

I hope these considerations are sufficient to suggest, even though they do not establish, that the possibility of inactivity is not a real one. Man is not inert: he is fundamentally and inescapably 'ert'. And this conclusion requires a deep shift in our philosophy of man. A person is not a thing but a process. As George Kelly said, 'man is a form of motion'.[8] He is not a noun but a verb. He exists by happening, and if he stops happening, he ceases to exist in that state we call living. Birth presses the start button and death presses stop, and in between there are no shut-downs, no Bank Holidays, no rest. The direction of our energy changes constantly but its existence and its flux are unceasing. The mechanical analogies of car or clock are ill-chosen. Rather we should say man's activity is like his breathing. The only answer to 'What causes us to breathe? is 'Life itself'. Or like the babbling of a brook, to be more poetic. If the brook is to flow, it will flow through shallow places, and when it does so it will babble. Why? Because that's just the way it is. Babbling is a natural consequence of 'brooking'. Just so is the relationship of doing to living. The shift is like that encapsulated by Newton in his revolutionary First Law. 'A body will remain at rest *or travelling in a straight line with constant speed*, unless acted upon by an external force.' With one fine stroke of his intellectual scalpel, he declared that activity, motion was *not* a problem after all. No explanation, no internal force or energy was necessary. All that needed explaining was *change* – change of speed, change of direction – and for this we have to look at the interaction between the body itself (the crucial facet of which Newton called its 'mass') and the forces or influences to which it is subject. The psychologist J. McV. Hunt, though no pretender to the title of the Newton of the Mind, gives the animate equivalent of Newton's First Law. Living things, he says, are 'open systems of energy exchange with the environment, on which stimuli have a modulating, but not an imitating effect.'[9]

So the basic question of motivation becomes: what modulates or directs our activity? And thus, significantly, the real issue emerges as one of *priority* rather than of *impulse*. I cannot be impelled into activity because I am always active. But I can ask why I am doing one thing rather than another, or why I stop doing X and start doing Y.[10] Why did I turn out on such a foul night to sit in this lecture rather than stay at home with a can of lager and watch television? Why is Joe sticking chewing gum in Sandra's hair rather than doing his long division? And what caused him to stop doing that, and start whistling, banging his heels on his desk and staring out of the window? At any and every moment in my life there is not just one but many things it would be desirable to obtain, effect or avoid. And the strength or urgency of each of these needs is constantly fluctuating, so that its *priority* within the total repertoire is varying too. Sometimes eating is a low priority activity, sometimes high, and sometimes when it becomes a matter of life and death, it will rule out all other considerations entirely. So the job of the mind becomes a bit clearer. In order to find the best solution to the equation of the desirable and the possible, it has to take account of all my needs and their relative priorities, the range of possibilities that exist for me right now, together with the relative degrees of effort and likelihood of success of each of the courses of action I am allowed; and then select that action that maximizes satisfaction and minimizes the amount of effort required and the chances and costs of failure. It is turning out to be quite a tricky computation. We cannot say, for example, that I will always do the most urgent thing. The effort and risk involved may simply be too great. Rather I will do that relatively urgent thing that my circumstances seem capable of satisfying. More complicatedly still, the mind will, if it is working well, try to produce an action that will satisfy not just one but several of my priorities. A student may turn out to his lecture on a cold night out of curiosity about the lecturer, interest in the topic, blind habit, so that he can escape from the house, so that he can take a book back to the library, to meet people, to get the degree so he can get that promotion, to prove to himself he can still think after all those years in the classroom, to 'accidentally' bump into that woman again . . . for any *or* all of these reasons, and a hundred others besides. Freud called this 'over-determination': he surmised on the basis of his experience as a therapist that most of what we do is done to satisfy a whole set of different needs and desires.[11]

2.5 Hunger

We can illustrate the complexity of our motivations by looking at the one that has traditionally been studied as the most straightforward – hunger. Alfred Hitchcock was once asked if he was interested in psychic phenomena.[12] He thought briefly and then replied: 'Yes. Hunger.' And he was right. Even such an apparently simple and biological need *is* a psychic phenomenon. It is, when you dig into it, a complex and mysterious business.

And if we need to speak of theories, minds and priorities, rather than S–R associations and drives, to account for when we eat, then it follows *a fortiori* that these simpler concepts will not be up to accounting for anything more sophisticated or uniquely human.

In the first half of this century, the inert view of living organisms had produced a particular approach to motives such as hunger. From time to time, it said, physiological changes occur in the body that are not desirable. The level of sugar in the blood falls, or contractions occur in the stomach. If something is not done to eradicate these trends, they will get worse and worse until survival is threatened, and eventually life cannot continue. These sensations that all is not well constitute 'drives', or 'drive stimuli' which energize the search for and ingestion of food. When an animal is exploring under the influence of a drive it will learn from experiences and actions that turn out to be relevant to the removal of that drive. In the absence of the drive, it won't. It follows that there is a close relationship between hunger and eating and learning about eating. Hunger leads to eating. Eating is a response to hunger. When hunger stops, there is nothing to 'energize' eating, so eating stops.

Within experimental psychology itself, problems arose with this view soon after it was formulated. One of the most awkward was the pheno-menon called 'latent learning'.[13] Take a rat, let it eat its fill, and put it in an unfamiliar maze. What it will do is wander about a bit and then take a nap. Now remove the rat, put him on short commons so he gets peckish, and put him back in the maze again, having hidden some food somewhere in it. The rat learns to find the food faster than another hungry rat who has not had the previous exposure to the maze. Clearly Rat 1 learnt something about the maze on his first visit even though he was not 'motivated' to learn. So learning is not, as had been proposed, conditional on the presence of a relevant motive.

A different experimental assault on the drive theories comes from physio-logical research that shows that we eat not in response to hunger, but in anticipation of it. We in the 'developed world' very rarely get physio-logically hungry: we have learnt to eat *before* the body's reserves have been significantly, or noticeably, depleted.[14] For us, eating is triggered much more often by the perception of a certain juxtaposition of the hands on a clock-face than it is by any change in our tissues.

There are many real-life examples of the fact that whether we eat in response to hunger depends on what else is going on, and what our other priorities are. Sometimes a person may be hungry – really, physiologically, hungry – yet fail to eat. 'Coming', I mutter absent-mindedly in response to the call to table, not even lifting my eyes from the page in front of me: and emerge six hours later, the novel finished, and suddenly feeling ravenous. More extremely, ascetics, anorexics, and prisoners may ignore the increasingly urgent promptings of their own hunger because other goals are more important. By fasting the ascetic hopes for enlightenment, the anorexic schoolgirl tries to punish and confuse her parents,[15] and the internee seeks publicity for his demand to be treated as a political prisoner. On the other hand, eating sometimes happens in response to promptings other than those of hunger. It is a well-known way of avoiding boredom or stress, for example. I remember a teacher in a school I used to work in collapsing in the staff-room with a Mars bar and declaring 'I always feel hungry after 3C'. It is unlikely she actually felt hungry, but she certainly felt something that called for the instant comfort of a sweet. Psychotherapy is familiar with the grossly overweight compulsive eater who claims to want to kick the habit, whereas it turns out that making herself 'fat and ugly' is her way of eliminating any possibility of the sexual relationship that she craves, but dreads even more strongly.

Let us summarize these considerations by looking at a range of things that may cause eating to *stop*. First, the food may run out. There is a change in the World that is directly relevant to eating. Second, someone may spill red wine on the tablecloth. There is a change in the World that promotes a competing activity to a higher priority than eating. Third, you may be full up. The Body has changed so that eating itself is no longer desirable. Fourth, you may get stung by a wasp. The Body is suddenly subject to a need that over-rides the hunger. Fifth, you may remember a vital phone call. The intrinsic activity of Mind throws up a new priority that grabs control of the system. Sixth, someone says 'How are you enjoying the Pekinese cuisine?' and for an awful moment you are convinced you have been tricked into eating dog. Beliefs and attitudes are activated within the Mind that causes eating itself to be inhibited. Thus we may conclude that the control of what you do always depends on an *interaction* between what is happening in World, Body, and Mind. Drive theorists have tried to put the Body in the driving seat; cognitive psychologists have tended to say, It's All in the Mind;[16] and radical behaviourists, like Skinner, have ignored the innards of the person almost entirely and claimed that the World does it all to us. None of these three attempts at simplification is helpful. We need to keep the whole picture in mind if we are to do justice to the human actor and learner.

2.6 **Motives are Inferences**

So far in this chapter I have been offering some speculations about the actual mechanism that selects or constructs a course of action: what are the relevant momentary considerations that influence us, and how are they weighted and combined into a single outcome? But there is another whole domain within the study of motivation that we need to look at, and that is the reasons or causes of action that people consciously attribute to themselves and others. 'He only did it to show off.' 'I wanted to teach you a lesson.' And so on. These consciously formulated answers to the question why did I/you do that are stories that we tell ourselves in order to render actions intelligible or comprehensible to us, and they need not bear much relation to the actual considerations that were taken into account by the mind. The mind of which we have spoken up to now is not the seat of our conscious images and verbally formulated thoughts. It is the computer that integrates all the influences to which we are transiently subject, many of which are not available to our conscious awareness. The workings of the computer are not available at all to consciousness. Rather the contents of consciousness are one kind of print-out from this organismic computer. It generates actions, it generates perceptions, and it generates thoughts: and sometimes these different outputs seem to match quite nicely, and sometimes they don't. 'I think I'll take a bath', you say to yourself, and find that your feet have carried you firmly into the dining-room to pour another scotch instead. 'He only does it to annoy, because he knows it teases', says the duchess of the baby, only to discover later that his cries reflected not cussedness but a strangulated hernia.

Everyday life gives us many indications of the fact that motives are consciousness's attempt to infer the antecedents of action. Sometimes we admit, for example, that no plausible inference has occurred to us. All we can say in response to 'Why?' is 'I just felt like it' or 'It seemed like a good idea at the time.' Sometimes we confess that we are as puzzled as the next man. 'I don't know what came over me', we say; or 'I wasn't myself'. Conscious reason is in these cases unable or unwilling to explain our behaviour because it seemed out of character – callous or tactless perhaps. In other instances we are prepared to speculate about our motives – but acknowledge as we do so that they are only speculations. 'I'm sorry I was so grumpy last night, love. I *must have been tired*.' Here the story-telling is clearly admitted. And in fact the more honestly one looks at oneself, the more suspect these motivational stories seem to be. Yet it is a hard habit to break, because there is a strong motivation for this business of finding causes: the *conscious* part of the mind hates not knowing what is going on because without attributing reasons and motivations it is impossible for it to play its favourite game of judging, evaluating, distributing praise and especially blame. We shall have a lot more to say about this later. Let us just note in support of this position that when the cause of an action is completely obvious, we do not bother to seek for motives. The need to create the story is not there, because the element of choice, and therefore of personal responsibility is not there. If we are watching two huge policemen frog-march a student demonstrator into the back of a Black Maria, and I ask you 'Why is the student getting into the van?' it would sound a bit silly. 'He had no choice', you would be inclined to reply. But if the demonstrator is an aggressive and politically active protestant minister from Northern Ireland and the arresting officer one small policewoman, we might begin to wonder. Now in answer to my question you might speculate 'He *wants* to be arrested to become a martyr to his cause and to get publicity.' The antecedents of his action seem to have left other courses of action open, so we fill the gap of uncertainty by inventing other antecedents and then transplanting them into the object of our concern. If he *is* a publicity-seeker, we can now have a nice discussion about the troubles in Ulster and whether he is justified in wasting the court's time.

If it is difficult to be sure of your own motives, it is doubly difficult to be sure of somebody else's. One needs to be very cautious indeed. 'Why is Julie being so obstreperous in class today?' you ask a colleague. 'Oh, it's because her parents have just adopted a little boy and she's jealous', comes the confident reply. That may be significant certainly: but so may the fact that she has just had her first period, or that she doesn't think your last mark was fair, or that she thinks you deliberately ignored her outside the cinema the other night, or that she's cross with herself for forgetting her PE clothes again. If you just assume that the jealousy is the truth and the whole truth about Julie's bad mood, and respond to her on that basis, you may make more trouble than if you hadn't thought about it at all. Your exaggerated concern may confuse her terribly, and make her very unsure of what *you* are up to. If this causes her to withdraw from you even more, then a sticky web of groundless supposition falls over the interaction and it gets more and more difficult to disentangle yourself. The truth is it *is* possible to be sensitive and receptive to the significant promptings within ourselves and others; but to formulate a simple intellectual answer, and stick to it, is to run the risk of over-simplifying and distorting people and their situations, and of preventing ourselves from reacting freshly to their constantly changing complexity.

There is another common motive for playing the 'motive game'. As well as trying to bung up holes in our own conscious understanding of what's going on, it is a way of denying the fact that what someone else is doing is upsetting us. It is a common defensive ploy to dismiss a genuine conflict, and avoid the struggle and effort which its resolution might entail. When I say 'You're only saying that to make yourself feel better', or 'She's just doing it to hurt me', what I am really trying to do is avoid the painful content of what has been said by calling you names or impugning her integrity. When the true response is 'Ouch!' my actual response is to deny the hurt by questioning your motives. 'What right have you got to say such things to me? You're not perfect.' And while the immediate effect is to divert attention from my discomfort, the actual conflict is replaced by the sterile one of 'Who is right?' and 'Who has the right?' Within the context of school, these kinds of evasions are more often found in the staff-room than the class-room. The business of assuming you know what other people's motives are, without checking it out, applies as much between teachers as between teachers and children.

2.7 Teacher Words: 'Unmotivated' and 'Motivating'

In the light of all this, we can expose a couple of shady characters who are often called upon to do a bit of dirty work in everyday language – especially that of school teachers. The first is the word 'unmotivated'. This is used as a more respectable synonym for 'lazy' as a way of implying that a pupil's lack of interest or achievement in school is a reflection of a general trait of his personality. Why does Simon muck about in French? Because he's unmotivated. Used in this way, it is one of those words that seems to provide a cause or motivation for a way of behaving, whereas in fact it is simply another way of describing it. The lack of motivation is inferred from the mucking about, and then used to explain it. This verbal sleight-of-hand is a common one, and one to which B. F. Skinner[17] is particularly sensitive. He uses the example of a piece of rope. If it can take a lot of strain without breaking, we call it 'strong'. Then we say, if it is strong, it must have strength – to be precise, tensile strength. The adjective which describes the way it behaves is transmuted into a noun that is taken to refer to a hypothetical quality of the rope. Now we can 'explain' how it can take so much strain: obviously because it 'possesses tensile strength'. Language, and teacher language par excellence abounds with such bogus causes. 'Delinquent', 'maladjusted', and 'hyperactive' spring to mind alongside 'unmotivated'.

A more specific problem with 'unmotivated' occurs when it is used to name a trait of the learner, rather than a state he passes through from time to time. It suggests that Simon is not only slack at French, but at learning *anything* – because it is his nature. And, concomitantly, that if he is not learning French, then he is not learning anything else of value instead. But neither inference follows from his slumped posture or his vacant stare. All we can deduce is that his *priorities*, right now, in this French lesson, are different from those of most of his fellow pupils, and most importantly from my own. He is not doing what I want him to do, and what I judge it would be valuable or worthwhile for him to be doing. Physical inactivity and a glassy look do not mean that nothing is going on. It is quite probable, for example, that Einstein spent a fair bit of his time gazing at his office wall in exactly the same way. Simon's state does mean that he has got other things on his mind that are of higher priority than listening to you. And this is not altered by the fact that you judge his day-dreams about motor-bikes, or being a disco champion, to be a waste of time. Postman and Weingartner in their *Teaching as a Subversive Activity*,[18] tell a nice story about a teacher in a ghetto school in the United States who asked a young black child: 'How many legs has a grass-hopper got?' To which the little boy shook his head rather sadly and replied: 'Gee, man, I wish I had *your* problems.'

However, it is a big mistake to deduce from this that you as a teacher do not have any right to change, or attempt to change, Simon's priorities. That is part of your business: to try to 'turn people on' to things that they had not previously valued. It's your job to see if you can fix things so that learning French irregular verbs becomes a higher priority, at least during your lessons, than chucking things about or having fantasies about girls. Now you can't, however much you might wish to, get inside Simon's mind and twiddle little knobs to achieve your aim. But you can try to do it more indirectly by rigging the consequences of the two alternatives – learning his verbs or day-dreaming – so that the consequence of the one you want becomes more desirable than the consequence of the other. 'Motivating' means trying to change someone's priorities. It does not mean trying to increase someone's impulse or energy to learn French as if it were either that or nothing. You are working with a hierarchy of priorities, and this means you have to pay attention to the competition. It's not just what Simon *isn't* doing, but what he is, that holds the key. If there were only two motives operating, we might imagine them as weights on a pair of scales. As far as you are concerned, you want A to win, to be heavier, but at the moment B is the weightier. So what you do when you *extrinsically motivate* someone is add something else, C, to the side with A on, so that the balance shifts, and now A and C together gain control of behaviour. Or you can add a *negative* consequence, D, to B, so that B and D together are now lighter than A. It comes to the same thing. In everyday language we call C a *reward* and D a *punishment*. When we reward somebody, we are fixing things so that getting something they want is now conditional on doing something they don't want to do. When we punish, we fix it so that getting something they don't want is now conditional on doing something they do want to do. When people do things we want them to do without our having to mess about with the scales, we say they are *intrinsically motivated*.[19]

These words 'intrinsic' and 'extrinsic' are used somewhat confusingly in the psychological literature. Often people talk about intrinsic and extrinsic motivation as if they were quite different forces at work inside the person. They are not. From the learner's point of view all motivation is intrinsic. If he didn't care about money or his free time, your offer of 50p for every verb correct, or your threat of five minutes' detention for every one wrong, wouldn't make any difference to Simon's class-room demeanour. If the rewards and punishments are not intrinsically attractive or repulsive to the pupil, they will be no good as ploys with which to extrinsically motivate him.

A further distinction has added to the confusion surrounding these two words. Sometimes an activity is undertaken for the satisfaction it brings in itself. I can jog, swim, play a musical instrument, or read a novel not simply to achieve a result. It is not a means to an end: doing the activity is an end in itself. I don't run in order to get home again nor play the piano for the satisfaction of getting to the end of the sonata. The desirable consequences arise immediately from the sensations that the activity generates. But on some occasions I do do things as a means to an end. I run to get home in order to get out of the rain. I read my text-book in order to pass the test, in order to be allowed to sit for the 'O' level examination. The differences are clear in principle, though in practice they often go together. Most sports are played for the pleasure of playing *and* to win. But the problem is that psychologists have labelled an activity undertaken for its own sake an 'intrinsically rewarding activity', and one undertaken to get something an 'extrinsically rewarding activity'. J. S. Bruner has made things worse by confusing motives and activities. 'An intrinsic motive', he says 'is one that does not depend upon reward that lies outside the activity it impels.'[20] This is ambiguous, but it looks as if he is talking about intrinsically rewarding activities rather than intrinsic motivation. But we can keep a clear head if we remember: (i) all motivation is intrinsic; (ii) extrinsically motivating means rigging the consequences so as to change how somebody else behaves; (iii) intrinsically rewarding activity is done for its own sake; (iv) extrinsically rewarding activity is done for the result it produces.[21]

CHAPTER 3

LEARNING THROUGH EXPERIENCE

> You don't believe – I won't attempt to make ye:
> You are asleep – I won't attempt to wake ye.
> Sleep on, Sleep on! While in your pleasant dreams
> Of reason you may drink of Life's clear streams.
> Reason and Newton, they are quite two things;
> For so the Swallow and the Sparrow sings.
> Reason says 'Miracle': Newton says 'Doubt'.
> Aye! that's the way to make all Nature out.
> 'Doubt, doubt, & don't believe without experiment';
> That is the very thing that Jesus meant,
> When he said 'Only Believe! Believe and try!'
> 'Try, try, & never mind the Reason why'.

You never know what is enough unless you know what is more than enough.

Now that we have some idea about what our personal theory is, what its job is and how it does its job, we can begin to look at how it changes. In this chapter we will focus on the kind of learning that changes our skill, capacity, and competence; that is, at how we come to do things better and see things differently. Particularly we shall be interested here in how these changes come about as a result of direct experience. In a later chapter we will revisit this type of learning, but then from the point of view of instruction – that is the situation in which one person tries to help another to do something better by telling him things like 'Keep your eye on the ball', 'Why not try dividing all through by 2x?', or 'That passage should sound like a funeral procession, not the Teddy Bears' Picnic.'

3.1 Experiential Knowledge

So far we have looked at the Grand Design of the mind, but if we are to describe how 'it' changes as a result of experience, we need to have some clearer ideas about what 'it' consists of. We need a rather finer theory about experiential knowledge before we can say very much about experiential learning.

As an initial model, we can use the image of a landscape of dunes – a great network of hillocks, troughs, and channels, distributed over a wide area, and not fixed in form, but changing under the influence of sea and wind.[1] Some of the hills are large mountains, others are little humps. For any hill, some others are close neighbours that are easily accessible, others are remote and hard to find. These hills represent our concepts, schemes, rules, and generalizations – all the abstractions from our own experience that enable us to know what to do *now*, because we can analogize 'now' to a type or class of 'thens' that we know how to deal with. The hills consist of all the grains of experience patterned together that are diagnostic of significantly different types of event. Those grains – or 'features' or 'attributes' or 'associations' we can call them – that are at the top of the hill are the most useful ones, the ones that are most highly diagnostic of this situation, or discriminate most clearly between this and other similar but different types, or tell us the most important things about how it is likely to behave. Further down the hill we find other associations and attributes that are less relevant, or less frequently associated with this concept. They are less tightly 'bound' to this particular idea, we might say (see Figure 3.1).

Although the concepts within this dune-scape are not divided up into different sorts, it will help in seeing how they are interrelated, as we look down on it from above, if we assign them roughly to different groups. There are dunes that are mostly collections of sensory features. For a baby 'Mum' is one of the first *perceptual dunes* that begins to emerge – that is, Mum in the sense of what she looks like, smells like, sounds like, tastes like, feels like, and the sorts of contexts in which she is likely to appear. It is these perceptual dunes that help us to realize we are in the presence of familiar individuals, objects, or relationships, despite variations in size, distance, mood and hair-do. Then there are collections of connections to the body's muscles that specify certain kinds of recurrent action or skill. We can call these *motor dunes*. For a little child, the coordination of muscles involved in *crying* is an important one. For a test cricketer the motor dune called *cover drive* is a useful one. And so on. In addition we have two sorts of dune that

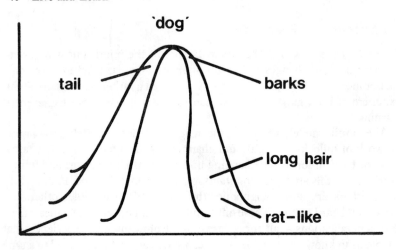

Figure 3.1

represent patterns of experience arising from within the body, rather than from outside. These are *motivational dunes* and *feeling dunes*. The former enable us to recognize states like hunger, thirst, and tiredness. The latter give us the conceptualizations we call sadness, joy or embarrassment.

One central characteristic of our experiential concepts is that they are never isolated; none of them stands alone. In fact, it is nearer the truth, though more difficult to express clearly, to say that the relatedness is primary, and that what we have called concepts, skills, and so on are aspects or facets of larger, more integrated patterns. To shift the metaphor for a moment, the basic unit of our experiential knowledge is a molecule, not an atom. And while we can talk about conceptual atoms, we need to remember that these never exist in the free state, but only as constituents of larger wholes, each of which contain other atoms.

Just as there are a number of different types of concept, so there are different ways in which they can be interrelated – different kinds of bond within the molecule, or different kinds of channel that run between the dunes. The most basic are those that link together things that have been found to go together in space or time. They tend to happen 'together', whether that means side by side or one after the other. Bread and butter, flame and smoke, sheets and pillows, teacher and pupil tend to be found in each other's company. Fire and ashes, night and day, pressing the brake and slowing down, pregnancy and child-birth, cooking and eating, setting the homework and marking the books tend to follow regularly, one after the other. But in addition to these neighbourly associations we develop a rather more sophisticated set of relationships for describing how different concepts are interacting. Much of what we perceive about the world is not simply 'A next to B' or 'A and then B': we want to be able to represent the function or role that A and B are playing within an event. In one system that has been proposed, for example,[2] the pivot around which events can be represented is the *action* involved. Then there might be an *actor* who is doing it, and/or an *experiencer* who is feeling it. There may be an *object* of the action, an *instrument* by which it is being carried out, a *location* in which it is occurring, and so on. The precise details of this categorization don't matter. The pundits disagree, and it is probable that the categories differ somewhat between individuals and considerably between cultures. For the moment it is sufficient to see that each concept we possess is inextricably entwined in this enormous network of relatedness.

3.2 Expectancies

From the point of view of experiential learning, one type of relationship, or rather combination of relationships, is preeminently important. Many of my hypotheses about the way the world works concern regularities over which I have no control. The sun rises and then sets. The tide ebbs and flows. The school holidays come and go. Thursday is early closing day in Slough. People are born and eventually they die. But if the function of my theorizing is my survival, then it is best if I pay attention to states and changes in the world that I can do something about. I need to learn that I can intervene in the course of history and alter it to suit my own ends or to satisfy my own needs. Thus my most important tool in my dealings with the world is the knowledge that when situation A is around, and I do B, then C is likely to result. And depending on which C happens to be a priority for me at the moment, so I can choose different Bs. If we let A stand for the Antecedent situation, B for my Behaviour, and C for the Consequence, then a very important part of my experiential theory is the linking together of Antecedent, Behaviour, and Consequence into molecules that give me reliable indications of how to get what I want in different circumstances. These Antecedent–Behaviour–Consequence, or ABC, sequences, we will call *expectancies*.[3] Slightly more generally, one can look at expectancies in terms of the functional relationships described in the previous section. They are interrelated sets of perceptual, motor, motivational, and feeling concepts in which the 'actor' is *me*. Experiential learning, then, is about building up a vast and accurate repertoire of ABCs that enable me to get to where I want to be from where I find myself as reliably and painlessly as possible.

Expectancies can be expressed as: '*If* such-and-such is the case, *and I do* so-and-so, *then* this is the likely outcome.' If I have a tickly nose and I take Beecham's Powders then my cold will be less severe. If I'm giving a lecture and I dry up then I will feel embarrassed. If I go to a party and I have a few drinks then I will have a good time. If I go to a party and I don't drink then I may feel lonely, isolated and introverted. If I have a raw egg, and I boil it for four minutes, then I will get a nicely boiled egg for my breakfast. If I find myself with 4F on a wet Friday afternoon and I give a poorly prepared and boring lesson, then there's quite likely to be chaos. If I find myself in a familiar maze and I turn right at the cross-roads, then I will find a few succulent pellets of Purina Lovely Pet Food in the little box at the end. Examples such as the latter, though of only minor interest to us, were very significant not only to laboratory rats everywhere but to Edward Tolman, an American psychologist, who first formulated the notion of expectancies.[4] B. F. Skinner[5] has done much research on the effect of experience on expectancies in simple situations, though he uses different terms. Instead of Antecedents, Behaviour, and Consequence he calls the components Stimulus, Response, and Reinforcement; and the three linked together he calls a 'contingency of reinforcement'. The main difference between Tolman and me on the one hand, and Skinner on the other, is that Skinner ties himself up by trying to insist that Stimulus, Response, and Reinforcement exist 'objectively' in the world, rather than (as we say) 'subjectively', as part of our theory about the world.

Expectancies represent regularities in the world that I can do something about so as to create new happenings that are of personal significance to me – to get what I want and avoid what I don't. Thus our experiential knowledge binds inseparably together 'What I can do' with specifications of 'When to do it' and 'What to do it for'. This must be so, because the best tool-kit in the world is absolutely useless if you don't know what to use each tool *on*, and what to use it *for*. To survive we must be able to deploy what we know and what we can do appropriately and effectively. So the kind of learning we are considering here can't be called 'learning to do more' pure and simple. It is also inescapably to do with testing out when to do it, and what the effects of doing it are.[6]

Though this seems obvious enough, it has often been ignored in both psychological research on how people learn and in education. Psychologists sometimes talk as if people have two separate kinds of experiential knowledge: concepts about 'things', and 'skills' which we use to manipulate things. So that what we know about things is in some way independent of what we can do with them, and what we can do is independent of the range of things we can do it to. The problem with this way of looking at it is that it leads people – especially educationalists – to suppose that when we learn a skill, be it mental or physical, arithmetic, talking or kicking things, what we have learnt will be available to be applied wherever it is relevant. What the expectancies view says is that this isn't so. What 'relevant' means has to be learnt just as much as the skill itself. Relevance, applicability, appropriateness, are not given: they have to be found out. Thus how well a person can do sums may depend crucially on whether he is in a maths class or out with his friends ten-pin bowling, or playing darts. $301 - ((2 \times 20) + (3 \times 18) + 12) = 195$ may be easy in one and hard in the other, depending on whether you are a darts champion or a professor of mathematics education. (I have verified this with at least one of each.) The fluency of a black child's language depends on whether he is talking to his best friend or a white educational psychologist.[7] Or, to come back to learning, when you are kicking a ball you are learning about 'kicking' and about 'balls' and about each in the context of the other.

Put slightly differently, we are inclined to think that when we are learning to do something we are learning a *verb*: to cook, to kick, to swim, to solve quadratic equations. What we ignore is that we are also, inevitably, learning the *adverbs* of time, manner, and place that go with the verb. Any sportsman, musician, or raconteur will tell you that his success depends on 'timing' and 'touch', on the suitability of the story for the audience or the stroke for the delivery. Just so, the good teacher is one who suits his approach and his pace to the subject and the class, not the one who ploughs on regardless.

To end this section on a philosophical note, we can be a bit more precise about object-concepts and skills now. An 'object' is a set of mostly perceptual features that is invariant across a number of expectancies whose Behaviours are different. And a 'skill' is a set of motor features that is invariant across a number of expectancies whose Antecedents are different.

3.3 Learning to Walk

Before we go on to look in detail at the processes whereby expectancies change, let me introduce some of the issues with a real-life example. About two years ago I found myself learning to walk. On the south coast of Crete, towards the western end, is the village of Agios Galini. East, some two hours walk away along the beach, lies the even smaller village of Kokinos Pyrgos. The beach is narrow, stony and sloping, and in places the cliff falls right into the sea, so that you have to paddle. I was making my way along carrying a heavy ruck-sack. It was 11 am, already very hot, and I had on my feet an old pair of sandals that got wet every so often, so that my feet tended to slide off them. I gradually became aware that I was learning how to walk: walking had become problematic and strange, and I was having to concentrate hard and pick my way carefully. I wanted a drink, but as I became more interested in the process of my own learning I sat down in a small piece of shade and started to make some notes about what was going on. These are some of the things I observed.

(a) *Perception and action change together*   What I had been doing, I noticed, was *detecting* those types of surface that made walking easier, and at the same time *selecting* my walking pattern so that I stuck to and made the most of those surfaces. The best stones were 6–9 inches across. Sand I sank into; little stones got inside my sandals; slightly bigger ones slid about too much as I walked on them; big rocks were no good because, although stable, they required climbing up and down, which was hard work. At the same time as my perception was beginning to make these fine discriminations, so my stride was becoming shorter, I was moving as smoothly as possible to avoid disturbing the stones, and keeping out of the water to stop my sandals getting slippery.

(b) *Learning is about gaining, or regaining, desired outcomes*   The gradual refining of my perception and my habit was not gratuitous. It was designed to achieve a specific outcome, namely getting along the beach as quickly and as comfortably as possible. More concretely, my goal became a seat in the shade with a long, cold drink. The criteria of comfort and speed were used to select and consolidate those changes in my way of doing and seeing things that worked best. In just the same way that 'natural selection' ensures the survival of the fittest animals, so 'functional selection' ensures the survival of the most fitting skills of perception and action.[8]

(c) *Some learning is refining what you already know*   Only rarely, as we shall see in a moment, do you have to start from scratch in learning something. More usually, as my walking illustrates, what is required is a refining or a modification of what is known to meet slightly changed circumstances. We shall call this kind of learning *tuning*.[9] Experience gradually tunes our expectancies more and more finely, so that they 'pick up' what is significant to us with increasing accuracy and reliability.

(d) *Learning depends on your priorities*   What you are doing, what you are experimenting with, and therefore what you are learning about depends on what matters to you at the moment. My circumstances on the beach afforded a variety of possibilities for action, of which two were getting to the bar as fast as possible, and sitting down and writing notes about learning. Initially the former was more desirable, so 'walking better' was my learning target. But after a while 'understanding learning better' became a higher priority, so I sat down and started writing notes. Learning about learning took over from learning about walking.

(e) *Learning depends on the general state of the learner*   When you lose your cool, you lose your concentration, and learning suffers. As I was walking, I began to get 'hot and bothered' and my attention was more on the present frustration and the future drink than it was on the stones and my developing walking skills deteriorated. This can lead to a vicious circle of frustration increasing incompetence which increases frustration – a downward spiral with which many school children and teachers-in-training are only too familiar.

(f) *Tuning can proceed without conscious awareness*   By the time I'd noticed what was going on, I had already learnt quite a lot. The unconscious, automatic nature of much of our learning often leads us to underestimate its ubiquity and its importance. Whether we are consciously aware of it or not, much of our everyday life is concerned with testing and tinkering with what we already know. And not only is consciousness not necessary: conscious thought sometimes seems to be a positive hindrance. My thinking about learning to walk didn't seem to improve my walking. And there are many learning situations where 'thinking about it' appears to conflict with 'learning to do it better' – situations of this sort are frequent in psychotherapy, as we shall see. It is as if the conscious activity of deliberating competes with, rather than supports, the processes involved in experiential learning.

(g) *Learning requires some awareness of what's going on*   Although it does not always help to cogitate on what's happening, I cannot learn if I am not attentive to, or aware of the success or failure of my actions at some, not necessarily conscious, level.[10] Though this sounds obvious it is very important, for much hangs on it in what follows.

3.4 Consequences

Our heads are full of expectancies about what to do when, and what the consequences will be. These constitute our experiential theory. At every moment analysis of the outside world suggests to us a range of possibilities – what we have called Antecedents. And the inside world tells us what would be desirable Consequences of action. It is the job of the theory to select or construct an expectancy whose Behaviour will produce the right Consequence. Will a rap on the desk do the trick, or do I need to shout, or give Ray and Charlie detention? Is it too soon to put my hand on her knee? If I give Mum some pink towels for Christmas will she be pleased? Mind's business is to come up with behavioural answers to this constant string of problems. But if it is to get better at doing this, if learning is to take place, one vital ingredient is necessary, and that is a comparison between the *expected consequence*, C_E let us call it, and the actual, *observed consequence*, C_O. Unless we register this match or mismatch, we won't know whether our action succeeded or not, and therefore we won't know whether the expectancy on which that act depended is in need of improvement or replacement. As we shall see, much of experiential learning can be seen as a response to the *recognized violation of expectancy*. We have an expectancy, it fails, we register its failure, and we then set about trying to improve the theory so this kind of upset doesn't happen again. The other major kind of learning is not in response to a wrong answer from our theory, but to its failure to come up with any answer at all. In this case no expectancy exists to be violated, so it can't be modified. A new expectancy has to be designed, built and test-marketed from scratch.

If there is an expected, desirable consequence, then the observed consequence may match it or it may not. If it does, the action is defined to be successful, and all that needs to happen is for the relevant expectancy to be consolidated. That conjunction of A, B, and C becomes more firmly cemented together, and your confidence in its value and accuracy increases. Holding and rocking the baby seems to be an effective strategy for soothing him, so that is the one you always try first. This class, you discover, reliably respond to your jokes, while that one like the firmer touch. The more it works, the higher your confidence in its working.

If what happens is different from what you expected, it can be different in a variety of different ways. It can be a lot different or a little different and, more importantly, it can be nice, neutral or nasty. The kind of learning that occurs depends on the nature of the relationship between C_E and C_O.

3.5 Tuning

The most common form of learning-to-do occurs when you do something, with a more-or-less confident expectation of what the upshot will be, and things don't turn out quite like that. You have an expectancy, the observed consequence isn't a disaster, but the match between it and what you anticipated isn't exact: there is room for improvement. In this case the contours of the 'dunes' involved need changing somewhat. The carefully chosen birthday present receives a rather absent-minded 'Oh, how nice, dear'. What was supposed to be a square cut streaks over the head of second slip. Doubling the quantity of coriander turned out to be not such a good idea.

In order to regain the consequence you desired, you need to modify your specification of what you did, or when you did it, or both. In my walking example, as in most real-life situations, both change together. But there are some circumstances where only a change in perception *or* a change in action is possible. If what you can do, your Behaviour, is fixed, then the only thing to do is try to tune your perception of the Antecedent, the trigger, more finely. Conversely, if the situation is so simple that there is no room for any insights, then it is the action that needs refining. Psychologists have investigated these two, rather artificial, learning contexts extensively, calling the first *classical conditioning* and the second *operant conditioning*. They have often assumed that these are two quite different types of learning.[11] They are not: they are the kinds of learning that result when you are forced to one end or the other of a continuum. Sometimes we reperceive; sometimes we react. Usually we do both!

(a) *Reperceiving*   In the classic classical conditioning experiment,[12] we start with a reflex response. A: dog sees a piece of meat; B: dog salivates in anticipation of C: meat being chewed. Then a bell is rung or a buzzer sounds in unison with the appearance of the meat. What does the dog do? He adds the feature 'sound of meat' (the bell or buzzer) to his specification of A, which already includes 'sight of meat' and 'smell of meat'. He does not have the biological freedom to tinker with B ('how to salivate') (although it does vary slightly), but he can tinker with 'when to salivate'. The buzzer serves as a useful predictor of meat in the same way as the sound of the front door bell or the sound 'Daddy' become, for a nine-month-old baby, useful predictors of Daddy. Or the sound of a key in the lock, an old record, the smell of perfume on a towel, or a voice on the phone come to evoke the same basic responses of fear or excitement. This gradual shifting and sharpening of the dune-scape is therefore not restricted to dogs and babies: it is a general process that operates throughout life. It enables us to generate all our perceptual categories, and without it the wine-taster, medical student, music critic, and chef would be out of business. One particular example of the triggering of emotional reactions by widening contexts is in the development of phobias. An originally neutral, or insignificant object or attribute becomes associated through contiguity with the responses of fear and flight. One intense feeling of terror as a geography teacher advances on you at the age of twelve, with his hand raised and hectoring voice, may become attached to 'male teachers', 'geography', 'this classroom', or even issue in a full 'school-phobia'. Many new teachers discover that traces of these associations still remain in the unbidden 'butterflies' that greet them at the school gates.

(b) *Reacting*   As classical conditioning is associated in the history of psychology with Pavlov, so operant conditioning calls forth the name of B. F. Skinner and his famous box. This box, into which rats and pigeons are put, though not together, in order to learn, allows the learner some freedom about what he can do, but very little about what he can see.[13] This is just the reverse of the Pavlovian situation where the 'response' is more or less fixed, but the 'stimulus' changes. Thus the problem for a rat may be to learn to press a lever down when a red light is on and not to press when a green light is on. For both of these 'correct' actions he is rewarded with a small pellet of something rats like. Throughout the learning session what changes is the nature, effectiveness, precision, frequency, and vigour of the action, B. A is clearly either red or green: there is no more useful information to be extracted however hard the rat pays attention. And the *internal* aspects of the Antecedent – the rat's hunger – also remain constant. (The pellets are small enough so that it takes a very long time for the rat to get full up.) His job is to experiment with his actions so that he eventually comes up with the 'B' part of an expectancy that will reliably produce 'C' – the pellets – in 'A' – the box illuminated red or green. When he first arrives in the Skinner box, the rat hasn't a clue what the game is, of course, let alone how to win. So if you left him to it, it would take a very long time for him, 'by accident', to press the lever with enough force to make the machine pay out. Much better first of all to give him a general very approximate expectancy and then help him to tune it more and more finely. Thus to start with, the rat, to his surprise and delight, gets a pellet whenever he wanders into the half of the box with the lever in. Then gradually the reward is restricted to his being in contact with the lever, pressing the lever, pressing the lever when the red light is on, and so on.

This process whereby someone is helped to tune an expectancy by successive redefinitions of what counts as a successful response, Skinner calls *shaping*. Parents use it extensively in guiding their babies towards such finely tuned performances as walking, talking, or the control of the bladder.[14] In the latter case, for example, an action that originally occurred in response to a single antecedent – the internal sensation of a full bladder – becomes associated with external sensations like the sight of a toilet, the sound of running water, and later, the absence of other people. These become so much bound in to the specification of when to urinate that their control is actually greater than that of the internal sensations. The failure to oblige with a urine sample in a hospital cubicle, or when someone else is present, is not an uncommon experience. Nor is the discovery that turning on a tap and listening to the sound may do the trick.

As we noted before, the mechanism of reacting is like natural selection. Mutations of existing expectancies arise, their actions are emitted as experiments, and the 'fittest' – that is, the most fitting – survive. A mutation that delivers the desired consequence is consolidated. Others are dropped. When expectancies are reasonably well developed, the deliberate attempt to tune them even more finely is called *practising*.

3.6 Investigating

Sometimes you are in a situation that looks familiar, action is required, you know what to do, do it – and it doesn't work. Your expectancy lets you down with a bump. The observed, actual consequence is quite different from your prediction. The feeling that tells you that this has happened we call *surprise*, or *shock* if it is more intense. Tuning often happens automatically, below conscious awareness. Surprise or shock is the grabbing of consciousness by the occurrence of something decidedly unexpected. The shock is due, in the type of learning we are looking at here, entirely to the unexpectedness. What actually happens is not in itself painful or harmful to the learner. (Painful consequences we will look at later.)

Under these circumstances, when there is a sudden conflict between The-Way-It-Spozed-To-Be,[15] according to your theory, and The-Way-It-Is, the best solution is to approach the situation, get involved in it, *investigate* it in order to find out what went wrong and why. Other priorities are shelved for the moment in the interests of updating the theory. Out come the Research and Development team with their microscopes and slide-rules and conical flasks, analyse the conflict, and suggest alternative ways of looking at it that might resolve it. I assume that you will be pleased to see me, so I bounce through the door with a cheery 'Hallo'. Your response is 'Can't you shut the bloody door?', without even raising your eyes from the newspaper. Shock. So I say 'Hey, what's going on? What's the matter?' trying to investigate the antecedent of the upset, and resolve my sudden conflict.

We could if we wished distinguish between relatively passive investigation – simply paying closer attention to the occurrence or thing in question, and a more active attempt to get the strange thing to reveal itself – what we shall call in Chapter 8, when we look at it more closely, *prodding*.

Berlyne, in his *Conflict, Arousal and Curiosity*[16] has proposed a mechanism for the resolution of conflict through investigation. Conflict, he says, increases our arousal, and animals and humans don't like to be over-aroused. So the heightened energy enlists activities that are designed to reduce the arousal level (see Figure 3.2). These activities Berlyne calls rather grandly 'epistemic' or knowledge-seeking. The problem with proposing 'arousal' as the active ingredient in the learning process is that it is not at all easy to measure, and it isn't clear that it is necessary. It looks rather like another answer to the question 'Why do people learn?' that we exposed as being unnecessary in Chapter 2. It has the petrochemical smell of the other redundant activators such as libido, drive or *élan vital*. If we could actually measure it directly, then we would be getting somewhere. But people have proposed lots of different indicators of arousal level that unfortunately don't seem to measure the same thing. Pupil-size, heart-rate, brain activity (EEG), sweatiness (GSR) and physical effort have all been proposed, and all been found wanting.[17] Physical activity, just to take one,

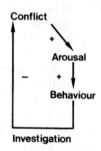

Figure 3.2

sometimes *follows* resolution of a conflict rather than accompanying it. Archimedes leapt out of his bath in response to the solution, not the problem.

It is important to see that investigation is a strategy for reducing a felt conflict between theory and data. If the recognition of the 'violation of expectancy' doesn't happen, no amount of apparent novelty or strangeness in your situation will evoke learning. Most school lessons are novel to the pupils, and many present information that potentially conflicts with what the pupils know or believe. Yet the occurrence of spontaneous approach and investigation is all too rare an event. The conflict has to be felt, it has to *matter*, it has to involve the nonappearance of a desirable consequence, before the learning mechanism grinds into action.

3.7 Dropping

Quite often the most salient thing about an actual consequence is not that something happened that you didn't expect, but that what you did expect *didn't* happen. The feeling that accompanies this experience is therefore not shock but *disappointment*. A hundred times before you have pressed the lever, and a hundred times your delicious pellet has appeared. This time, it doesn't. Every day for the last twenty years you have caught a 14 bus to work. From today, unbeknown to you, they have changed the route. The problem is not a matter of tuning. You can turn up earlier and wait longer, but the bus still won't come. You have to realize that this expectancy doesn't work any more, and drop it. For only if you accept that the old way isn't going to work do you start investigating and experimenting with alternative new ways.

It is very common for us to go through a *sequence of learning strategies* when things start to go wrong. First we try *tuning*. If you stop laughing at my jokes, I try to find funnier stories, or improve my timing, or see if it's something about your mood. (When you are worried about something, you find my humour irritating.) If none of this seems to regain your laughter and affection, I have to *drop* being witty as a way of pleasing you. And, if that is what I want, I have to *investigate* new ways of making sure that you find it worthwhile being with me. Ultimately, if nothing cheers you up, I may have to drop the general expectancy that I can get your love at all, and acknowledge that if love is what I'm after, then I have to look elsewhere – and that may be a very difficult thing to accept.

Rats in boxes do the same. When the pellets stop coming, first they try modifying the previously successful behaviour. They hit the lever harder, or more often, or with their nose instead of their paws. Then they gradually stop pressing altogether and start investigating alternatives. Then if nothing works, they eventually give up.

This process, which Skinner calls 'extinction', demonstrates that the basic function of our theory is to work, to assist us in getting what we need, want or desire. In order to do that it selects and associates recurrent features of the world that predict these significant outcomes. If an expectancy stops working, if it fails to predict, then it is gradually dropped, dismantled or eroded. In other words, C is the major partner in every ABC expectancy, and if C pulls out, then A and B fall apart.

In the early years of 'the psychology of learning' two so-called 'laws' were proposed. The Law of Contiguity said that when things recurred together in your experience, they became stuck together in your mind. More precisely, William James in 1890 proposed: 'When two elementary brain processes have been active together or in immediate succession, one of them, on recurring, tends to propagate its excitement into the other.'[18] This *is* the basic learning mechanism, but it is not, we can see now, the whole story. We do not pick up and register all the possible regularities and patterns in our world. There are far too many, and we don't need to. What we do need to pay attention to are those particular features that are significant to us, and this is caught in the second law, the Law of Effect, which says: if it *works* do it again; if it doesn't, forget it. The two laws are thus complementary. The Law of Effect tells us *when* experiential learning happens, and the Law of Contiguity suggests *how*. Like an umbrella, the significant consequence is the shaft onto which the diverse elements of experience and habit are attached. No shaft, no focus – no expectancy.

Out of Skinner's insights about learning has grown a technology of personal change called 'behaviour modification'.[19] If my actions are controlled by my perceptions of Antecedent and Consequence, then I can change my own or other people's behaviour not by struggling with B directly, but by changing A and/or C. The attempt to change myself through the exercise of 'will' alone is misguided, on the present view, for it ignores the embeddedness of my habits within a complex and deeply intuitive network of associations with their occasions and purposes of use. Let us take an example. Leroy, aged fourteen, a pupil in your class, possesses the following expectancy:

A = You turn round to write on the board
B = He throws things about
C = You attend and speak to him

(For almost everybody, being attended to functions as a desirable consequence some of the time.) What can you do to reduce B? First, you can change A, so that the ABC isn't triggered. You learn the teacher's trick of writing with your back to the board instead of to the class. While this may be effective, note that the ABC remains. It is not unlearnt, just unelicited. Second, you can change C, and there are a number of options open to you. You may stop attending to Leroy when he's naughty, hoping that the expectancy will drop as a result. The trouble with doing just this, as we have just seen, is that the learner's first response to his disappointment is to try tuning, and this means that he will experiment with variations on the theme of B before he gives it up. Now one general expectancy we have learnt, a strategy for coping with disappointment or frustration, is to do what we did before but *more* – harder, faster, longer. 'I wasn't trying hard enough', we believe, or 'More effort will be rewarded: *per ardua ad astra* as they say.' So the first response to your attempts to ignore Leroy may well be an *increase* in his disruptiveness. If a teacher is not alive to this possibility, he is likely to abandon his strategy, and this is disastrous, for Leroy's confidence in his ability to provoke you if he is naughty enough is thereby enhanced, and the expectancy correspondingly strengthened. The way out of this is to offer Leroy an alternative way of getting your attention by making it conditional on a different, incompatible action like sitting down quietly. You don't just ignore him being bad; you notice him being good. The third possible way of changing C is to remove the nice result of doing the original B and replace it with something nasty – a punishment. The whole domain of how people cope with painful consequences is very complicated and we begin to look at it in the next section.

There is another way of altering expectancies which Skinner doesn't recognize, but which follows from my point of view. The relationship between awareness and learning is complicated, as we saw in the example of my learning to walk; but it appears that the more receptive we are to what we are doing, and especially to the match or mismatch between what we expected and the way it actually turned out, the better we learn.[20] The learning mechanism is fuelled not by energy but by awareness, and the degree of awareness that we exercise is variable. Thus an interesting recent development in the Behaviour Modification camp is the promotion of self-awareness in learners. If Leroy can be persuaded to pay attention more closely to his own actions and their consequences – perhaps by getting him to keep a log of them – then he may come to notice that he is generating other consequences, as well as your attention, that are not so desirable, and the expectancy will begin to alter 'naturally', without any more machination on your part. Many programmes for helping people to give up smoking, or eat less, use the device of getting them to record accurately the triggers, both internal (anxiety) and external (meeting strangers), and the physiological consequence of the action to be changed.

People sometimes object to the idea of 'manipulating' other people's behaviour through the explicit use of such techniques. It sounds to them rather sinister and Brave-New-Worldly. It helps to be aware that this is not a new weapon for controlling others, but just a more explicit recognition of what we are doing, naturally but implicitly, all the time. Every time you smile at your husband, your baby, or your class you are saying, 'I like what you just did' and hoping that your approval will be a desirable consequence for them. All our interactions are shaped by the constant trickle of 'rewards' or 'punishments' that we offer to each other. Teachers especially cannot afford to feel too squeamish about altering the course of their pupils' development. It is, after all, what they are paid to do.

3.8 **Rejecting**

Survival is about getting what you need or want, and one of the things we want most is not to get what we don't want. We need to learn to keep away from the nasty stuff just as much as we need to learn to get the nice stuff. And sometimes we get it wrong. We get clobbered, and it hurts. This section is about how we react in the face of unexpected pain – emotional or physical. Aged six, you are playing with the family Dobermann and teasing him, as you have done dozens of times before, by trying to hang from his ears. Suddenly there is a loud snarl and a violent pain as his teeth slice through your jumper into your upper arm. Aged thirty-eight, you arrive home ready to apologize for the things you said and find a note from your wife saying she has had to get away to 'think things out'. In psychology such painful consequences of action are often called *punishments*, even though there may be no intention on anyone else's part that you should suffer, nor any moralistic notions around that you have 'done wrong' or 'broken the rules'.[21]

The problems with punishment stem from the fact that it has a dual nature. On the one hand, it certainly gives you information about how the world works that is worth trying to fit into your theory. It is, objectively, worth investigating in order to find out how it came about, what went wrong, and how to avoid it in future. But on the other hand, it hurts, it has an emotional impact that makes you want to *escape without learning*. It would be stupid of the six-year-old to bite his lip and experiment with the amount of ear-pulling that the dog will tolerate. Depending on which of these two tendencies predominates, we will either adopt the learning solution (approach and investigate) or the no-learning solution: escape from the situation by eliminating the source of the pain (kill the dog) or by running away. These two strategies – fight and flight – are our way of ensuring survival but without improving our theory. As we shall see, the human being possesses a variety of other ways for neutralizing his painful experience without learning about it. The abandoned husband is quite likely to drink himself to sleep, for example.

Out of this conflict comes a variety of different effects that people, especially those like teachers who use punishment deliberately, should be aware of. First, as we saw with phobias, punishment can lead to generalized aversion to teacher, subject, books, or school. Whether this will happen and to what extent is very hard to predict in any particular case. But it is a risk. Second, punishment leads to suppression of an expectancy, not its dissolution. The expectancy is rejected lock, stock, and barrel, but it is not unlearnt. Skinner's understanding of this, as expressed in Bower and Hilgard's *Theories of Learning*,[22] is very clear. 'A response cannot be eliminated from the organism's repertoire more rapidly with the aid of punishment than without it. Permanent weakening comes about only by nonreinforced elicitation – and this weakening process may be prevented if punishment suppresses the response. This is in line with clinical findings about forms of aggressive or hostile responses which have come under parental or other social punishment. They are not eliminated until they can be brought to free expression, when the behaviour can be appropriately redirected.'

When a person rejects a part of his theory, rather than retunes or dismantles it, what happens is that one expectancy becomes overlaid by another, stronger one. By 'overlaid' I mean that they share the same A, the same trigger, but because the C of the new expectancy is painful, the B that is immediately attached is 'escape' or 'neutralize' or 'avoid' – or, if all else fails, 'ignore'. The major principle becomes the successful avoidance of hurt, even if this entails the loss of the previously valued outcome. Being deeply hurt by being abandoned by a loved one, for example, may lead to a lifetime's avoidance of a repetition of that experience, but we cannot do this without also suppressing our deep desire for love and intimacy. The risk is just too great. The only way out of this trap is to decrease the fear of the hurt so that the buried desire has another chance to be tried out and, if necessary, adjusted to fit more successfully with reality. Only if I overcome my fear of all relationships can I begin to update my experiential feel for those that work. This process is what therapy is about, and we shall have a lot more to say about it later.

A third effect of punishment is that it creates a behavioural vacuum: it tells you forcefully what not to do, but it does not on its own tell you what to do instead. It can lead therefore, if no clues are given, to a dithery, nervous way of being in which one doesn't know what to do, and dare not find out. Fourth, as we have pointed out already, being punished may lead to an *increase* in the ineffective or undesired activity. This is especially likely if a teacher does not realize that what he considers to be aversion is actually attractive. To him it's a detention: to the student it's attention, and an opportunity not to have to be alone at home, before Mum gets back, with her older brother who teases and bullies her.

Fifth, the act of punishing someone else changes the way the punisher – the teacher, say – behaves, and this may have counter-productive side-effects. Suppose the children's naughtiness is a way of making you anxious, and your anxiety is their desired consequence. You respond by shouting at them and reprimanding them, but the confrontations involved make you even more anxious. The change in you as you try to change them undermines your intention, and actually delivers to the class what they want – on a plate. Difficult classes become very skilled at winding teachers up in this way.

Sixth, punishment, especially prolonged punishment, can have a long-term detrimental effect on a learner's self-esteem, and therefore on his ability as a learner. To get punished is to fail – to fail to predict and avoid a nasty consequence. Often there is no way you could have done so. The teacher may have had a row with his wife, or last night's staff meeting agreed a general 'toughening-up' on trouble-makers. But some people choose to blame themselves for their 'failures', even the unavoidable ones. 'It failed' becomes 'I failed', and 'I failed' becomes 'I'm a failure'. Thus one's theory about oneself as a learner incorporates this perception, and one comes to see oneself as a helpless victim, rather than a fallible changer of the course of events. If the punishment is dished out inconsistently – that is, in a way that does not depend on what you are doing – then this *learned helplessness*, as it has been called, is the only thing you can learn.[23] You learn that nothing you do works, so you might as well do nothing. The problem with this depressing conclusion is that if your world starts being consistent again, you neither notice nor exploit the consistency. You remain locked up in a cage of resignation, even though the jailer has withdrawn the bolts and gone away. It has been suggested that the state that we call *depression* is actually a manifestation of this learned helplessness.

3.9 Floundering

In our discussions so far we have focused mainly on what happens to expectancies that don't work: they get modified, they get dismantled, or they get suppressed. Now we need to redress the balance by looking at strategies we possess for throwing up possible improvements. We have acknowledged that an expectancy has let us down, we want to sort it out, and we are prepared to investigate and experiment. Or quite frequently we want to achieve something, but our theory doesn't have an answer at all. We are moving into terrain that is as yet uncharted. If we have enough time, resources and self-confidence for the expedition, the feeling-signal is *interest*. But if the world is pressing us for the solution to a problem that we don't feel sure of coming up with, then we experience *anxiety*, or perhaps more commonly we say we feel *nervous*. To 'suffer from nerves' is to feel that immanence of being found wanting as a recurring theme in one's life. The constant suspicion of one's own incompetence is a staging-post on the way to the firm belief in one's own incompetence that underlies the depression which we have just discussed.

Except in such situations as being tortured for information we do not possess, this pervasive sense of despair is a matter not of fact but of belief. But we all experience this nervousness quite appropriately whenever we are about to do something *for the first time*. Your first lesson as a teacher, your first day at primary school, your first date, your first time on skis, all present you with a situation that you do not yet know how to handle. There is an Antecedent, a desirable Consequence, but no B to get you from one to the other. What do you do?

The simplest, but most inefficient thing to do, is just *flounder*. Thorndike, in the early days of psychology, put cats in a box and looked to see how they learnt the trick of getting out. What they did was wander around, or thrash about until, by accident, they pulled the catch that opened the door. When they had done it once or twice, they began to investigate the catch rather more intently, and gradually developed a more organized and economical solution to the problem. We do just the same. First we flounder around till we generate an expectancy that works, however vaguely, and *then* we can start to investigate and tune it. You can experience this sequence quite readily for yourself by learning a new skill like roller-skating or diving backwards. Initially you don't have any expectancy about how to do it, or even what it would feel like if you did it right. But you *do* have the ability to imagine what it would feel like if you did it wrong. You will land on your bottom, or do a nasty belly-flop; people may laugh, and it will hurt. So there is an incentive to get it right, but you don't know how. In these examples, you can't even rely on other people to help you. The first time I went ice-skating I was taken by my eleven-year-old cousin. 'How do I do it?' I asked. 'It's easy' she replied. 'Like this . . .' and sailed off. 'That's all very well,' I said when she glided back, 'but what do I do?' She looked exasperated. 'It's easy. You just do it!'

In this kind of learning the moment when the first expectancy is formed comes with an almost audible click. The dive *feels* right, or just for a few moments you *know* you are skating. The subsequent processes of tuning and experimenting may take years, but the division between believing that you can't, and knowing that you can, is very often stark and unforgettable. If the pain, either physical or psychological, of failure is too great the first attempt may be literally make-or-break. If it's a disaster, you give up. But if it sort-of-works, then the hope of success will outweigh the fear of failure, and a star (or at least a trier) is born. Of course, how much failure you can take before chucking it in depends on who you are. Not only your will to succeed but your whole personality is important. But more on that later.[24]

3.10 Experimenting

The more common situation is one in which your theory generates some possible leads, some *experiments* to try, but without much confidence in any of them. Floundering is a vital strategy for babies, but as we get older it is not common that we find ourselves in the position of 'not having a clue'. Instead we have to emit trial actions that have some basis (normally unconscious) in existing theory, but for which the proof of the pudding can only be established in the eating. There being no clear favourite, you have to bet on an outsider; play your hunches. This sort of learning is more like the early stages of a scientific inquiry, where the scientist is guessing, trying out different ways of looking at the problem and different times of attack, than it is like the careful testing of well-formulated hypotheses.

Where these hunches come from, and what their rationale is, is a tricky question. We shall have more to say about this when we talk about creativity and 'gumption'. But two ways of generating guesses are fairly easy to spot. They are *bridging* and *imitating*.

3.11 Bridging

This strategy is a kind of problem solving or deduction, but we have to be careful about the use of these terms. Usually they refer to processes that are conscious, deliberate, logical, and very often verbal. Here I am talking about processes that are experiential, automatic and, for the most part, tacit. The problem that we face is: given A and a desirable C, but no ready-made or readily modifiable ABC to link them together, can we create a *bridge* between them from existing ABCs? If the present situation is A1, and the desirable consequence is C*, can I find a bridge like this:

$$A1 + B1 \rightarrow \begin{cases} C1 \\ A2 + B2 \rightarrow \begin{cases} C2 \\ A3 + B3 \rightarrow C^* \end{cases} \end{cases}$$

B1 will produce the consequence C1, which is a situation which enables me to use B2 in order to get C2. This in turn provides an appropriate context for the application of B3 which – if all goes according to plan – should result in C*. The process is like trying to work out how to get by car from Harrods to Waterloo Station: you may be able to do it, even though you have never been over that exact route before, by piecing together different sections that you do know. Sometimes this results in a high confidence solution that works; sometimes you will try it out and find that it works with modifications (you forgot that you can't turn right going east along the Strand across Waterloo Bridge, so you have to make a detour around the Aldwych); and sometimes it only gives you a long-shot. But you may be able to avoid the insecurity of the pure flounder.

The Gestalt psychologists such as Köhler claimed to observe this kind of learning in animals – especially apes and monkeys.[25] For example Sultan, Köhler's brightest ape, was provided with two short sticks that would fit together to make a longer one, and a banana was left outside his cage. Neither stick alone was long enough to reach it, but the longer composite stick would. After a while Sultan fitted the two sticks together, raked in the banana, and solved the problem. A1 is the two short sticks; B1 is fitting them together; and C1 is the longer stick. Now C1 becomes A2 which enables B2 – raking in the banana – to get C2, the banana in the cage. Sultan can then rattle off a well-learnt string of ABCs which involve picking up the banana, peeling it, and so on, to obtain C*: banana inside Sultan.

Whether or not any of this went through Sultan's consciousness is an unanswerable question, but it is certain that adult people can construct complicated bridges in conscious awareness as well as tacitly. When this happens we call it *imagination*, and it seems to be a strategy that is valuable but under-used in our present culture. Sports coaches, for example, are increasingly making use of imagination to help people improve their skills. To take time to construct internally as clear a sense as possible of what the right shot would look like, sound like and feel like seems to be a good investment.[26] Some sportsmen and sportswomen know that they use this strategy automatically. Tony Jacklin described in an interview in *The Sunday Times* some years ago how a vital part of his golf was to create the right 'mental model' of every shot. To put it in computer terms, what he first has to do is write the appropriate program for his shot, and then 'run' it – that is, actually hit the ball. Unless the intention is right, the right action can only arise as a fluke. And imagining the perfect drive appears to be a most valuable way of ensuring that the intention is as clear and as accurate as possible.

3.12 Imitating

The second useful strategy for avoiding the risks of total trial-and-error is to use someone else as an example. If you don't know how to get X, watch how somebody else goes about getting it. Children derive a lot of useful hints from their observation of adults; and adults too are well advised to spend time watching skilful exponents of complex arts like teaching and batting, or listening to top-class players of instruments they are trying to learn. There are a number of points to be made about this 'observational learning'.

First, like the other strategies we have considered, doing what others do is by no means an infallible guide to success. A young child, wanting his Mummy's attention at the dinner table, notices that when Daddy swears Mummy puts her hand on his arm and looks at him. So Junior tries it, and gets a lot more attention than he anticipated. Often when the learner is small and the model is big, imitation doesn't work, because many of the background conditions that enable the adult to perform successfully are not present for the child. His strength or authority or use of language may let him down, his relationship to those he is trying to influence is quite different, and so on. In general we need to distinguish observational learning, as a useful but fallible strategy for generating ideas about how to achieve particular goals from rigid imitation, where the habits of the model are not taken as clues but are snatched off-the-peg in an unreal attempt to 'become' the model. It is a vain hope that, by apeing the hair-style, voice, walk, clothes and mannerisms of *Kate Bush* or *Barry Sheene*, one will automatically reap the rewards of fame and wealth that the models have obtained. This is a step away from reality, for it prevents my more modest exploration of what-works-for-me. It ignores the considerations of *my* character and *my* circumstances.

Secondly, to take someone else as an example, especially in the long-term transmission of a skill, requires a particular kind of relationship between Master and Apprentice. The Apprentice has to trust and respect the Master for his ability and judgement: the Master has to be patient and perceptive about the apprentice's progress, and (hopefully) has the latter's development at heart, rather than wishing to keep him in the role of tea-boy or slave. Michael Polanyi in *Personal Knowledge* spells this out:

> To learn by example is to submit to authority. You follow your master because you trust his manner of doing things even when you cannot analyse and account in detail for its effectiveness. By watching the master and emulating his efforts in the presence of his example, the apprentice unconsciously picks up the rules or the art, including those that are not explicitly known to the master himself. These hidden rules can be assimilated only by a person who surrenders himself to that extent uncritically to the imitation of another.

Observational learning is, I believe, undervalued by adults in our culture. They do not think that anything worthwhile is happening unless they are *doing*: their trust in the learning process working 'of itself' is not high enough. Sitting quietly and receptively watching a good model at work is an enormously productive inactivity, for we are constantly absorbing, at a tacit level, hints and notions, finesses of touch and timing, that inform and enhance our own practice. In religious instruction, for example, the principle of absorbing the Master's wisdom, serenity, and style just through observation is of paramount importance. A Zen story tells of a Master who accepted a boy as a disciple and for three years gave him no 'instruction' at all. When at last the boy complained that he wasn't being taught anything, the Master turned on him in (probably mock) astonishment. 'What?' he said. 'When you bring me my tea, do I not acknowledge you? When you bow to me, do I not return the bow? I have done nothing but teach you for these three years.' The Christian Mass or Communion should remind us of the same thing, for it celebrates the essential characteristics of observational learning: the surrender to an example; absorbing and digesting, rather than learning explicitly or intentionally; and its organismic, physical rather than cerebral or intellectual basis. Christ's metaphorical instruction to his disciples captures all of this. 'Take, eat, this is my body which is given for you . . . feed on it in thy heart by faith with thanksgiving.' Learn how to be like me by feeding on my example.

3.13 Off-duty Learning

Most of the learning situations we have looked at up till now occur when we are 'on-duty'. We are going about our business and suddenly learning is required. We cannot say 'Stop the world, I want to get off': we are on-stage, sometimes a very public stage, and when our theory dries up, we cannot take time out to look at the script. We have to improvise, muddle through, carry it off as best we can. It is these upsets to our illusion of omniscience that are signalled by the 'negative' feelings of shock, threat, disappointment, and anxiety. Happily we possess another strategy which we can use to minimize or circumvent these upsets: when the world is demanding very little from us, and we therefore feel quite safe, we can create mock-ups of potentially disturbing events, and *play* with them. In these off-duty, self-initiated and self-selected situations we can keep the uncertainty within tolerable limits, and so feel freer to try things out and run the risk of making a mess of it. We can rehearse in front of the mirror, practise in the nets, sing in the bath, and try out new recipes on our families.

We might distinguish three different forms of play, depending on whether we start out with a clear specification of a desired consequence or not, and on what we are trying to refine. When we know where we want to go, and are experimenting with different ways of getting there, we are voluntarily creating contexts within which to use the learning strategies that this chapter has described. But when we take a jump 'just for the fun of it', or 'just to see what happens', the outcome is to some extent uncertain, and we call this *exploration*. Berlyne, whose little diagram we used in Section 3.6, has proposed that we explore when our arousal level falls too low.[27] He suggested, you remember, that people do not like to be over-aroused. But conversely, we do not like to be under-aroused either. So we can add another side to his picture (see Figure 3.3). Deprivation of stimulation leads to a lowering of arousal that we seek to redress. But the solution this time is not to investigate in order to resolve discrepancies, but to explore in order to generate some.

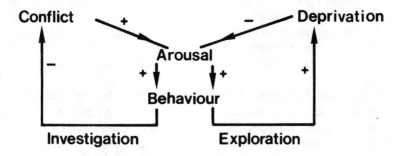

Figure 3.3

Up to a point, we look for uncertainty. Especially if we anticipate real threats to survival, we may seek to generate safer analogues within which we can play with ways of coping. Thus children who grow up in tough neighbourhoods may develop a pseudo-tough act at a very early age in order to create small-scale replicas of the confrontations they fear they will meet in adolescence. In these rehearsals they can develop the skills of physical and verbal assault that the adults they admire use with considerable panache and success. Young animals of all kinds, who will need to be aggressive adults, indulge in such conflict-generating explorations.

The other two strategies, both aimed at off-duty tuning of existing expectancies, we might call *playing* (proper) and *practising*. Practising involves the attempt to replicate a successful action so that all the relevant features of doing and sensing are consolidated. Playing I will define here as the deliberate variation of an expectancy, so that irrelevant 'superstitious' features are discovered and dropped. Thus practising makes an action more *effective*, while playing makes it more *economic*. These strategies are described in more detail in Section 8.6.

3.14 The Feel of Learning

Those aspects of our conscious awareness that we attribute to the outside world we call 'perceptions'. Those that we assume to be internal in origin we call 'body sensations' or feelings, emotions, and moods. Usually 'emotion' is treated in psychology in two ways; as separate from other areas, like thinking or learning; and as a phenomenon that can be treated as a unit, so that when we have explained 'emotion' we have explained all the varieties and shades of emotion. Here I want to deal with emotion in exactly the reverse way: by starting with particular experiences that we call feelings, and by linking them explicitly to thinking and learning. Several of our most common, everyday feelings are best seen as awarenesses that certain kinds of learning are actually taking place or are imminent. It is on these that we shall focus here.

We have already mentioned some of these learning-feelings, but now we can tie them together. At the same time we can give some indication of how the different learning modes that we have identified are used. We can give the strategies and feelings a place in an overall picture of experiential learning that is presented as a flow diagram in Figure 3.4. (This is not meant to be definitive, nor could it be. The precise strategies used, their sequence and their emotional timbre will vary from person to person and task to task. It is illustrative only of the kind of way in which the substance of this chapter could begin to be formalized.) Let us follow it through. First, I keep asking myself what I need or want to do. Usually there will be a stack of such goal-orientated priorities, each specifying a desirable consequence to be obtained. If, at the moment of my asking, there is no such specific goal, then there will always be some general priorities that 'bridge the gap'. Two of these are recuperation (REST) and EXPLORATION. If nothing much is going on, I can take the opportunity either to allow time for the physiological processes that require inactivity to repair me, or I can go looking for some action. Through play and exploration I can create conflicts that will themselves require action, resolution and learning. The feeling of having no specific needs that one is willing or able to do anything about, but without feeling tired, we call *boredom*.

If there are some things on my agenda, then I have to check out which of them have a chance of being fulfilled within the confines of my present circumstances. This process of selecting an expectancy on the basis of the external and internal inputs to my theory we discussed in Chapter 2. The question to be answered is: can I find an expectancy that will enable me to produce, with a reasonable degree of *confidence*, one of the states of affairs that will *please* or *satisfy* me? (In this section, strategies I can adopt are indicated by capital letters; feelings are in italics.) If I find an acceptable expectancy off-the-peg, then I can ACT it out. The state of awareness in which I execute such an action is *security*: I feel safe, at home, *comfortable*.

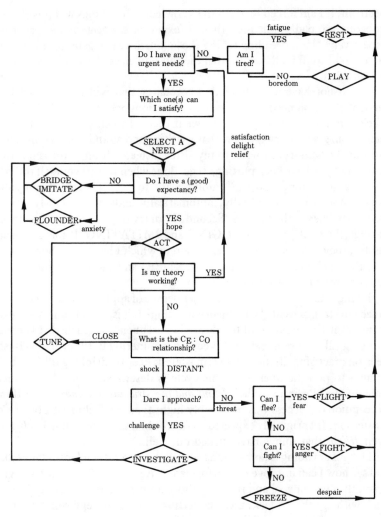

Figure 3.4

Everything is routine. But if the action that I eventually emit is not gilt-edged, then the feeling changes. When my confidence is quite high, but tinged with doubt, I feel *hopeful*. The feeling of hope always contains an awareness of at least the possibility of failure. If I act without much confidence at all, I feel *anxious, insecure*, or *nervous*. At the other end of the spectrum, if I am forced to act in the knowledge that things will possibly or probably go badly for me, then I experience *apprehension* or *dread* respectively. 'I am dreading taking those fourth years again' means I have got to, and I confidently expect that the consequences of my doing so will be *un*desirable.

If I do not have a ready-made expectancy that will reliably satisfy a particular current need, then I have three options open to me. The first is to check through the other needs, to see if there is an easy way of satisfying them. I can give up struggling with my writing and go and make a cup of tea, sort out the laundry, or write to my sister instead. (It often turns out that things that you have been putting off get done when you set yourself the task of doing something you *really* don't want to do.) The mind-computer usually does this very rapidly, automatically and unconsciously, so no feeling attaches to the process. Second, I can try to generate an expectancy through the strategies of BRIDGING and IMITATING. If these are successful, they will come up with an action in which I have some hope, but if not, the final alternative is to FLOUNDER, and the uncertainty of the outcome manifests itself to me as *anxiety*.

Having acted, with a greater or lesser degree of apprehension, I then have to see how things went. Is my theory working? If it is, then I simply keep on doing what I'm doing until the desired consequence is reached. I keep on studying till the exam is passed, keep on hammering until the nail is flush, keep on practising till the sonata is mastered, keep on drinking till I am bold enough to pop the question. This cycle is described in detail by Miller, Galanter and Pribram in their *Plans and the Structure of Behaviour*.[28] If my expectation of success was reasonably high, then my feeling will be one of *satisfaction*. If I originally expected some trouble, then the feeling is *relief*, or even *delight* that things have turned out well.

If what I am doing is not working so well, however, then I must take stock and see how I can improve my performance. Again, one possibility is to give up on the current goal and turn my efforts towards a different one. But if I stick with my chosen task, then the feeling and the strategy will depend on how severe I judge my failure to be. If I can, I will try to get away with TUNING my expectancy. If not, if I have experienced *surprise* or *disappointment* or *shock* of a more persistent or recurrent or dramatic kind, then the next decision I have to make is: How safe is the situation now? Dare I approach and become involved, or should I say 'Thanks but no thanks' to the learning opportunity, and remove myself from it rather than try to master it?

When I dare to engage with the conflict, my feelings are *interest*, *involvement*, *intrigue*, *fascination*, and *absorption*. In general, I feel the learning as a *challenge*. On the borderline between approach and avoidance there is a complex feeling of uncertainty that may alternate between *excitement* and *anxiety*. Many of the fast-moving attractions (or repulsions) of the fairground are masterfully designed to induce this state. And if the answer to 'Dare I?' is 'No', then the situation is felt to be not a challenge but a *threat*, and the strategies of avoidance come into play. If possible, I will take to FLIGHT – run back to Mummy, cover my eyes in the scary bits of the movie, or leave the examination hall after the compulsory half an hour. The feeling that accompanies flight, or the intention to flee, is *fear*. If flight is blocked (either physically or psychologically) the next line of defence is FIGHT. If I can't escape from it, I can try to destroy it. The energy flips, so to speak, from the legs to the arms – instead of running, I punch – and the feeling may likewise flip from fear into *anger*. These two sides are seen clearly in animals' territorial disputes.[29] My territory is that place, by definition, from which I cannot run: so long as I see it *as* mine, I have to fight. The intruder, on the other hand, does not have this conflict: if things get too tough, he can leave. Thus it is, to move back to the human world, that home wins in football are more common than away wins, and the points scored for predicting a win at home correspondingly less. The final strategy for escaping from threat, if it cannot be avoided or destroyed, is to neutralize not the source of the threat but the experience of it, by FREEZING one's awareness of the disturbing emotion. We shall have much more to say about this in Chapters 6 and 7.

An interesting shift in the feel of learning occurs when we bring other people into the picture. The feelings we have discussed so far are appropriate regardless of the object or circumstances of learning. But what happens, for example, in the particular case when we perceive, rightly or wrongly, that someone else is determining, or at least influencing, the outcomes of our actions? Now our feelings begin to get entangled with our beliefs about how others ought to treat us. I ask you, a friend, to lend me your loudspeakers for a party, expecting you to say 'Yes'. You refuse. The basic feeling for this event is disappointment, but because you are human, it all gets more complicated than that. I *resent* your not complying with my request and *blame* you for letting me down. I feel *estranged* from you, I *distrust* you, I feel *hurt* by you, *confused* about what your refusal means. (Have I *upset* you? Do you *dislike* me? Are you being *spiteful*? Are you *angry* with me?). I am inclined to indulge in a convoluted process of attribution and rationalization (described in Section 2.6), all of which makes me feel worse for longer and all of which is quite irrelevant to the problem of getting the party organized. Friendships frequently founder on less than this. But somehow it must be worth it. The friend is lost, the suffering protracted, the party ruined – and for what? For the sake of my belief that friends do not refuse each others' requests. And if they do, then my belief can only be salvaged from the scrap-heap by scrapping the friendship. By refusing to accept the transient feeling of disappointment, I have bought myself a permanent sense of disillusionment instead.[30]

Our over-reaction to shock when it involves another person whom we hold to be responsible is nicely shown by the Zen story of the empty boat. A young man was rowing across a lake when his boat hit something. Startled, he turned round and saw that he had run into an empty boat that had drifted into his path. Shrugging his shoulders he rowed on until, a few minutes later, there was another bump. Turning round, he saw another boat with an old man in it. This time the young man was furious and shouted at the old man for minutes on end. (The question that a Zen Master now asks his students is: 'Is it possible to *be* an empty boat?')

If people fail to live up to our Pollyanna attitude that it is their duty to protect and assist us, we punish them with our resentment. If they do deliver us from evil and deliver us the goods, we reward them with our *gratitude*, our *trust*, and our *approval*. We may even award them ourselves, and insist that they play our game, and be the Fairy Prince, forever. Sheldon Kopp's marvellous book *An End to Innocence*[31] subjects many of these myths about how others are to behave towards us to an eloquent and penetrating analysis.

Let me comment further on a few of the emotions that have particular associations with learning. *Frustration* is the name we give to the mounting sense of irritation and incompetence that accompanies a succession of disappointments. Bruner, Goodnow, and Austin comment on this: 'One characteristic of cognitive activity is that it has associated with it some rather unique affective states. The sense of tension that occurs when we cannot "place" someone . . . the malaise of the trained mind faced with a seemingly causeless effect . . . are as characteristic of frustrated cognitive activity as desire is of blocked sexual activity.'[32] On the other hand there is the equally characteristic sense of satisfaction that accompanies the solution of such a puzzle – when we recall the name, resolve the paradox, or 'do it right' for the first time. 'Got it!' we say with a smile, or 'Ah Ha!', or 'Eureka!' even. It seems that Nature has endowed us not only with signals for when learning is required, and of what kind, but also with intrinsically pleasurable signals of its successful completion. When we hit the jackpot of learning, our feelings pay out automatically. We don't just become more competent: we feel good too.

We have mentioned *boredom*, but it is worth contrasting with *indifference*, and that kind of pseudo-boredom that is a form of *disdain*. Boredom is an uncomfortable state that is removed by the initiation of exploration and play. If there is no overlap at all between the things I find desirable and the things I find possible at the moment, then I am temporarily stuck. A solution is to shuffle the set of possibilities by changing my circumstances. But if this too is denied, as in the padded cell of a Jumbo jet, then the boredom is felt. In contrast, indifference is the feeling we get in the face of events that are so predictable and familiar, and are of such little moment to us that there is to all intents and purposes no learning to be done. Prolonged indifference leads to boredom. The third member of this trio is a form of disdain or contempt that has its roots in fear and masquerades as boredom. Its focus is not on the inclination to find something else to do, but on the disinclination to do whatever is currently on hand, because it is threatening. People affect to be bored with things that they suspect they are failing, or might fail, at. I have caught myself, for example, professing boredom with fixing my motor-bike, playing bridge and bar football – all things that, on closer inspection, I see I actually don't feel confident about. And I cope with the discomfort that this causes by denying the value of the activity, or my interest in it. School children use this ploy a lot. 'It's *boring*, Sir' they chorus, whether it really is or not.

These different feelings are the 'feel' of learning: they are the way learning feels to us. They are not optional extras, any more than the feel of the wind against my skin, or the sweet taste of sugar are optional. I can be aware of the sensations of anxiety or coolness or sweetness, or not, but I cannot choose to have them go away. They are of the essence. It follows that anxiety, fear, disappointment, and the rest are not nuisances to be resisted. They are inevitable and useful facets of learning. They are the way learning signals itself to us. Your theory has just been found wanting, they say: if you want to improve your chances of survival, or simply of getting on with the notoriously difficult Deputy Head, you had better engage your learning strategies. Thus anxiety is not something to be fought or denied or hidden or ashamed of. If you accept the fact of your own recurrent incompetence, it is an ally, not a foe. It is stupid to feel threatened by noticing that the petrol gauge reads almost empty: it is not out to get you but inform you. Just so, the feelings we have been talking about are 'learning gauges'. Yet for reasons we shall explore later we have all been brought up with the contrary attitude. These affective indicators of our fallibility *are* threatening, and we turn our eyes away, put on a bold front, bluster, and ignore them. We assure our colleagues that everything is fine, and keep the depression and the tears, when they cannot be contained any longer, for the privacy of our rooms.

Anxiety, we have said, lies at the boundary between challenge and threat. But we need to say something about where this boundary lies, and how it shifts. First, we should note that the decision as to whether any learning opportunity constitutes a challenge to be taken up or a threat to be eliminated is a subjective one, and therefore depends on such cloudy variables as self-confidence, self-esteem, and self-image as well as on the 'actual' disparity between theory and data. A challenge is a conflict that I hope I can resolve, and feel some confidence in my ability to do so. A threat is a conflict or problem that I do not anticipate being able to sort out through my own efforts, and whose solution is important to my survival. Thus while some problems are threats for almost everyone (remember the nightmare problem of being tortured for information you do not possess), the variations between people, and between an individual's perceptions at different times, are immense. If I have been told that my last essay was excellent, I may feel up to querying the pontifications of the lecturer who *nobody* interrupts. Paradoxically (and unfairly), if I know that Elaine thinks I'm terrific, I may feel good enough about myself to risk rejection by Lizzie. If I see that Sarah, who in my estimation is no great brain-box, has mastered Rubik's Cube, then I may feel spurred into having another go at the damn thing myself. (This effect accounts for the snowballing popularity of the Cube, by the way. When it first appeared it was perceived by most people as far too difficult to attempt. But as more and more people mastered it, so others reassessed their own chances of success, and began to fiddle with it too.)

David McClelland[33] has identified two relevant and antagonistic feelings which he calls 'hope of success' and 'fear of failure'. If hope exceeds fear, you have a shot at it. If the fear wins, you don't. For confident learners, hope generally wins; for unconfident learners, fear generally wins. In one study, McClelland showed that these two groups of people had quite different attitudes to *actual* success or failure at a task. The confident ones attributed success to their own ability, and failure to a lack of effort or bad luck. The unconfident ones, however, put their successes down to good luck, and their failures to lack of ability. As Hazlitt said (in an epigram quoted in a recent advertising campaign for vodka), 'As is our confidence, so is our capacity.' Some unfortunate people's estimates of their own chances of learning are so low that they will not even experiment with chop-sticks in a Chinese restaurant, and dare not deviate from the syllabus for a moment lest something unexpected happens. (Hazlitt is not perfectly right, of course. Reckless optimism is as counter-productive as groundless pessimism. The ideal state is one in which our feeling is an accurate predictor of our ability. When it is not, we either give up too soon, or waste our time and effort bashing our heads against a brick wall.)

The feeling that accompanies giving up is *despair*.[34] Giving up may mean either dropping the problem entirely, or, if that is not possible, continuing, but in an unintelligent, slack, going-through-the-motions kind of way. Even were we to stumble on a solution in this frame of mind we probably would not recognize it. Sometimes in the course of solving a problem an unexpected setback can flip us from the hope-of-success state, in which we are approaching the task with awareness and resourcefulness because we think we can do it, into the despairing and despondent, 'I'll never be able to do it' state that is dominated by fear of failure. In fact this fear becomes a self-fulfilling prophecy because we have lost our *gumption*. Gumption is an old-fashioned word that has been revived by Robert Pirsig in his *Zen and the Art of Motor-Cycle Maintenance*,[35] and it means, roughly, the ability to remain intelligent in the face of temporary frustration. It means being able to review and reevaluate the new situation, so that I can discover ways of achieving the desirable consequence other than the one that has just failed. It means, as Tony Jacklin said recently of his lengthy exile in the golfing wilderness, not giving up the whole game when you miss another three foot putt. Pirsig calls these upsets *gumption traps*, and illustrates their operation nicely with the example of fixing a motor-bike. All is going well until you ruin the head of a screw, and it now becomes impossible to shift with a screwdriver. Or, to take another case, a well-prepared lesson with a usually friendly class begins to go wildly wrong. Frustration wells up, you are unable to look reasonably at what might be required, and all you want to do is set fire to the bike or machine-gun the wretched class. In such cases we become so identified with what is desirable that we lose touch entirely with what is possible.

Gumption traps are so powerful because they are more than disappointing: they are invalidating. Suddenly I am exposed as less than I hope or believe myself to be. Less competent, less knowledgeable, less powerful, less in control. If I have a deep investment in seeing myself in a certain way, as 'capable' or 'attractive' let us say, then even a joke about my class control or the size of my ears may feel like a body blow. As we have seen, fear and anger and despair are feelings that accompany nonlearning, self-preservation responses to threat. When even a wrecked screw or a good-natured jibe evoke such responses, something has gone wrong with our learning mechanism. Somehow the subjective definition of survival has become too broad. We shall return to this later.[36]

CHAPTER 4

REMEMBERING AND UNDERSTANDING

A MEMORABLE FANCY

I was in a Printing house in Hell, and saw the method in which knowledge is transmitted from generation to generation.

In the first chamber was a Dragon-Man, clearing away the rubbish from a cave's mouth; within, a number of Dragons were hollowing the cave.

In the second chamber was a Viper folding round the rock and the cave, and others adorning it with gold, silver and precious stones.

In the third chamber was an Eagle with wings and feathers of air: he caused the inside of the cave to be infinite; around were numbers of Eagle-like men who built palaces in the immense cliffs.

In the fourth chamber were Lions of flaming fire, raging around and melting the metals into living fluids.

In the fifth chamber were Unnam'd forms, which cast the metals into the expanse.

There they were receiv'd by Men who occupied the sixth chamber, and took the forms of books and were arranged in libraries.

The eagle never lost so much time as when he submitted to learn of the crow.

Intricate though it has turned out to be, we have as yet told less than half of the story of human learning. In fact, although most of my examples have been to do with human beings, nearly all of what we have covered so far is equally applicable to at least the higher reaches of the animal kingdom. Animals learn solely through their experience, and they have at their disposal all of the apparatus that we encountered in the previous chapter.

Although it is anthropomorphic to attribute awareness to animals, and ultimately unprovable, I see no good reason for not doing so. But human beings alone, with the arguable exception of a few chimpanzees, possess language.[1] Certainly animals communicate: the moth and the musk deer through the sense of smell, birds through their calls, monkeys through their touch and their posture. And they can learn from each other, as humans do, through observation and imitation. But they do not code their theories into complex strings of symbols and trade them with anything like the ubiquity, sophistication, and enthusiasm that we do. Indeed when we think about human learning it is often the commerce in these symbols that we automatically assume to be the key. Contemporary psychological theory and educational practice place a much greater emphasis on the acquisition of verbal knowledge than on the development of skill. Linguistics has even tried to understand our use of language solely in its own terms, without reference at all to the nonlinguistic, experiential knowledge on which, it seems to me, it must be parasitic.[2] Thus when we turn to the study of learning through words we need to address the following questions. What is the nature of language? What is its relationship to our nonlinguistic knowledge? How do we learn through language? And how is language itself learnt? The last of these we shall leave till we look at the learnings of young children in Chapter 8. The remainder are what this chapter is about.

4.1 The Map of the Map

The shifting dune-scape of our experiential knowledge is a theory about how the world works. More accurately, it is a theory about how me-in-the-world works, for, as we have seen, I cannot separate my perception of my world from the things I want from it and the things I can do to it. To be more accurate still, the dune-scape is not the theory: it is a way of representing or talking about the theory. I cannot exhibit my theory or anybody's theory *directly*: I have to turn it into words and pictures and, through offering you these pointers and allusions, hope that you can recreate an understanding that is not too far from my own. I can never tell you my theory: all I can do is tell you about it, and 'about' is always approximate. Just as my experiential knowledge, my complex mesh of expectancies, is an approximation to reality, with its own inertia and distortions, so my verbal knowledge is an approximation to that approximation, yet more rigid and inexact. Language is a map of a map. The position is reminiscent of Alice's infuriating conversation with the Knight about his beautiful song.[3] ' "The name of the song is called *Haddocks' Eyes*". "Oh, that's the name of the song, is it?" Alice said, trying to feel interested. "No, you don't understand", the Knight said, looking a little vexed. "That's what the name is *called*. The name really is 'The Aged Aged Man' ". "Then I ought to have said 'That's what the *song* is called?' " Alice corrected herself. "No, you oughtn't: that's quite another thing! The *song* is called '*Ways and Means*': but that's only what it's *called*, you know!" "Well, what *is* the song, then?" said Alice, who was by this time completely bewildered. "I was coming to that", the Knight said. "The song really *is* 'A-Sitting On A Gate': and the tune's my own invention" '.

Even with such a keen set of symbolic scalpels as that provided by quantum theory, we cannot match exactly what we sense to be the case with what we can say. Werner Heisenberg describes Neils Bohr as using 'classical mechanics or quantum theory as a painter uses his brush or colours. Brushes do not determine the picture, and colour is never the full reality; but if he keeps the picture before his mind's eye, the artist can use his brush to convey, however inadequately, his own mental picture to others. Bohr . . . (has formed) an intuitive picture of different atoms; a picture he can only convey to other physicists by such inadequate means as electron orbits and quantum conditions. It is not at all certain that Bohr himself believes that electrons revolve inside the atom.'[4]

If we understand that the-way-we-*say*-it-is is likely to be even more unlike the-way-it-is than the-way-we-*perceive*-it-is, and respect its limitations, then language is a blessing. The ability to converse and learn through language means that as individuals we can benefit from the researches and experiences of others, and as a species our knowledge becomes cumulative. We do not have to keep reinventing and rejecting scientific notions like phlogiston, or recreating philosophical arguments that Plato or Descartes have already worked out. We can describe imaginative variants on the world which we inhabit (though both are works of fiction, of course). We can leave notes for our friends telling them where we've gone, and write shopping lists to combat the fallibility of memory. Truly words are a boon in all sorts of ways.

But if we forget Korzybski's famous dictum that 'Whatever I say a thing is, it is not', and lose sight of the gap between the reality and the model, then language is a bugbear too. Aldous Huxley explained why: 'Every individual is at once the beneficiary and the victim of the linguistic tradition into which he has been born – the beneficiary inasmuch as language gives access to the accumulated records of other people's experience; the victim insofar as it confirms him in the belief that reduced awareness is the only awareness and as it bedevils his sense of reality, so that he is all too apt to take his concepts for data, his words for actual things.'[5]

Everything that we earlier discussed about the relationship between map and territory therefore applies *a fortiori* to language itself. For example, our experiential theories pick out and accentuate differences that are just one-among-many in reality. And they create types of relationship like cause-and-effect, or actor-and-action that may have no objective basis at all. It is, as we saw, in the nature of theories to do this. But language has to create conventions and symbols that are totally unlike their referents. If we are drawing a real map of Great Britain, let us say, we can use a variety of scales, perspectives, shadings, and colours to convey what we want. With the English language all we have to play with are twenty-six letters, or forty-odd sounds, and their order. All the complexity of life has to be reduced to this linear print-out: two dozen kinds of beads and a long piece of string on which to thread them. No wonder that simplifications have to be made, distortions allowed, the various forms of our experience chopped and squeezed in order to fit into the pattern of what can be said. Given this, it is astonishing that communication works as well as it does. It would be quite unrealistic to expect the liquid evanescence of our experience to be caught completely in any net of words, however fine the mesh.

4.2 Prototypes

One of the basic simplifications that language must have is to make things much more definite, clear-cut, solid, and stable than they are. The image of dunes is a good one for our experiential theory, because dunes are not clear-cut and not stable. But language cannot tolerate all this fuzziness and probability, and impatiently divides 'black' from 'white', 'town' from 'country', 'gentleness' from 'weakness', as if there were no question about it. When a thing is named, it is hard not to succumb to the illusion that it is thereby well defined. When words are used in context their meanings are shaded by the different elements of the context in which they stand. Adjectives and adverbs modify our understanding of nouns and verbs explicitly. Other currently active ideas, tone of voice, the preceding dis-course, all merely modify a word's meaning implicitly, as we shall see. Yet even so the impact of language is stark, skeletal, and prototypical compared with the rich and variegated effect of direct experience. It is the constant struggle of the writer and especially the poet to twist language in such a way that she escapes from the seductive hold of these prototypes and is thereby able to create in her readers the taste of the dish rather than merely a list of the ingredients.

The dunes or mountains are models of our experiential concepts, showing them to be constellations of features or associations, some of which (those at the summit) are central to the concept, and others (on the foothills) are more loosely or optionally related. When we perceive something directly as an example of such-and-such a concept we usually attribute to it most of the central features and many of the optional ones.[6] This cat sitting beside me certainly has fur, four legs, a tail, a cat-like shape and likes fish. She is also white, small, moulting, has one tawny eye and one blue one, likes having her ears pulled but not her tail and is much more friendly than her brother. In fact Pushkin is not only much more than my prototype of 'cat': she is different from it. Unless I discover to the contrary, it is part of my prototype of 'cat' that its eyes should be the same colour. Yet the fact that Pushkin has odd eyes does not make me doubt her cat-hood. Any particular cat may be bald, three-legged, mute, turn its nose up at fish, or even all of these, and still be an acceptable cat. But in the absence of information of this sort, we tend to fill in our central features of 'cat' quite automatically. Marvin Minsky[7] has called these central features *default-values*. They are the bits and pieces that we attribute to all cats (or teachers, or tape-recorders, or olympic athletes) by default: that is, unless we specifically discover otherwise. Thus it is that, because the evidence is often incomplete, we tend to perceive things as more normal, usual, prototypical than they actually are.[8]

This tendency, present in our experiential process, is exaggerated a hundred-fold by language. A word is a device for activating a prototype. When I say 'The cat sat on the mat', your understanding is probably rather humdrum. A tabby on a door-mat, you might imagine. But when I tell you that both cat and mat are Persian, you can replace some default-values with these, *a priori* less likely, features. Now I tell you that the mat is a flying carpet and the cat is a CIA agent on a secret mission to assassinate a Central American Head of State by scratching him with a surgically implanted poison claw – and your original prototype, skeletal though it was, is shot to pieces. We can use language to convey the shadowy uniqueness of experience, but both speaker and listener alike must guard against the constant subversion of 'what is meant' by their own stereotypes.

There are even times when we insist on filling in a default-value, of hearing what is usual, or desirable, rather than actual, even though there is clear evidence that it is not appropriate. George Kelly calls this *preemptive construing* (i.e. what is so is preempted by what we expect). More generally we call it *prejudice*. If someone is Christian, she must also be unthinking, go to church every Sunday, be middle-class and have a limp hand-shake. If he's conservative he must approve of hanging, hunting, profit at any cost, and speak with forked tongue. His denial of any of the first three simply furnishes me with evidence of the fourth. English girls on holiday are after 'a bit of fun', so when Carol says 'No' to Luigi, what he hears is 'Yes'. And similarly the relative coarseness of everyday language means that people's opinions are often not a very reliable guide to how they behave. 'Liberated' males may revert to type when it comes to getting up in the night to feed their own child. 'I *always* return books' I tell you, in good faith; but somehow, just this once, it gets overlooked.

Of course, words vary in how well specified they are: how much of their meaning is skeletal and how much nebulous. The more tightly specified, the less malleable a word is by its context. Specialized or technical languages in particular tend towards more precise definition. In normal usage the word *hit*, for example, is sufficient to convey what is important about the interaction of an actor and an object. 'Dominic hit Linda's spaniel' is sufficient to evoke the desired understanding – and attendant disapproval. But in a cricket commentary the listener wants more detailed information, and a wider repertoire of terms has been developed to indicate in what direction, with what force, and with what success the ball has been hit. The batsman can *drive*, *hook*, *cut* or *sweep* the ball. He can *stroke* it, *snick* it, *edge* it, *push* it, *pull* it, *smother* it, *loft* it, *turn* it, *smash* it, *sky* it, *steer* it, *punch* it, *hammer* it or *prod* it. In such monologues or discourses, though it remains, the margin for personal interpretation and possible misunderstanding is reduced.

4.3 Flags and Nets

We can develop our simple picture of how our mental theories are organized by imagining words to be flags planted at the summit of some of our dunes. When we hear the words that enables us to locate the flag, and then, for concrete words that refer to experiential concepts, we can slide down the flagpole and discover what the dune consists of. From the flag *Mum* we can retrieve what she looks like, sounds like, feels like, how she behaves, how I can influence the way she behaves, and what other kinds of things (like *Dad*) are associated with her, (see Figure 4.1). Note that when I land on the dune,

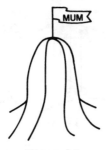

Figure 4.1

at its summit, what I see first when I look around are its default-values, or central attributes. If the context demands it, I explore further; otherwise not. The features at the summit are those that form the skeleton of the word's meaning. It is this relationship between flag and mountain that predisposes our linguistic understanding to be stereotypical and conventional.

Flags, like dunes, do not exist on their own. They too are linked with other flags to form what we shall call *propositions*. Propositions are the verbal equivalent of expectancies and, like expectancies, they express relationships, like 'Mum loves Dad', 'I'm a bad boy', and 'The beaver is an amphibious rodent'. Thus, overlaid on the experiential dune-scape there is a verbal 'flag-scape' of interlocking propositions: 'Mum loves Dad', and 'Dad thinks I'm a bad boy' and 'Dad works at the Zoo' and 'Dad says they have beavers at the Zoo' and 'Beavers are amphibious rodents', and so on. The overall picture now looks like Figure 4.2.

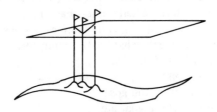

Figure 4.2

There are connections *within* each plane, and *between* the planes. We shall refer to this picture from time to time, so in order to simplify it, we shall just represent dunes by circles and the flags by dots, as in Figure 4.3.

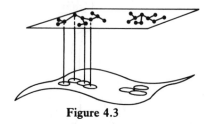

Figure 4.3

Learning within the two planes emerges as being rather different. In the experiential plane, the topography is shifted as a result of experience, as described in the previous chapter. In the verbal plane, learning is 'putting out more flags', and constructing elaborate nets of bunting between them.[9] At first when we are beginning to learn language, the relationship between the two planes is very close. Words label dunes that have already developed through our prelinguistic learning, and the simple syntax of the Actor–Action–Object sort is based on our analogous 'syntax of experience'.[10] But then the mapping between the two planes starts to become imperfect. For one thing, the terrain in which the flags are planted is itself changing rather fast for the young child. As experiential concepts develop, therefore, the peaks of the dunes move, while the flags, already locked into a network of other flags, tend to stay put. What we say, our descriptions of our experience, begins to be dislocated from the experience itself. Second, the conventions of the syntax that we have to learn become more remote from the organization of our experiential theory. In experience, the earlier of two events always happens before the later. In language, this is not necessarily so. We can say 'E2 *after* E1' or 'Before E2, E1' ('He slammed the door after getting into the car'. 'Before we had dinner, Father always said grace').[11] In experience, Actor–Action–Object combinations always occur together, simultaneously. In language they have to be strung out, and worse, they can be strung out in a variety of orders:

The goat ate the rubbish.

The rubbish was eaten by the goat.

It was the rubbish that the goat ate.

What the goat did to the rubbish was eat it.

Having eaten the rubbish the goat slept.

Being eaten by the goat, the rubbish was gone.

Third, we learn words like *it, the, was*, and *nevertheless* that have no fixed experiential referent at all. Fourth, we develop the ability to link flags together to create definitions and descriptions that do not themselves correspond to anything in our experience. We can create mythical entities like unicorns, justice, God, Hamlet, the Great Pumpkin, and my intimate friendship with the Princess of Wales. We can create and discuss verbal conceptions without bothering to see whether they have any connections with experience. This is what philosophy has become. We can create conditional sentences that might be true or false, depending on what Reality is up to. 'If England win the Ashes, I shall make a lot of money': the conjunction of England's victory and my sudden wealth make this true. But what are we to say to the truth or falsity of 'If Queen Victoria dies tomorrow, I'll eat my hat'? Because of my fallacious presupposition there is *no state of affairs at all* that could make this true or false. We can create nonsense like Chomsky's famous 'Colourless green ideas sleep furiously'. We can even invent new words that have a glow of meaning but no definition: 'Twas brillig and the slithy toves . . . .' And the attraction of *Jabberwocky*[12] exists precisely because of its daftness. It is somehow beside the point to know that a *tove* is a cross between a badger, a lizard, and a corkscrew that nests beneath sundials and lives on cheese. We can lie, by putting words together in such a way as to deceive ourselves or others, 'I didn't mean to'. 'Please, Sir, it was Stephen, Sir'. 'The recession is over'. And finally we can construct for ourselves rules about what can and cannot be said that prevent us from fully expressing our experience. When Aristotle suggested as a basic rule of thought that a thing could not be both A and not-A, he was just as entitled to do so as the man who dreamed up cricket. But we get into trouble if we take this principle to be a law of nature rather than the foundation of an interesting game called 'reason'.

In short, the verbal plane originates, in both its content and its organization, in the expression of concepts and relationships that have already developed experientially. But it becomes in large measure autonomous: it develops its own rules, its own concepts and its own prohibitions, many of which have no basis in an individual's experience, and some of which are directly contrary to that experience. There is much that we know, intuitively, that we cannot express; and there is much that we express of which we have no personal knowledge.

My verbal theory differs not only structurally from my experiential theory; it differs functionally, too, in terms of how it works and what it is for. We saw that the twin pivots around which my experiential knowledge turns are 'What I need' and 'What I can do' – my survival, and my ability to resist or avoid threats to it. While some of my verbal fact-finding springs from a real need to know, most of it does not. The whole culture of school and of the mass media seems designed to fill people up with news and views that they have not requested: answers for which they have no questions.[13] To be well-informed becomes a virtue in its own right. So although much of our verbal knowledge is of no use to us in itself, nevertheless we go on hoarding it, because we have been brought up to believe that ignorance is a sin. Not to know is for many people an uncomfortable experience. There is a game that people play at parties and in universities called 'Have You Read . . .?' 'Have you read *Tomorrow's New Yesterday*?' 'No'. 'Oh, you should. It's marvellous. Perhaps you've come across *Bridlington Mon Amour*?' 'No'. 'Pity . . . absolutely brilliant . . . startling insights into the plight of the unemployed gay community . . . what about Shillingford's new one on attitudes to lunch in the Austro-Hungarian Empire?' 'Er 'fraid not'. And so on. It takes a very sanguine personality not to be either intimidated or enraged by this. In school particularly, as we shall see in Chapter 9, not to know is unacceptable for teachers and pupils alike.

4.4 Processes of Verbal Learning

The existence of the verbal plane makes available to us a whole variety of new learning methods; new ways of amplifying our ability to find things out. They are represented diagrammatically in Figure 4.4. First of all we can add new knowledge to the giant 'molecule' of our verbal knowledge through the processes of *tuition* – listening to people and reading. The most common, and most important, of the ways in which this happens is *understanding* or comprehension. We listen to or read a string of words and swiftly and automatically they lock together with each other and with the relevant branches of what we already know. Sometimes, however, this process does not proceed so smoothly, and in these cases we have three other strategies available to us. If what we are being told doesn't make any sense, if it is short enough, if we only have to hang on to it for a few seconds, and if nothing much else is going on, then we can *rehearse* it – repeat it over and over under our breath. If it doesn't make much sense, but repeating it silently won't do, then we have to *remember* it. In school the word 'learning' is often applied to just this process, as when a teacher says 'I want you to learn these formulas (or these irregular verbs) for homework tonight'. The third strategy is to stick with the process of trying to make sense out of something that is resisting making sense. This comprehension we can call *grasping*, as in trying to 'grasp' the meaning or the point. Grasping relies heavily on a more

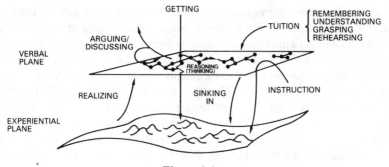

Figure 4.4

well-known process called *reasoning*. When we reason, we are not receiving new information from outside, but are extracting and making explicit relationships that are already present implicitly in what we already know. This is the verbal equivalent of the 'bridging' strategy that operates within the experiential plane. And likewise there is a verbal equivalent of the experiential 'practising', where we turn what we know into an overt action and see how the outside world responds to it. It is called *arguing* or *discussing*.

There are two general points to make about the kinds of verbal learning mentioned so far. First, formal education at the secondary and under-graduate levels is characterized by a mixture of these strategies. We are told things; we try to remember or understand them; we talk about them; and we try to work out what their implications are. Second, all these processes can operate without any contact with the experiential plane. Over the last twenty years or so educationalists have asserted that learning is 'better' when efforts are made to integrate the verbal and experiential domains,[14] and this philosophy has altered quite markedly the conduct of primary schools at least. But despite Nuffield Science and the Humanities Curriculum Project, the dominant tradition in secondary schools remains that inherited from the public and grammar schools – learning through words for verbal understanding. While critics of education often seem to assume that there is something wrong with such a regime, the question we shall pursue here is: what are the kinds of learning that result from different teaching methods, and when and where are they appropriate? This pragmatic approach seems to me a necessary preliminary to the application of ideological or moral standards.

When we come to look at the ways in which verbal and experiential knowledge *interact* with each other, a further set of strategies for teaching and learning need to be considered. Sometimes a string of words has an immediate experiential effect – often an explosive one, as, for example, in *getting* a joke, which is quite a different experience from understanding it. Understanding happens, but it is a transitional point on the way to a deeper, more pervasive experience. The train does not stop there. Then, sometimes, we feel the impact of something we have been told not at the time but later, perhaps years later. We can call this more gradual penetration from the verbal to the experiential planes *sinking in*. When we hear or read something with the intention that this new input should make a difference to what we do, what we express in our actions, rather than to what we profess, then we talk about *instruction*. Understanding the role of language in instruction is a considerable problem, because the effect of instruction is so variable. Compare 'Don't touch that', 'Don't take your eye off the ball', 'Don't cry', and 'Don't worry'. Finally there is a type of learning that is in some ways the reverse of sinking in. It occurs when something that we have known tacitly, at an experiential level, surfaces into conscious awareness in such a way that it can be caught and expressed in words. This process is central, as we shall see, to an understanding of both 'creativity' and 'personal growth'. I call it 'bubbling up' or *realizing*.

4.5 Understanding

We understand when a string of words click together sensibly and without any sense of strain. Hopefully you just did it. If our accumulated verbal knowledge can be likened to a giant molecule, then understanding is a chemical reaction which 'goes' easily. A little bit of new information is tipped into your mind, and bonding occurs just like that. No extra energy, or catalyst is needed. Or, to change the metaphor, understanding is like feeding an animal familiar and digestible food: it is assimilated spontaneously.[15] Both these metaphors are useful in showing that when we understand something, we do not just add it to our store of knowledge. It becomes *integrated* with the system of what we know and thereby changes the properties and potentialities of the whole system, sometimes only slightly and sometimes profoundly. Learning that a whale is a mammal changes what we know about mammals. Learning that space and time are not separate but different projections of a four-dimensional unity, changes one's whole view of physics. And learning that your father is not your *real* father may change your whole life.

For this integration to occur, two general conditions must obtain, one structural and one dynamic. First the new information must bear a sensible relationship to the existing 'cognitive structure', as David Ausubel[16] calls it, of the learner. The input has to be integrated with something, and if no suitable foundation exists, no integration can happen. A child of five will not comprehend Schrödinger's Wave Equation or the economic foundations of monetarism. There is no more point in trying to teach him than there is in trying to feed a newborn baby with raw carrots. Second, for the reaction to go, the 'energy' must be right. If the learner has a will or a need to complete or add to a particular part of his memory molecule, the chances that what he learns will stick are much greater. As with experiential learning, the process of verbal learning is always contingent on the anticipation of a desirable consequence. Though the *strategies* of learning in the two planes are rather different, the *conditions* are not. In short, if I give you a piece of a jigsaw puzzle, there may be two reasons why it doesn't get incorporated into your puzzle. It may belong to a different puzzle, and/or you may not care enough to find out whether it fits or not.

Ausubel calls integration 'subsumption', and distinguishes two kinds: *correlative subsumption* and *derivative subsumption*. Correlative subsumption occurs when new information 'is an extension, elaboration, qualification or modification of previously learned propositions', that is, the input serves to develop the molecule. Derivative subsumption occurs when new information 'constitutes a specific example of an established concept in cognitive structure'. In this case the specific details of the example, being illustrative, may be readily lost, and only a general confirmation or consolidation of the preexisting idea remain. As well as these, there are several other kinds of integration that need to occur if real understanding is to result. We shall look at these briefly now.

(a) *Integration with referents*   For a sentence to make sense the individual content words (nouns, verbs, adjectives, and adverbs) need to be recognized. 'Arthur sank his gargleblaster and made for home' will resist comprehension unless you know that a gargleblaster is a kind of drink (as opposed, let us say, to a kind of boat). Recognizing a word means locating it in the existing verbal network so that the verbal *and* experiential features that are associated with it can be retrieved. In the case of a simple concrete word like 'cat' both sorts of association will be plentiful. For 'monetarism' the associations will be, for the man in the street, much less profuse and predominantly verbal. In either case what the word makes available is a skeletal stereotype plus a whole cloud of possible associations and attributes that can be drawn on to aid the integration of the word with its context.[17]

(b) *Semantic integration*   As these fuzzy constellations of possible meaning are retrieved, so they have to be fitted together with each other. Sometimes the bare prototype will be sufficient, as in 'The cat sat on the mat'. Even here our options for 'cat' 'sat' and 'mat' are limited by each other. Probably a domestic cat, probably a small door-mat, we are likely to assume. In other cases our understanding of a word varies widely, depending on the company it is keeping. Compare what you understand by 'ran' in the following sentences:

John ran the race.
John ran the bookshop.
The car ran well.
The road ran from London to Dover.
Reagan ran for President.

And it gets worse if we consider idioms like:

John ran up the wall.
John ran up the dress.
John ran up the bill.

Or

John ran down his neighbour's cat.
John ran down his neighbour's achievements.

Or

John ran over the mouse.
John ran over the script.
John ran over for coffee.

Yet so skilled are we at selecting interpretations and shades of meaning that will complement each other that we can comprehend such sentences, and thousands like them, in our everyday discourse without batting an eyelid. V. I. Pudovkin, a Russian film maker in the 1920s and '30s, said in his book *Film Technique*: 'To the poet or the writer, separate words are as raw material. They have the widest and most variable meanings which only begin to become precise through their position in the sentence. . . . The single word is only the raw skeleton of a meaning, so to speak. . . . Only in conjunction with other words, set in the frame of a complex form, does art endow it with life and reality.'[18]

It seems to me, though I am not sure, that if words are skeletons which can support a wide variety of possible forms, then the richness of our comprehension is to some extent a matter of whether we focus on the bones, or on the wealth of possibility that each skeleton creates. How we comprehend is therefore influenced by our deep attitude to the nature of language. If we see only the essential framework, then we shall be forced to create an angular and spartan 'Mondrian' of an understanding. But if we see, as Pudovkin does, clouds of possibility, then we may create a more 'impressionistic' picture – a Turner or a Monet, say – that despite or even because of its lack of definition, captures more of the shade and texture of what was meant. Thus it is perhaps that one person becomes a philosopher and another a poet.

(c) *Syntactic integration*   The order and the structure of the words, the way the beads are strung, contributes to the meaning, too. 'Mix substances A and B slowly and heat to 180 °C' may be crucially different from 'Mix substances A and B and heat slowly to 180 °C'. More generally the order and inflections (variable endings) of the words indicate their *role* in the picture that the sentence is trying to paint. In Chapter 3 we mentioned one attempt to identify these notes – that of Charles Fillmore – that assigns functions like Action, Actor, Experiencer, Object, Instrument, and Location to the words. One of the simplest codes, for instance, that children use for a while is 'Identify a Noun–Verb–Noun sequence as Actor–Action–Object'. This strategy will work for sentences like

John hit Bill.
The cat scratched the furniture.
Daddy took off his socks.

But it breaks down for

Bill was hit by John.
The cat eyed the fish.
It was the socks that Daddy took off.

The strategies we use to assign these functional roles are very complex for adults, though we are so skilled that we don't even know it.

A grammar like Fillmore's is much more use to us here than the more well-known one of Noam Chomsky.[19] Our use of language is grounded in our wish to communicate our experience to each other, though, as we have seen, as language develops more abstract terms, it does take on a limited life of its own. Thus the basic set of relationships that our syntax encodes for us must be compatible with the relationships that our experiential theory uses to represent our nonlinguistic experience. Notions like Actor, Action and the rest make sense in both domains, whereas more traditional linguistic functions, like 'subject' and 'predicate' do not. People do not look out of the window and say 'Hello, there goes a predicate'.

(d) *Integration with linguistic context*　As well as fitting words together into sentences, sentences have to be fitted in with the discourse that surrounds them. If this cannot be done, then our understanding is incomplete. Take this passage:

> With hocked gems financing him our hero bravely defied all scornful laughter that tried to prevent his scheme. Your eyes deceive he had said: an egg not a table correctly typifies this unexplored planet. Now, three sturdy sisters sought proof forging along sometimes through vast calmness yet more often over turbulent peaks and valleys. Days became weeks as many doubters spread fearful rumours about the edge. At last from nowhere welcome winged creatures appeared signifying momentous success.[20]

There is nothing problematic about the sentences here; but it is not until one realizes, or is told, that the passage is about Christopher Columbus discovering America, that it all fits together, and the egg, the sisters and the edge can all be comprehended together.

(e) *Integration with nonlinguistic context*　What we understand and how we understand also depends on what else is going on besides the language. If I like the look of you, and reckon you 'know your stuff', then I will fill in gaps and correct small mistakes in what you are telling me, as I interview you for the job, quite readily. If my attitude is different then the depth and 'indulgence' of my understanding will be different. I may be less inclined to make allowances. My comprehension of a narrative will depend on whether it is told in the pub or from a hospital bed. Sometimes, without an appreciation of the nonlinguistic context, my understanding cannot proceed very far at all. Take this passage, devised by Bransford and Johnson.[21]

> If the balloons popped, the sound wouldn't be able to carry since everything would be too far away from the correct floor. A closed window would also prevent the sound from carrying, since most buildings tend to be well insulated. Since the whole operation depends on a steady flow of electricity, a break in the wire would also cause problems. Of course the fellow could shout, but the human voice is not loud enough to carry that far. An additional problem is that a string could break on the instrument. Then there would be no accompaniment to the message. It is clear that the best situation would involve less distance. Then there would be fewer potential problems. With face to face contact, the least number of things could go wrong.

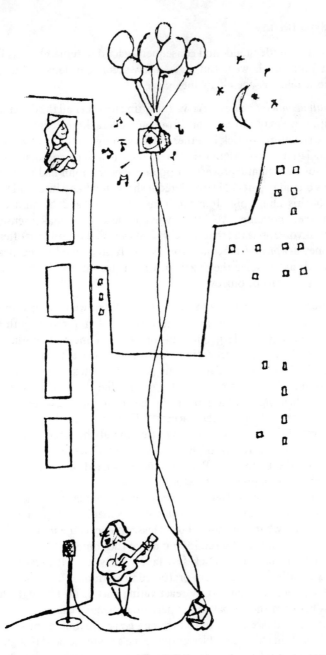

Figure 4.5

This is hard to understand, and consequently hard to remember, as Bransford and Johnson showed. But given a few seconds to look at Figure 4.5 again the whole passage clicks into place.

(f) *Integration with inferences*   As well as fitting together all the different bits of the input, we may add extra bits from our general knowledge if they help the whole structure to stick together. This fleshing-out of what we are told with associations and inferences of our own is a very common and frequently quite automatic process. Suppose we hear: 'John had been invited to Katie's birthday party. He wondered if she would like a kite, and he went and shook his china pig. It made a healthy noise and he smiled. . . .' Without even noticing, we fill in what is needed to make sense: that birthdays involve *presents*; that presents cost *money*; that children often keep their money in a *piggy-bank*; and so on. Not only do we modify the meanings of the words as we solve the puzzle of what is meant, we often contribute whole propositions of our own.

(d) *Integration with autobiographical context*   When we read or hear something, we do so in a personal context: a strange living room, with lots of other people, with two large gin-and-tonics inside me and another in my hand, with certain preoccupations, sitting in a certain posture, feeling apprehensive and lonely. Part of this ambient context may relate to my understanding of what is being said. Feeling slightly drunk and sorry for myself has a bearing on what I make of what you are saying to me. But other parts, like the pattern on the carpet and snatches of the music that is playing, which happens to catch my attention at the same time, also get bound in to my total record of the event.[22] Your views on Hermann Hesse and mine on the Boomtown Rats become associated in this record simply because they are happening together.

These autobiographical connections are important because they form the basis of our ability to *recall* and *recognize* events that have happened to us. If I want to recall what you think about Hesse, it may come to mind directly, or you may prompt me by reminding me of the context. 'Remember? We were sitting on the sofa at Dick and Jane's party. . . . It must have been about six months ago. You were pretty fed up, I think. . . .' The recall of a whole event can be triggered by reactivating part of it. Through the connections between the verbal and experiential planes I can retrieve content from context and *vice versa*. In fact the *vice versa* situation is the one we call recognition. You show me a face or quote me a sentence, and recognizing it requires me to find an episode in my autobiography within which face or quote is embedded. Sometimes this context becomes conscious. 'Oh yes! I remember her. She was the woman who was dancing with Ian. . . . Didn't she come with that friend of Dick's, you know, the one who works for Hambro's?' And sometimes this nexus of personal associations is only reactivated tacitly, so that all we get is a feeling of familiarity, but without (consciously) being able to 'place' the thing recognized.

Thus the interlinking of verbal content and experiential context plays a large part in our ability to remember what we have learnt. Specifically, the more I can recreate for you the actual context within which the learning took place, the more likely it is to come to mind.[23] Names, faces and events from your schooldays, that had seemed irretrievably lost, may resurface with a vengeance when you return, years later, to stroll around the playground. Any part of the record can be used to reactivate any other part. If you sit down quietly and recreate, in minute detail, a class-room in which you were taught at age thirteen or fourteen, you will find other feelings, perceptions, memories, and learning begin to flood back. You can reexperience what it was like to be adolescent.

But this interpenetration of experience and language is problematic. If the context is significantly changed between the learning-event and the remembering-event, recall will suffer. The greater learning achieved in an informal, friendly class-room or seminar group may well be offset by the disparity between these social and relaxed conditions and the formal, isolated anxiety of the examination hall. Likewise learning can be 'bound' to the physiological state of the learner. Students who learnt a route on a map after a few drinks recalled it better when they were drunk again than when they were sober.[24] It may be that the use of psychoactive drugs to relieve chronic depression, so that psychotherapy can be attempted, while it seems a good idea, may be misguided if the benefits of therapy then remain bound to the bodily presence of a hefty dose of monoamineoxidase inhibitor.

Some of our linguistic knowledge remains connected to its context of acquisition, and some does not. What I was told about Sam's summer holiday is still associated with the event of running into her in the King's Road. But 'The 1944 Education Act introduced a three-tier school system for all children' is now free of any record of how I came to know it. 'The whale isn't a fish: it's a mammal' is part of my knowledge about the world in general. But the statement 'The whale isn't a fish . . . it's an insect' is still tightly bound to memories of Peter Cook sitting on a park bench boring John Cleese with 'amazing facts', and to the event of going to see 'The Secret

Policeman's Ball' (the film in which this lunacy is featured) with my sister and my elder niece in Hobart.

Psychologists (including myself) have invested a disproportionate amount of effort in experimenting on and theorizing about our ability to retain and recapitulate bits of language. John Anderson and Gordon Bower's *Human Associative Memory*[25] is good on recall and recognition, and on verbal learning in general. Endel Tulving has discussed autobiographical and general verbal memories, which he calls 'episodic' and 'semantic' memories respectively.[26] Jerome Bruner calls them 'memory with record' and 'memory without record'; which is clear enough.[27] The literature is vast.

4.6 Grasping

This and the next section look at variants on understanding. The first occurs when comprehension is possible, but does not proceed as smoothly or automatically as it usually does. The passages about Christopher Columbus and the balloons in the previous section were of this sort. So often is reading an academic text-book, especially in a new area where the terms and the ways of writing and arguing are unfamiliar. So, in microcosm, are the sentences

The notes were sour because the seams split.
The trip was not delayed because the bottle shattered.
The haystack mattered because the cloth ripped.[28]

In all these cases the skeletons of the words seem not to fit together, and some time and effort must be taken to explore their extended families of nuances and associations to see if some legitimate but unusual or metaphorical sense can be discovered that will work the trick, and allow integration to occur. If the new input cannot be *assimilated* to what is already known, then for comprehension to happen, what is known has to alter somewhat in order to *accommodate* the new input. The balance between assimilation and accommodation, terms borrowed from Jean Piaget, is determined principally by the disparity between existing and new knowledge. To use the feeding analogy again, some things we hear are like baby food: they are ingested and absorbed almost without effort. Others are like big chunks of tough steak: they need a lot of 'chewing over' and an increased production of digestive juices before they can become part of the body. Both input and organism have to change for them to become compatible, sometimes minimally, sometimes by a greater amount over a longer time. Just as with the experiential process of 'bridging', so *grasping* involves trying out different meanings for the words involved, dropping some features and adding others, until either a connection is made, the bridge is built, or we give up. In the three examples above, for instance, bridges can be found *via* the concepts 'bagpipes', 'launching', and 'parachute' respectively. These act as 'catalysts' which enable the reaction to go, and the old knowledge and the new knowledge to mesh together.

4.7 Getting

Getting is what happens when we understand something in such a way that it has a personal, experiential significance for us. It is what happens when we *get* a joke, or really *get* what someone is on about. Instead of being solely an intellectual matter the whole person in both their thinking and feeling aspects becomes involved. Part of the definition of 'get' in my dictionary[29] is 'to succeed in coming into touch or communication with: to grip emotionally, take, captivate, hit the taste of exactly'. When we get a joke there is the pleasure that always results from solving a problem, like fitting the last piece into a jigsaw puzzle, but which is heightened by the fact that not until the very last piece is in place can we see the whole picture. Suddenly our understanding clangs shut, and the sound it makes is laughter. But in addition, with many jokes there is a momentary apprehension of some aspect of human frailty or stupidity that we normally prefer to ignore. And this apprehension is experiential, not intellectual. An elephant says to a mouse 'My! You are small!' and the mouse replies 'Yes, I know. I've not been well'. And in laughing at the mouse, we can acknowledge our own propensity for self-deception and rationalization.

When we get what another person is saying, then too there is a feeling of understanding deeply not just the words but the experience of the person behind the words. Therapists call this rather grandly 'empathy', though it is not something so esoteric. Whenever we are sensitive to the other person's posture, tone of voice, hesitations, eye contact and the rest, we can integrate our intuitive responses to those with our intellectual comprehension of what they are saying. Thus we clothe the skeleton of their verbal message with an outfit that is appropriate. When we listen only to the words our understanding either remains skeletal (Mondrian-ish), or we select its habit from our own idiosyncratic wardrobe of associations and concerns, memories, fantasies and judgements.

4.8 **Remembering**

This section is about remembering in the sense of *rote learning*. 'I've got to remember these dates for tomorrow.' When school children say 'I hate learning' or 'I can't learn these' this is what they usually mean. It is a pity that the word *learning* is maligned in this way. This sort of learning has been extensively studied in psychology. In fact for the first sixty years of this century verbal learning was synonymous with rote learning. Ebbinghaus,[30] who started this tradition in the 1880s, wanted to investigate 'pure' learning. He had the idea that we had a learning machine inside our heads, rather like a letter-sorting robot. If it was asked to learn anything that 'meant something' – if it recognized that the address on a letter was where it used to go for its holidays as a robot-let – then it got confused and its performance became impure, clouded with these pesky personal associations. So the answer was to feed it nonsense to remember: that way its past experience couldn't get in the way. Ebbinghaus invented a particular form of nonsense called the 'nonsense syllable' – things like PUK or WAJ – lists of which were used to delight psychology professors and torture their students for decades. At the same time as the Noble Experiment was prohibiting alcohol in North America, so psychology's own Prohibition was directed against meaning and understanding. (Perversely, a psychologist called Noble did experiments to rate the 'meaningfulness' of this nonsense.) The job of the mental robot was to sort this rubbish into appropriate pigeon-holes, so that it could later be recovered. Unfortunately, because it was rubbish, no sensible person had bothered, at the start of the experiment, to build such a set of pigeon-holes. So the first job was to get an idea of what kind of rubbish it was, then knock up the right number of holes, and then sort them. Towards the end of Prohibition people began to use lists of unrelated *words* as the memory task. In this case the pigeon-holes were there already: you just had to sort the words into them. If at some later date you couldn't recall something, one of three things might have happened. You might never have put it in. You might have put it in but it had decayed or changed with the passage of time. Or it may still be there but you just could not find it – buried under all the subsequent mail, perhaps. It's like trying to find the soap in the bath. Either it isn't there, or it has dissolved, or you can't get hold of it.

The trouble with this picture of 'verbal learning' is not that it is wrong, but that its priorities are wrong. The kind of learning machine that we are is one that thrives on meaning. Our preferred strategy, both experiential and verbal, is to use new information to modify our existing theory. Ebbinghaus' learner is like the old-fashioned scientist who just 'collects data' and 'makes observations' without (as far as is possible) any hypothesis testing or theoretical speculation at all. He views theorizing, the attempt to integrate and make sense of things, what Sir Frederic Bartlett[31] called the 'effort after meaning' as suspicious and subjective. But suspicious or not, that is the way we are. Thus integration is our primary *modus operandi*. And only if the material is such as to prevent or inhibit integration, do we resort to the tedious strategy called remembering.

Remembering actually boils down to two sub-strategies. The first is the same kind of extended search for *something* meaningful that we met with grasping and bridging. If I can associate this bit of nonsense with something meaningful, and that bit of nonsense with something meaningful too, then I can use my giant memory molecule of the 'verbal plane' and/or my experiential dune-scape to find a path between the two. Sure enough, in 1969 a researcher called Prytulak[32] found that the way people tried to remember nonsense syllables was by finding what he called Natural Language Mediators. The easier it was to turn the nonsense into a real bit of language, the easier it was to remember. Thus PUK is well remembered: it readily turns into 'puck' or 'puke'. WAJ isn't so easy to convert, so it tends to be harder to learn. This is the first stage: the next is to find some way of using your prior knowledge to link things together. If you can link different ideas together, then the problem of finding them subsequently is solved. We possess two common strategies for doing this. The first is to have a ready-made, well-known, easily retrievable piece of rope on to which the originally separate ideas can be pegged. These handy clothes-lines are called *mnemonics*, and a simple one is the rhyme 'One is a bun; two is a shoe; three is a tree; four is a door; five is a hive; six is some sticks; seven is heaven; eight is a gate; nine is a mine; ten is a hen.' Suppose I am given a list of ten random words to remember, like MOUSE, ASHTRAY, TENT, HIPFLASK, CUSHION, MEMORY, COPPER, BISHOP, CHERRY, POUND. What I do is peg MOUSE to *bun* – (with an image of a mouse eating a bun, say); ASHTRAY to *shoe* (with a memory of a large wooden clog that a friend used to use as an ashtray); TENT to *tree* (easy one, that); and so on. Later on I can run through the rhyme to myself and pick off the images I find there. An alternative mnemonic is the 'orator's walk', used by Greek and Roman public speakers: you imagine a familiar building, let us say, and then stroll around it placing eye-catching symbols for the successive points of your speech at various points.

The alternative to this clothes-line strategy is the freight-car strategy. Here the things to be remembered are linked directly to each other, like the wagons on a freight-train. Imagery is again a very successful way of creating the hook-up. Using this strategy to remember our list of words we might create in our mind's eye a cartoon about a Tom and Jerry MOUSE who is sleeping rough using an ASHTRAY as a TENT, and his little padded HIPFLASK as a CUSHION to rest his head on . . . and so on. Many experiments have shown how effective these strategies are in enabling us to make sense of and string together apparent nonsense – when we have to. They solve most of the problem of remembering.

But as well as integrating the separate items with each other as well as you can, you also need to attach the whole package to the autobiographical context in which the learning is taking place. Without this, when I say 'Recall those words', you can only say '*What* words?' This 'contextualizing' occurs easily: linking to context is something that happens automatically because we are doing it all the time. People shown 2,500 slides can recognize them later with 95% accuracy:[33] the contextual associations must be created quickly and reliably.

The last ditch strategy of all for retaining rubbish is *repetition*: if you can't fit it in, stamp it in. Even things that cannot be made any sense out of at all (like the 'times tables' to a six-year-old) can be retained if they are repeated often enough – either out loud or under your breath. With things like the multiplication tables, the effort may be worth it, justified by the usefulness of what is learnt in helping us to understand and retain other information. Rote learning is not a bad thing in itself: it certainly isn't 'wicked' or 'stupid' to use it as a teaching or learning technique. But it is an inefficient use of the mind's learning apparatus, that is probably justified considerably less often than was common in schools twenty years ago, and somewhat more often than current liberal educational dogma asserts.

Rote learning is adding a new isolated patch to the verbal plane, and isolated patches are not what the mind likes best, because they do not nourish it. The new knowledge has not been absorbed into the fabric and process of understanding, and it neither changes our understanding nor is changed by it. It is simply appended, unincorporated. It is not nourishing, therefore, in the sense in which food retained undigested is not nourishing. However full his cheeks a hamster will die unless he allows himself to 'let go' of his food in the form in which it arrived, and permit it to be transmuted, by digestion, into his own body. A bellyfull of undigested food does not 'become' you – in either sense of the word.

4.9   Rehearsing

We have a special strategy called 'talking-to-ourselves' or *rehearsing* that has two functions. First it helps us remember things (as in the previous section) by providing repeated exposure to their association. Even though a word, let us say, has only been spoken once, I can strengthen the association between it and its context by repeating it to myself as often as I can before the next word arrives. Second, rehearsal can simply keep things alive for a short period, so that, even though I cannot make a permanent record of them, I can hold them in my mind's eye until I have used them. Here is another analogy. Imagine the letter-sorting robot is faced with the problem of pigeon-holing a stream of letters (or small parcels would be better) that are arriving faster than he can cope. Someone is throwing him these parcels at a rate of one every second, but it takes him two seconds to sort each one. Worse, all the parcels contain glass and are marked HIGHLY FRAGILE, and the robot knows that if he drops one it will smash. Under these circumstances he has one last trick to fall back on: he can *juggle* with the parcels, while trying to flick the odd one into its pigeon-hole, and hope that the stream stops before his juggling limits (he can manage about four to five parcels) are exceeded. If they are, then he can't help some of the parcels getting broken (i.e. forgotten.)

This specialized, short-term holding strategy has aroused intense excitement amongst experimental psychologists, the reason for which is not at all clear. In everyday life we use it to remember unfamiliar telephone numbers between looking them up and dialling them, and precious little else.[34]

CHAPTER 5

THOUGHT, INSTRUCTION,
AND ILLUMINATION

Then Suction Ask'd if Pindar was not a better Poet than Ghiotto was a Painter.
'Plutarch has not the life of Ghiotto,' said Sipsop.
'No,' said Quid, 'to be sure, he was an Italian.'
'Well,' said Suction, 'that is not any proof.'
'Plutarch was a nasty ignorant puppy,' said Quid. 'I hate your sneaking rascals. There's Aradobo in ten or twelve years will be a far superior genius.'
'Ah!' said the Pythagorean, 'Aradobo will make a very clever fellow.'
'Why,' said Quid, 'I should think that any natural fool would make a clever fellow, if he was properly brought up.'
'Ah, hang your reasoning!' said the Epicurean. 'I hate reasoning. I do everything by my feelings.'

I attempted every morning for a fortnight together to follow your Dictate, but when I found my attempts were in vain, resolved to show an independence which I know will please an Author better than slavishly following the track of another, however admirable that track may be. At any rate, my Excuse must be: I could not do otherwise; it was out of my power.

The cistern contains: the fountain overflows.

'Well, I sort of make it up,' said Pooh. . . . 'It comes to me sometimes.'
'Ah!' said Rabbit, who never let things come to him, but always went and fetched them.

(A. A. Milne: *The House at Pooh Corner*)

The focus of attention in this chapter is not so much on registering new information and ideas as on developing the potential of what we have already got. Not eating but body-building. In some of the kinds of learning we shall look at, the process starts with the input of a problem, say, but what is important now are the internal machinations that ensue.

5.1 **Deliberating**

Most of our conscious mental activity is taken up with thinking, reasoning, figuring things out. This kind of verbal and symbolic problem-solving is what this section is about. It is the same kind of process as the bridge-building that we have met before, but its 'feel' is different. The bridging that happens at the experiential level is not conscious: we may be consciously aware of the *product*, when we find ourselves trying out a newly formed expectancy, but the *process* is not open to observation. Many of the solutions that we produce to our daily problems are of this sort: 'It just came to me' people say, or 'I just had to wait and see which way my feet pointed.' 'I couldn't think what to do, and then I just found myself dialling your number.' Very often the experiential plane comes up with actions that seem to fit the bill without any effort of will on my part. But when we deliberate, the bridge is built out of a series of propositions: the destination is reached by travelling on a 'train of thought', the separate carriages of which have to be connected by links that are, or at least seem to be, logical and rational. Not any kind of wild association will do. I feel bound to follow the rules of the logic I have been taught. If I do not then I cannot expect the bridge of my argument, my 'chain of reasoning', to be stable. It is in danger of being 'knocked down' by questions, of 'letting me down' if I pin my hopes on it.

When is this strategy of deliberating called into play? What counts as a suitable case for treatment? Obviously it is unnecessary when the 'problem' is so trivial that it is 'no problem'. I do not have to work out a plan for getting from here to the kitchen: I do it literally without thinking. Nor, at the other extreme, is it a problem for me to get from here to the kitchen *without moving*. My mind plays briefly with the fantasy of having the house reconstructed around me so that it is moved seven yards south, while I remain at my desk – and then rejects the 'problem' as impossible. I do not see my situation as a problem unless (i) I have no immediate and appropriate response to it, but (ii) I feel the need for some action or decision, and (iii) I anticipate that I am capable of finding a solution. And as we saw in Chapter 3 the boundaries between the trivial, the problematic and the impossible are set as much by my feelings and beliefs as they are by the actual disparity between current knowledge and desired outcome.

With respect to this fluctuating band of problems, we might identify two strategies – we can call them *start-to-finish* and *ends-to-middle*. Some problems are amenable to both of these, and some to only one. Start-to-finish problem-solving means working outwards from the problem, exploring possible associations and implications, fitting assumptions end-to-end, until we reach a position that we recognize as a, or the, solution. Crossword puzzles and brain teasers are good examples of problems that demand this sort of approach. You start from one bank and gradually build your bridge outwards until you get to the other. You bolt on one section, then crawl along that and bolt on the next one, and so on. In fact the analogy is improved by imagining the construction work being carried out in a thick fog: you don't know where the other bank is till you get there. And if one bridge doesn't seem to be getting anywhere, you may abandon it and start work on another. 'Simon and Nancy leave Farnham and Alton, ten miles apart, simultaneously, and cycle towards each other along the dead straight A31, both at 10 mph. As Simon leaves Farnham a fly takes off at 16 mph from his handlebars, flies until it meets Nancy and then back and forth between the two cyclists at constant speed until they meet. How far has the fly flown?' The first bridge people often try to build involves working out where Nancy is when the fly first gets to her; then where Simon is by the time the fly gets back; and so on, gradually adding up all the distances. But this rapidly gets complicated and very tedious. So they abandon that and see if there is a simpler way – which there is. When Simon and Nancy meet, the fly has been on the go for a half hour. At a constant speed of 16 mph he *must* have done eight miles. Easy.

Other problems allow you the possibility of building the bridge outwards from both banks together, and hoping they meet. (This reminds me of a 'news' item created, I think, by Tony Buffery. 'There were rowdy scenes today as the Prime Minister officially opened the escalator joining the 12 mile English Channel Bridge to the 12 mile French Channel Tunnel. . . .') The clearest example of this is mathematical problems of the sort:

Show that $\sin 2\theta = 2 \sin \theta \cos \theta$

Prove the identity: $e^{\pi i} = 1$

But we also use the ends-to-middle strategy in tackling more informal problems, like where to eat. We can propose a variety of *possible* solutions, and then link them up with where we are and what we want, in order to come out with a *good* solution. 'I'm starving. Where can we get a cheap meal?' 'Well, there's the *Shalimar*'. 'No, I don't fancy that. It's too far and the last time I went we had to wait ages to be served. . . .' And so on. This strategy only works, of course, when you either know the solution ('OK.

The Chelsea Pot it is. Now, how do we get there from here?'), or can generate a limited number of candidate solutions. Note, too, how these problem-solving techniques can be combined with others, like exploring. If we decide we would like to eat at *Ma Cuisine*, which is always very popular, we can supplement our reasoning with hard data by ringing up, before we set out, to see if they have a table. Or if my problem is to know whether I need to turn the bath off yet, I can either *work* it out (if I know how long it has been running and how long it takes) or *check* it out, by going to see.

There are a number of ways in which rational problem-solving seems to go wrong, many of which have been well documented by psychological research.[1] We may start trying to build the bridge from the wrong place. When we look at a problem, we make a decision to see it *as* a problem, but we also make assumptions, often intuitively and automatically, about what kind of problem to see it as. What previous problems does it look like? What preconceptions can we make about how to tackle it, and what information that we already possess is or isn't going to be relevant? And so on. One of the most general conclusions that emerges from the research on deliberation is that it is surprisingly difficult to 'undo' these assumptions, once made. For example, the sentence: *The horse raced past the barn fell* is difficult for most people to comprehend.[2] If you tell them that it *is* a perfectly good sentence, and can be understood (without adding quotation marks, capital letters or tricky punctuation) it becomes a problem that is quite hard to unravel. The trouble is in the initial assumption we make about its syntax: it looks very like the similar sentence 'The horse raced past the barn' – but if we interpret it this way, 'fell' dangles awkwardly on the end, obstinately refusing to be integrated. If you suggest to the puzzler that a more fruitful analogy to work from is the sentence: 'The horse *sent* past the barn fell' the troublesome sentence suddenly reorganizes itself and all is well. Starting to build the bridge between the different parts of the sentence from an inappropriate point prevents, in this case, its ever being comprehended.

Another example. Try first to divide the square with one quarter removed into four pieces of equal shape and size (see Figure 5.1a). Having done this, now try to divide the whole square in Figure 5.1b, with the missing corner replaced, into *five* identical pieces.

What happens quite frequently is that people try to extrapolate the solution to *a* to the solving of *b* – and get into rather a mess. They subconsciously assume that the 'shape' of the bridge connecting problem and solution in the two cases is the same.

So far we have illustrated three 'problems with problem-solving'. We

a   b

Figure 5.1

may start to build the bridge in the wrong place. We may be unable to dismantle or abandon a bridge, once started, and look at the problem in a different way. And we may mistakenly assume that the way of solving one problem is the same as the way of solving another. We try to build the wrong *kind* of bridge. Another error occurs when we start from an appropriate place, but prejudge the direction in which the bridge has to be built, so that we refuse to explore ideas and hypotheses that, while initially not very promising, actually turn out to be the way to the solution. Consider this problem. Suppose you are given a chess-board that has had two opposite corners removed, as in Figure 5.2, and in addition a number of domino-shaped pieces of cardboard, each of which exactly covers two squares of the chess-board. The problem is to say whether you can exactly cover the mutilated board with the bits of cardboard without cutting, bending or overlapping them. There are two common nonsolutions that people try. Some insist on doing it by trial-and-error, and discover that it is quite hard to do. This fact alone however does not justify the conclusion that it cannot be done: for that, all possible permutations would need to be tried, and that would take even a computer a very long time. Alternatively, people realize that, as each bit of cardboard covers *two* squares, there must be an even

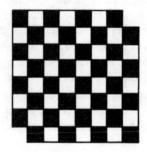

Figure 5.2

number of squares on the board. They work out that the board has 62 squares and conclude that the problem can be solved – without appreciating that the number of squares being even is a *necessary* but not a *sufficient* condition. Rarely do people spontaneously play with what they know about the *colours* of the squares on a chess-board. Yet herein lies an easy solution. Each domino must cover one black and one white square. So there must not only be an even number of squares: there must be an equal number of black and white. But the two corners that have been cut out must be the same colour – leaving either 30 black and 32 white or *vice versa*. Thus the solution to the problem is to see that it cannot be solved. A successful and solid bridge can be built out of knowledge that *a priori* seems irrelevant to the problem.

This is one form of 'jumping to conclusions'. Another is literally to jump from the problem to an assumed solution, and then try to build the bridge backwards in order to prove that this assumed conclusion is right. Sometimes this works. Often it doesn't. One of Peter Wason's puzzles will illustrate this.[3] He told his student guinea-pigs that he had in mind a rule that linked together a series of three numbers – one such series being 2, 4, 6. It was their job to generate other series, to which Wason would reply 'Yes' or 'No', depending on whether they conformed to his rule or not, until they felt sure they knew what the rule was. They could then announce the rule to see if they were right or not. A typical exchange would go:

'3, 5, 7?'   'Yes'
'6, 8, 10?'   'Yes'
'19, 21, 23?' 'Yes'

'The rule is X, X + 2, X + 4' 'No'.

At this point the subjects experience a rude shock, because they felt sure they knew what the rule was more or less from the word Go, and having received three or four confirmations are stunned to be told they are wrong. They are forced to experiment more daringly with the series they generate . . .

'2, 4, 8?'   'Yes'
'3, 7, 11?'   'Yes'
'6, 4, 2?'   'No'
'1, 2, 10?'   'Yes'
'90, 91, 89?' 'No'

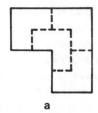

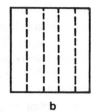

a   b

Figure 5.3 Solutions to the two puzzles above in Figure 5.1

. . . until they eventually realize that the rule in Wason's mind is '*Any* ascending series of three numbers'. This tendency that we possess, to reason backwards from what we believe, rather than forwards from what we know, would not be of much consequence if it were confined to such simple examples of our deliberations. Unfortunately we shall see in the next section that it is more widespread than this, and in Chapter 6 that it is in fact a ubiquitous and maladaptive feature of people's approach to life.

Another way in which our deliberations frustrate themselves is by going round in circles. We start by building a bridge, but we lose our sense of direction in the fog, and it turns back on itself and becomes an endless loop from which we cannot escape. This state, wherein as Alan Watts has put it 'thought whirls wildly around without issue', we call in everyday language *worrying* or *fretting*. We know that we are getting nowhere, yet we cannot stop. A relatively unimportant example of this is the 'tip-of-the-tongue' state, where we are trying to recall, let us say, a particular name, and we know that we know it, but somehow cannot quite retrieve it. Instead, an alternative name, that is like it but not it, keeps forcing itself on us again and again. More seriously a similar see-sawing backwards and forwards between argument and counter-argument is likely to occur when we pose ourselves such problems as 'Why did she leave me?' or 'Should I give him his ring back?' 'Perhaps . . .' we say to ourselves, and 'But then again . . .' and 'On the other hand . . .' chasing our tail round and round, constantly invalidating whichever tentative conclusion we have just reached.

Certain particular pitfalls are present when we are trying to solve problems that require strictly logical deductive reasoning. The most simple and well-defined of such problems are called *syllogisms*, and involve the extraction, or evaluation, of a conclusion from two premises. 'All normative sciences that deal with the problem of order may be considered to be branches of mathematics. Logic is a normative science dealing with the problem of order; therefore logic is a branch of mathematics.' It does not matter whether you *agree* with the definition of logic, or whether you *believe* the conclusion. The question is: Does the conclusion *follow* from the two earlier statements? 'Birth control interferes with a woman's natural instinct to reproduce. Any interference with nature is an evil which should be prohibited. Therefore, birth control should be prohibited.' The conclusion remains valid whatever your feelings about birth control or the manipulation of nature. It does not make it *true*, or *desirable*, or *practical*, or *likeable*; but if you accept the premises, then you cannot at the same time reject the conclusion. That is what 'valid' means. Logic is like civil engineering. It does not tell you what colour concrete to build your bridges out of, nor where to build them. It tells you what makes a bridge strong, and how to build it. Its considerations are of structure, not of aesthetics, purpose or location. The logic of deductive reasoning is therefore a tool for building useful arguments: it is secondary, a helpful means to the primary goals of solving personally relevant problems. And for this reason it is a fallible means.

When people are asked to reason logically under unfavourable conditions these failings become apparent. First, 'valid' is a judgement that it is difficult to make independently of *other* judgements like 'true', 'desirable', 'workable', or 'congenial'. Thus in the slightly unusual situation where the evaluation of validity becomes the end, rather than a means, it is not surprising that these other considerations – the more normally preeminent ones – intrude. We tend to accept as a good argument one that results in a conclusion that we believe to be true, or with which we are in sympathy;[4] whereas valid reasoning that leads to a distasteful or false conclusion we tend to reject. Although I have introduced this well-documented fact as a pit-fall, it is only such when we suddenly elevate the servant to the role of master. It is not surprising that the Lord of Misrule makes 'mistakes'. The errors are not inherent in the system, but in the application of the system to a task for which it was not principally designed. Reason and emotion are meshed together: it is inevitable that we get a grinding noise if we try to turn one without the other.

'Errors' also appear when we try to isolate the process of reasoning from familiar content that we are used to reasoning about. The misconception that human beings contain a faculty of 'pure reason' that we can apply to any content is similar to the one we encountered when looking at the early work on memory. Ebbinghaus, you remember, thought we had a 'pure learning' ability that could be studied free of past experience, and we criticized that in

Chapter 4. The critique of pure reason is analogous. A famous example of an abstract reasoning task is 'Wason's Four Card Problem'. Imagine you are shown the four cards in Figure 5.4. You are told *for sure* that every card has a letter on one side and a number on the other, and then asked which cards you would want to turn over in order to say anything about the truth or falsity of the statement: 'If there is a D on one side, there is a 3 on the other.'

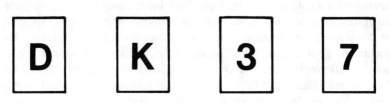

Figure 5.4

The 'pure reason' answer is D and 7, whereas people usually choose D and 3. (You can figure this out for yourself.) On the other hand, when the same logical task is presented in a guise that recruits people's past experience in an appropriate way, the 'logical' answer is much more commonly given. In this task,[5] you imagine that you have to enforce the licensing law. 'If a person is drinking alcohol they must be over 18 years old', and are shown the four cards in Figure 5.5: someone drinking beer, someone drinking coke, a 16-year-old and a 22-year-old. In this case the 'logical' solution – that you have to find out who is drinking the beer *and* what the 16-year-old is drinking, is readily perceived by the experimental subjects (see note 3).

Figure 5.5

5.2 Discussing

When we talk to other people, we do so often to elaborate what we already know, instead of, or in addition to gathering new information. We reason publicly as well as privately. The declared intent of such discussion, in a seminar, for example, is to explore communally the further implications of our current understanding. I build a trial bridge, and you expose flaws in its design, or suggest a neater one. Theoretically we are both engaged in a search for true or useful ramifications of our knowledge.

Sometimes this happens, and when it does, it is subject to the strategies and conditions we have already discussed. But frequently the real game of conversation is quite different: not an assault on the truth but a defence of it. Argument becomes the business of building any kind of flimsy bridge between certain premises and a conclusion that you already believe or want to be right, while at the same time mining or undermining other people's bridges, when they lead them to different positions. The process of arguing, as evidenced by politicians, trade unions officials, literary critics, senior management, and bar-room devotees of certain football teams – but especially politicians – is not start-to-finish, but ends-to-middle, or even finish-to-start. Often the bridge consists of no more than a string of verbal associations designed to con speaker and listener alike into believing that an argument has been made. Yet this semblance of a bridge consists only of overlapping girders without any logical links or ties.

In order to carry on this business of pseudo-discussion we develop a repertoire of sleights-of-hand for conjuring the illusion of a logical train of thought. Many of these tricks are described by Anthony Flew in his book *Thinking About Thinking*.[5] Just one example is what Flew calls the No True Scotsman technique. Jimmy (a Scotsman) and Bill are chatting about a newspaper story on a series of vicious late-night attacks on bus conductors in Glasgow. The story suggests they were all the work of the same man, and Jimmy delivers himself to Bill of the conviction that no Scotsman could have done such things. It must be an Englishman or an Irishman perhaps. Whoever it is, it can't possibly be a Scot. A week later Jimmy and Bill meet again, and Bill confronts Jimmy with the news that the villain has just been caught, and indeed turns out to be a native Glaswegian. What of his claim now? Without a pause Jimmy retorts: 'That's as may be. But no *true* Scotsman could have done it. That guy's not a *real* Scot.' This statement looks similar to the original one – but it is in fact crucially different, because it can't be proved wrong. The first claim is a substantial prediction: it asserts something about the world. The second one does not. It is not what philosophers call a 'contingent' statement: it is instead a definition of what a 'true Scotsman' is, that cannot be falsified by any experience. A 'true Scotsman' is necessarily a Scotsman who does not attack people on buses. By making such a move, Jimmy seems to be modifying his position without

admitting defeat. That is the point of it. It does not enhance our understanding of Scotsmen, or even *true* Scotsmen, because the definition is
infinitely flexible. A true Scotsman can be whatever we need him to be in
order to get ourselves out of a hole. Likewise 'true communists', 'real
aristocrats', and 'typical psychologists'. The most dangerous and infuriating
thing about these devices is that they are usually shock-proof. If you try to
show Jimmy what he is up to, he will either not know what you are talking
about, pretend not to know what you are talking about, or respond with a
counteracting smokescreen like 'Who the hell do you think you are – bloody
Plato or something?' Arguments begin to get heated when the participants
sense the imminent exposure of their conclusions as articles of faith, and
themselves as less than rational. And to avoid the discomfort, we reach into
our bag of tricks, and reason is twisted to suit our ends and preserve our
illusions. We change the subject ('Good grief! Is that the time?'); question
the other's motives ('You're only saying that because you're jealous of that
promotion I got' – as if your reasons for arguing have anything to do with the
validity of your arguments); appeal to a (usually unobtainable) authority ('I
think you'll find that Robbie Burns held much the same opinion. . . .');
and so on and so on.

5.3 Sinking in

Deliberating is an activity that happens within the verbal, symbolic plane of
our minds. Discussing and arguing reflect the interaction of *two* verbal
planes. The kinds of learning that are the subject of the rest of this chapter
all involve, in differing ways, interaction between the verbal and experiential planes within a person. As we have seen, verbal and experiential
knowledge, though somewhat different and partially independent of each
other, are closely interlinked. They are, in fact, components of an integrated learning system. Traditionally in psychology the two domains have
been studied separately, as if they coexisted in the mind but without
collaboration. So far I have respected this approximate split, but now we
need to look at learning that involves the modification of one form of
knowledge through the other. How, on the one hand, do verbal tuitions or
instructions come to alter what I see and do, as well as what I say? And on
the other, how does my tacit, intuitive, experiential knowledge come to be
represented in conscious thought? How is it that I can 'know myself'?

Let me take the problem of how the verbal plane penetrates into and
modifies the experiential plane first. How is it that by altering the flags I can

change the conformation of the dunes? The key observation that requires explanation, as I have indicated already, is the great variability of the effect of words on nonverbal action and experience. When I hear 'cat', the experiential referents and expectancies can be accessed and activated with ease. I can talk to you about cats in reply, but I can also draw one, look around for one, imitate one, put its food down or remember previous cats I have known. If you say 'the minimum lending rate', my responses are more impoverished and predominantly verbal. The words, to use Vygotsky's evocative phrase,[6] are not 'saturated with experience' in the same way as 'cat', 'pub' or 'Ian Botham' are.

The effect of statements and commands – tuition and instruction – are if anything even more variable. 'There is a tiger behind you' (spoken in plausible circumstances) percolates immediately from the level of verbal understanding to the control of action. So does the exclamation 'Fire!' So, in a rather different way, does the message 'I would like to make love with you'. I may not move very sharply, but all of a sudden I find my cheeks burning, my knees a bit wobbly, a stammer creeps into my voice and a foolish grin spills across my face.

At the other end of the scale there are statements that have no such effect on me. Most of what I hear on the news is of this sort. Were I an Estonian baker, news of the Soviet Union's wheat deal with the USA might literally be life-or-death to me. As it is, there is nothing I can do, need to do, or even want to do about it. However, in between the extremes of urgency and indifference there fall an interesting intermediate class of statements: those that have potential relevance to my life, but which somehow do not make spontaneous or immediate contact with my vitals. In such cases the 'news', though deeply significant cannot affect me experientially because I lack the experience to make deep sense out of it. 'The Kingdom of God is within you' is, I surmise, about the best news it is possible to have. Yet I cannot connect with it. My organism as it is, is not equipped to digest it, so, though rich, I cannot be nourished by it. It is like giving cellophane-wrapped fillet steak to a tadpole.

Fortunately we are better off than the tadpole, for we possess a way of storing such food until we are ready for it: we can preserve it in verbal form, much as a hamster can accumulate seeds that it cannot eat, but will not waste, in its cheeks. Language presents us with experience that is 'canned', so to speak, and if we are unable to use it immediately, we can pile it up in our verbal larder. When I first learnt that 'the best way to be of value to another person in distress is to listen', it was an attractive but rather lifeless idea, and I put it on the larder shelf. Gradually, over the years, this truth has *sunk in*, helping me to make sense of, and integrate, experiences that might otherwise have seemed isolated and fortuitous. Thus one way in which words can influence the growth of experiential knowledge is by providing a nodal point through which apparently disparate experiences can be inter-related. Bridges can be built between locations in the experiential plane *via* the verbal plane. The ultimate 'decision' as to whether two such experiences do belong together, whether they are to form the foundation of a new and useful expectancy or not, is itself an experiential one. But our verbal knowledge comprises another vast array of clues and suggestions about the direction that experiential learning might take. Words can point to signifi-cant areas of overlap between experiences that might otherwise have been missed. When we discuss the nature of instruction we shall consider more deeply what is already apparent: namely, that verbal learnings can *guide* experiential learning, but they do not *create* it. When a part of the verbal plane is well connected to an elaborated set of expectancies, hearing the words will activate them directly and immediately. Where this is not so, where some dislocation between the two planes exists, the receipt of a new set of words, however wise, does not cause an instantaneous alignment of the associated expectancies. Learning in this case can only happen in the indirect, more protracted, fashion I have just described. This is not clearly understood by teachers, who often become impatient with the lag between verbal tuition and experiential (usually behavioural) shift. Their impatience is inappropriate and counter-productive.

'Sinking in' in a slightly different sense occurs when a well-known statement – a cliché for example – suddenly reveals other *linguistic* inter-pretations through which experience can be contacted. The resonance of the two meanings often creates a deeper sense of understanding than either alone. A potent example is Donne's 'No man is an island', which has always meant to me that all mankind is essentially interconnected, interdependent in some way. 'And therefore never send to know for whom the bell tolls: it tolls for thee', Donne continues, expressing the same kind of thing. Every-body's joy is my joy. Anybody's death is my death. It is a pretty basic mystical notion. But a little while ago I realized that you can read Donne's line a different way, as ' "No" – man *is* an island.' The person who habitually says 'No' to his life, to other people's offers of intimacy and friendship, to the vicissitudes of his own experience, a man whose life-style is a struggle of resistance and denial – such a curmudgeon *is* an island, apparently disconnected, isolated and loveless. Putting these two meanings side-by-side, I saw that people, like real islands, seem to be separate but beneath the surface the connections are inviolable. Indeed it is the fact of unitedness that permits the appearance of division. And having seen that, it further becomes apparent that I, like everybody, have a choice as to whether I side with the unity or the diversity. If, like the curmudgeon that I am from time to time, I choose the latter, then I am, as Housman said, 'a stranger and afraid, in a world I never made', and it makes sense to be hostile, suspicious and fearful. But when I acknowledge that I have Life Membership, that is quite irrevocable, of a very intimate club indeed, then I can relax a little, for I am everywhere and always 'at home'.

5.4 Instruction

When I teach you *facts* in the hope that they will make a difference to how you are and who you are, I do so with the intention that you will discover for yourself that they provide a productive set of pegs and patterns on which to hang your own experience. The experience that I am referring to when I say 'pride comes before a fall' is not generated in the process. But when I give you an *instruction*, my intention is that you should create for yourself an action, so that you can evaluate directly or indirectly, its success in getting you what you want. 'Try dividing both sides by 2a' is such an instruction. So is 'Add the milk very slowly while stirring continuously.' In one case the outcome is a solved equation, in the other a lump-free sauce. The instruction does not make you want the outcome: that is presumed. But it does provide you with a suggested way of achieving it. As with statements, there are many commands or invitations that can be turned into action immediately. 'Don't pick your nose.' 'Press the button when the red light comes on.' 'Turn the oven down to mark 4 at a quarter past seven.' 'Look out for a 45 bus.' An adult may not perceive the value of such an instruction, in which case it will not be implemented. But there is no difficulty in principle in converting these words into deeds. For young children it is not so easy, because the necessary connections may not have been established. Even more basically, the child of one or two years old has to realize that it is *possible* for language to affect his own behaviour. He has to move from seeing language as solely descriptive, through the realization that his words influence other people's reactions to him ('Milk!', 'More'), to the reciprocal admission that it is useful for him to be on the receiving end of others' instructions. Verbal control of action has itself to be learnt. Thus A. R. Luria, for example, showed that two-year-olds could not really follow the instruction 'When the light flashes, press the bell.' And the more he exhorted them by saying 'Press *only* when the light is on', or '*Don't* press when there is no light', the more the children pressed their bells quite indiscriminately.[7]

More difficult to understand are the instructions that do not 'take' immediately. 'Keep your eye on the ball', 'Don't flash outside the off-stump', 'Try and drop your fingers onto the keys during this passage as if they were dew-drops rolling off a leaf into a still pond.' You can see what is required, but it takes time, practice and demonstration before the instruction becomes embedded in your spontaneity. Finally, there are instructions that are so nebulous that they may take a lifetime to be incorporated (in the literal sense of 'made flesh'), if indeed they ever are. 'Thou shalt love the Lord thy God with all thy heart and with all thy mind and with all thy strength' is a fairly tricky one to get hold of. In cases such as this, the instruction works by guiding the learner towards a goal that is way beyond what he can currently achieve, and which may even be beyond his ability to conceptualize, except in the haziest of possible terms.

Thus instructions serve two possible functions. They can help to *generate experiences* whose value the learner can assess for himself, and they can provide an *external standard of evaluation*, a temporary scale against which to measure progress, when the learner is not capable of doing this experientially. B. F. Skinner has pointed to both these in his *About Behaviourism*.

> We ourselves often acquire a deeper understanding of a rule . . . through exposure to the natural consequences it described. Thus if we have memorised a maxim and observed it, we may begin to be modified by the natural consequences. We discover for example that it 'really is true' that procrastination is the thief of time, and we then understand the maxim in a different sense. The understanding gained by moving from rule-governed to contingency-shaped behaviour is usually reinforcing, in part because the reinforcers in the latter case are less likely to be contrived and hence less likely to work in the interests of others.

Skinner illustrates the second function of instruction with the example of learning to drive a car.

> The instructor has not 'communicated' his knowledge or experience to the learner. The final uninstructed behaviour is shaped and maintained by the natural contingencies of car and highway. The instructor has made it possible for the learner to come under their control speedily and without harm . . . (Instructions) are often especially effective because many of the advantages of the behaviour they strengthen are long deferred and do not function well as reinforcers.

Note that neither of these roles for instructions produces learning. Their effect is to guide and facilitate the 'natural' (to use Skinner's word) learning processes and learning energies that we discussed in Chapters 2 and 3. They function with respect to these in the same way as a pea-stick functions for the growing pea.[8] It is in the pea's best interests (as well as the gardener's) to grow upwards, but on its own it may never get to the stage where it appreciates what a good idea it is. However, the gardener can utilize the energy of growth, and the pea's proclivity for winding itself round things by inserting a stick up which it will climb. When unskilled the learner may not appreciate why the instructor says 'Do it this way'. But if he takes it on trust, and wraps himself round the instruction, he is able to advance to a point where he can see in retrospect the justifications that he could not understand before. The young pianist, trusting her teacher, practises fingering and scales that are not much fun, but which will issue in the dexterity and intuition that she hankers for.

The image of the pea-stick can help us see a number of potential problems with instruction. First, if the pea is given not one but a host of sticks to follow, all leading in different directions, it may well, as Michael Flanders and Donald Swann wrote 'just go straight up – and fall flat on its face'. The more good advice we receive, to help us become good teachers or good parents, say, the more confused we get. Dr. Benjamin Spock, author of the famous 'bringing up baby' books, publicly recanted all his wise words. His honest observation was that the net effect of his good advice (and its goodness is not the question) had been to undermine parents' faith in their own native intuition and ability, and thereby to increase, rather than allay, their fears. Second, the stick may, by accident or design, lead the pea away from its natural direction of growth. A pea-stick in the form of a big croquet hoop, that starts taking the pea up and then turns it back on itself, is not assisting the pea; it is perverting it. Teachers in training, new parents, but especially young people, are bombarded with suggestions about how they ought to be that takes no notice of their individual needs and inclinations. Third, the pea's growth will be stunted if either it or the stick or the gardener misunderstand their relationship. Eventually the pea will be as tall as the stick, but it will get there in its own time. Yet, as we saw before, learners are all too frequently made to feel guilty if they cannot achieve the standard set by the instruction instantly. If the gardener derides the pea-shoot for being so small, or if he is constantly digging it up to see how it is getting on, he is inhibiting the growth he wishes to see. Either kind of dig is counter-productive. 'Really, Anna! If I've told you once I've told you a hundred times. How can you be so stupid? Even Jeremy's got the hang of it and he isn't exactly the class Einstein – are you Jeremy?' Neither peas nor children are elastic: they cannot be stretched by force.

Actually there are some people at some times who do respond to judgements about the disparity between pea and stick; whose growth rate or productivity is increased by being called lazy, weedy, or inadequate. But such goads, unless used by someone who knows that the learner *can* do it, and in whom the learner has some trust, are much more often undermining. A good example is provided by the way Mike Brearley handled the different temperaments of Bob Willis and Ian Botham when he was captain of the England cricket team. Willis needs no winding up, because when he bowls he is already tight as a drum. Any criticism or well-intentioned mickey-taking is likely to tip him over the top into the debilitating agony of self-doubt. However, when Brearley wants a little more out of Botham, he instructs mid-on and mid-off to have a go at him as he walks back. 'Come on, Woodentop,' they will say, 'I've seen my granny look more dangerous than that taking the top off a boiled egg.' And Botham paws the ground, his eyes turn pink, and he thunders in with new venom.

The fourth problem revolves around the trust that the pea has to place in the stick. For the instruction to be accepted as an aid to growth, the learner has to accept that the instructor knows what he is doing, that he has his best interests at heart and that when the skill is learnt the responsibility for future growth will be handed back to him. The danger, as Jerome Bruner has pointed out, is that the Master may be into a power-trip, and refuse to let you go. 'Instruction is a provisional state that has as its object to make the learner or the problem-solver self-sufficient. Any regimen of correction carries the danger that the learner may become permanently dependent upon the tutor's correction. The tutor must correct the learner in a fashion that eventually makes it possible for the learner to take over the corrective function himself. Otherwise the result of instruction is to create a form of mastery that is contingent upon the perpetual presence of the teacher.'[9]

Fifth (and here the metaphor begins to get a bit too fanciful, perhaps), a pea-stick that is rough and knobbly is easier to get a hold on than one that is smooth and shiny. 'Be firm but fair', or 'Try to be accepting of the children without getting too involved', are clear enough in their own way, but difficult to get a good grip on experientially. It often helps to roughen up such slippery maxims with anecdotes, examples, parables, and jokes, so that the learner's 'feel' for what the maxim means is increased. In order to get the hang of it, he needs something to hang on to. This is a facet of instruction that is under-valued, it seems to me, in the world of formal education.

Sixth, instructions are sometimes phased as Don'ts rather than Do's, as dams rather than conduits, and they are less effective and more confusing as a result. Dont's are the verbal equivalents of punishments, and most of the doubts that we aired about the latter are applicable to the former. Particularly a Don't instruction prevents you from validating it experientially, for it forbids you from doing exactly those experiments that would enable you to learn for yourself that it is a good idea. Some experiments are too risky to be allowed, and the corresponding prohibitions have to be enforced: 'Don't run out into the road', or 'Don't play with fire', and so on. Others endanger the lives or treasures of other people: 'Don't drink and drive', or 'Don't touch Auntie Rachel's Ming vase, darling.' But in general Don't is a poor instruction as far as the learner is concerned, not least because it develops a slavish dependence on or obedience to the commands of other people, and an unquestioning 'Why? Because I say so' attitude. The depth and ubiquity of this obedience-to-authority syndrome have been amply demonstrated by the well-known experiments of Milgram, Zimbardo and Adolf Hitler.[10]

To understand the seventh problem of instruction we have to leave our useful pea-stick behind. It is as much to do with how instructions are generated as it is with their reception. When we discussed experiential knowledge in Chapter 3, we saw that skills, things we can do, do not exist on their own, but are deeply embedded in a fine web of considerations about *when* to do it, *where* to do it, *what* to do it for, and exactly *how* to do it, under various conditions, in order to achieve the best effect. All our habits, we said, are contextualized with respect to the time, manner, place, and purpose of their use.[11] Even if it were capable of being absorbed undamaged by the learner, there is no way that this delicate filigree of ability can be rendered into words. Thus an instruction can only be a caricature of what the skilled exponent knows. It is at best a guide, an approximation, a hint about where to look for an understanding that can only be established through experience. Robert Pirsig in *Zen and the Art of Motor-Cycle Maintenance* describes the problem in the context of trying to teach the art of good writing to college students.[12]

> It seemed as though every rule he honestly tried to discover with them, and learn with them, was so full of exceptions and contradictions and qualifications and confusions that he wished he'd never come across the rule in the first place. . . . What he really thought was that the rule was *pasted on* to the writing after the writing was all done. It was *post hoc*, after the fact, instead of

prior to the fact. And he became convinced that all the writers the students were supposed to mimic wrote without rules, putting down whatever sounded right, then going back to see if it still sounded right and changing it if it didn't. . . . But how do you teach something that isn't premeditated?

And the insight that Pirsig is groping towards as he tries to teach 'rhetoric' is elegantly expressed by Michael Polanyi in *Personal Knowledge*.[13] He calls instructions 'maxims'.

> Maxims are rules, the correct application of which is part of the art which they govern. . . . Maxims cannot be understood, still less applied by anyone not already possessing a good practical knowledge of the art. They derive their interest from our appreciation of the art and cannot themselves either replace or establish that appreciation. . . . Maxims can function only within a framework of personal (i.e. experiential) knowledge.

This is the basic reason why ability cannot be transmitted directly.

The eighth problem with instruction follows from this. It is that an ability cannot be fully established by learning 'off the job'. Instruction and practice must take place at least in part in the context in which the skill is ultimately going to be exhibited, otherwise the subtle triggers and modulations will not be established. Some time in the nets, alone in the practice room, or experimenting with micro-teaching is valuable. But the learning process must at some stage be pursued in front of a class or on the concert platform. It is not possible to complete your learning before your first public performance.

5.5 Guided Discovery

A particular kind of instruction called 'guided discovery' has been a popular subject of debate in education for some time.[14] It usually involves leading people to a predetermined concept by providing them with a series of planned experiences. The teacher's role is not to communicate the understanding in words (tuition), nor simply to ask people to act in ways that will generate valuable and digestible feedback (instruction), but to orchestrate the learners' experience for them, and nudge their comprehension in the 'right' direction. Frequently this process is used to teach people concepts by showing them a range of things that are, or are not, good examples of it. Or the learners are allowed to generate *possible* examples and guess whether they are good examples or not. The words Yes and No, or some symbolic equivalent, are vital tools for accomplishing this. Guided discovery is useful for the acquisition of many concepts: for some it is essential. Without the assistance of someone else who already knows what the concept is, the strategies of the learner would be inadequate. The type of concept for which outside help is vital is that which only works when it is exactly right. This means that, very often, when we are in the process of discovering a new ABC expectancy, we try out an approximation to the right action (i.e. the one that will eventually turn out to be the most effective one), in an approximation to the right context, and what happens is that we receive back an approximation to the right consequence. The 'observed consequence', as we have called it, contains some but not all of the features that we wanted. Thus the success of the developing ABC is mirrored by the degree to which we get what we want. Gradually the taste of the sauce, the noise level in the class-room, the time on the stop-watch, the fun we have together, becomes more the way we would like them to be.

But there are other concepts that are not more-or-less but all-or-none. Like a lock, unless you have exactly the right key or exactly the right combination, nothing happens. One digit wrong is no more use than all digits wrong. (I am assuming that we cannot hear the tumblers fall.) The learning problem here is that we don't know how far off we are. The observed consequence does not lead us gently by the hand towards the ideal solution, and we need an alternative source of feedback. That source is most likely to be another person who can take over the guidance role when Nature refuses to play it. If there is nothing in the natural consequences of an experiment that tells us Right or Wrong, Yes or No, then a person can tell us. But in addition, if Right or Wrong is *all* that Nature will say, then a teacher can supplement that minimal information by telling us how far and in what way we are wrong. We can clarify this with examples of each kind of human intervention: those that tell us *whether* we are right or wrong; those that tell us *to what extent* we are right or wrong; and those that tell us *in what regard* we are right or wrong.

In 1956 Jerome Bruner published his researches with his colleagues Jacqueline Goodnow and George Austin in a book called *A Study of Thinking*.[15] The research investigated the ways people came to discover concepts when the only feedback they were given was Right or Wrong. The concepts that they used were 'artificial' ones: artificial in the sense that they were specifically invented for the experiments, rather than being naturally occurring; artificial in being well-defined rather than fuzzy;[16] and artificial in that the learner's job was solely to find out what the rules or features defining the concepts were, rather than to act on them in any significant way. The examples of the concepts were drawn from a big stack of cards that differed in the *shape* of the figures drawn on them (squares, circles, or crosses), the *number* of such figures on each card (one, two, or three), their *colour* (red, green, or black) and the number of *borders* to the card, which were black lines drawn round the edge (one, two, or three). Within this total set of cards, the experimenter would pick out a sub-set, like 'all cards with red squares', or 'all those cards with either two borders or three figures'. It was the learner's job to find out, by being told Right or Wrong about individual cards, what the concept in the experimenter's mind was.

The results of the research (which are summarized in almost every psychological and educational–psychological text-book) showed that people possess a variety of strategies for helping them to use the feedback to deduce what the concept is. Unfortunately, these types of concept, and this pure Right/Wrong kind of guidance, are rarely encountered in everyday life, so the usefulness of these strategies in everyday learning is somewhat limited. This way of guiding discovery is rather inefficient and teachers do not use it very much. The most prevalent real-life analogues of Bruner's tests are party games such as 'Twenty Questions', where you have to find out what I'm thinking about by asking questions, and all I will reply is Yes or No. Such games are entertaining precisely because Yes and No are not very rich responses, so that the questions have to be rather cunningly designed. These quizzes are more like mental press-ups than actually trying to get somewhere you want to be.

The second method of guiding discovery is to tell the learner something about how his attempts and conjectures are missing the mark. A good example of this is another popular game, a development of the Twenty Questions format, called 'Mastermind'. In Mastermind (which is not to be confused with the stress-inducing television quiz show of the same name) one player chooses a row of different coloured pegs – in the 'easy' version, four – which he or she hides from the other player. The chosen row might be White-Yellow-White-Red, for example. It is the second player's job to discover what this sequence is by suggesting a succession of guesses, about which the first player gives feedback. If the second player uses this feedback wisely, he can deduce the target sequence after only five guesses or so. This is possible because the feedback from Player One is not just Right or Wrong about the whole sequence that Player Two has proposed: it indicates how many of the pegs are both the right colour *and* how many of them are both the right colour and in the right position.

These games are fun because they both permit and challenge our rational, deliberate, deductive bridge-building abilities; but, as with the Bruner studies, the strategies that they require are applicable to only a small range of concepts – specifically those that are defined by a small, known range of dimensions (like colour and position), each of which has only a small, known range of values (e.g. white, yellow, red, blue, and black, or first, second, third, and fourth position). You could not teach someone what an elephant was, nor how to love, using the Mastermind technique.

In a more general way, however, the strategy of guiding other people's learning by pointing out to them in what ways their actions and conceptions are failing is, as we saw in the previous section, a useful, and widely used one, because their experiments become focused on these areas where learning is most necessary. And these instructions can facilitate intellectual as well as practical mastery. But Twenty Questions and Mastermind are not good models for this more general function, operating as they do solely within the domain of verbal reason.

The third type of guidance uses language (or some other code that the learner understands) for indicating how far away he is from hitting the right combination. 'Getting warm', we say, or 'No. I'm afraid you are way off.' Patrick Winston, a computer scientist, has shown just how valuable such information, particularly about 'near misses', can be.[17] His computer program can learn simple physical concepts, such as what an 'arch' is, for example, very quickly if it is shown things that *might* be arches, but aren't. The five examples in Figure 5.6, together with the information that they either are, or aren't quite, good arches, are sufficient to give us a pretty good idea of what an arch is.

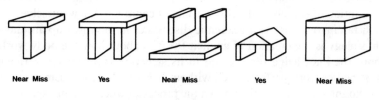

Figure 5.6

One block must be *supported* by *two* other blocks, between which there must be a *gap*, and the top block can be a *variety of shapes*.

These forms of tuition enable the network of concepts that we develop through our direct experience of the world to be aligned with the conventions and conceptualizations of the culture within which we are growing up. And unless we become a party to this consensus, we will find ourselves talking at cross-purposes with those around us. With the guidance of parents, teachers, and others who have already been initiated into the mysteries of 'being English', say, our world view becomes attuned to social contingencies in addition to those that have emerged from our interactions with the physical world. Likewise, as we learn a subject like 'chemistry', we are not only learning to conceptualize matter in more detail, but also to talk about it and even perceive it in the particular way that modern, Western chemists have developed and accepted. If I choose to be the kind of chemist described in Joseph Needham's *Science and Civilisation in China*,[18] my understanding may or may not be as deep, but my language will certainly be foreign to most Fellows of the Royal Society. As we shall see in the next chapter there is no problem about this social alignment unless the concepts, habits, and beliefs towards which I am guided contradict rather than supplement those that have grown in the soil of my own personal experience.

5.6 Realizing

To conclude our survey of the ways the two planes of our knowledge – the verbal and the experiential – interact during certain types of learning, we need to look at one more way, which I call *realizing*, or 'bubbling up'. Previously in this chapter we have been concerned with the filtering down of knowledge and understanding from the verbal to the experiential level. Realizing is the reverse process, where experiential knowledge that had hitherto been held tacitly becomes consciously conceptualized, and a verbal description of it is created. This activity of coming to know ourselves is of such fascination that vast academic disciplines have grown up around it. Physiology is the creation of explicit theories about how the body works, about the knowledge represented in its structure and function – though most bodies work perfectly well without being understood. Linguists and psycholinguists try to make known the processes whereby language itself is produced and comprehended. And the whole of psychology is the business of rendering people's actions, feelings, needs, perceptions, and thoughts intelligible to the intellect. Philosophy, too, is (or at least used to be) part of the same endeavour.

Now there are three ways to find out about people's experiential knowledge. You can do it experimentally, by prodding them in various ways, seeing what happens, and then trying to work out how come that prod produced that reaction. This is the psychologist's approach. Or you can just sit down in a deep armchair and try to figure out rationally what people must be like. This is what philosophers do. Or you can tune in to the experiential machinations inside yourself, so that the evidence on which you base your developing consciousness is your direct perception of yourself. This is the way of psychotherapy and of mysticism, and it is also closely linked to what psychologists have called *creativity*. The fundamental process is one of receptivity to the tacit workings of the experiential plane, or rather to its products. And this receptivity occurs naturally provided one is willing to allow one's existing conscious theory to be challenged and to be changed, not so much by the receipt of new information but by the promptings and intuitions of one's own tacit knowledge.

Though the process of bubbling up is one, its products, those things that we can become conscious of, are many. Sometimes they are aspects of ourselves – our meanness, small-mindedness or prejudice, for example – that we had previously managed to deny. Such insights into self are discussed in the following two chapters. What we shall concentrate on here are the products of unconscious processing that represent potential solutions to problems – the traditional domain of creativity. Carl Rogers has recognized the underlying process behind both problem-solving and personal growth.[19] He calls it 'openness to experience', and defines it as 'a lack of rigidity and permeability of boundaries in concepts, beliefs, perceptions, and hypotheses. It means a tolerance for ambiguity where ambiguity exists. It means the ability to receive much conflicting information without forcing closure on the situation.' Of course it takes courage to say 'I don't know' when the need to know is strong, or when others are pressing you for an answer. And fear is therefore one of the pressures that mitigates against creativity.[20]

The other inhibiting factor is a matter of habit – the habit of focusing our attention exclusively on the bridge-building, route-following activity of the verbal, rational mind, and ignoring the faint clues, hints, hunches, images, and intuitions that bubble up from the tacit depths. It is true that some problems can be solved by the logical bolting together of propositions, the earnest exploration of the tram-lines of rational thought. But there are other, more profound problems, whose solution is not to be found in the diligent application of familiar patterns of thinking, because it is precisely those patterns that are problematic. The theory with which we think has itself to be altered before a resolution to our dilemma is possible. An earthquake has to change the contours of the verbal plane, and the force is generated 'below', in the domain of the tacit and the experiential. The value of being able to switch from intellect to in-tuition (i.e. tuition from within) has been expressed by many writers on creativity. Arthur Koestler says: 'The temporary relinquishing of conscious controls liberates the mind from certain constraints which are necessary to maintain the disciplined routines of thought but may become an impediment to the creative leap; at the same time other types of ideation on more primitive levels of mental organisation are brought into activity.'[21] Whether thought has to die down before intuition starts up is a moot and perhaps unanswerable question. Although it seems otherwise, the stars shine throughout the day, and it is only the simultaneous presence of the stronger sun that obscures them. So it may be that Koestler's process involves not a new activity, but simply a new receptivity to what has been there all along. Richard Jones, in *Fantasy and Feeling in Education*[22] talks about the same problem. 'We often choose to be unimaginative in order to be effectively conventional, and we do so by remaining aloof from the collateral and emotional references which orbit preconsciously around our conscious lines of thought. This is obviously all to the good: nothing less than civilisation depends upon it. The trouble comes when the vague sense of choice wanes and we find ourselves being unimaginative for no very good reason. I need hardly add that people are as frequently miseducated into this dilemma as they are not educated out of it.'

Of what exactly does the sun of intellectual habit consist, that it blinds us to our intuitions? First, it may insist on the use of concepts that are inappropriate. As we saw before, the bridge cannot be built if it starts from the wrong place, pointing in the wrong direction, constructed from inadequate materials. If you insist that the relevant tool is a hammer, you will be unlikely to invent the screw-driver. Second, reason requires that each section of the bridge be secure before the next is built. You have to be right at every stage. The creative leap, on the other hand, may say 'To hell with reason' – for the time being – and arise from toying with images and ideas that are quite illogical, improper, and fantastic. Creativity often requires that one abandon civil engineering for the sand-pit, and, by giving up solemn reason, allow oneself to take nonsense seriously. The books of Edward de Bono contain many examples of such fruitful play.[23] One of his tricks is to place on end in front of a class, an opaque black cylinder. After a few minutes it suddenly, without any outside influence, falls over, and the audience is invited to speculate on what happened. What turns out, again and again, is that absurd ideas, like 'It got tired', 'It's got pins and needles in one leg', or 'It shot itself', far from being useless, often lead their authors back to workable and rational hypotheses – ones that they would not have found had they insisted on being reasonable.

The third damper that reason places on creativity is its preoccupation with language. Yet, as we saw in Chapter 4, language is *sharp* and *serial*, rather than fuzzy and wholistic, and is therefore an uncongenial medium for hanging on to ambiguity and not-knowing. Of much more value are images, and it is not surprising that solutions often bubble up, 'occur to us', 'pop into our heads' in this form. The danger is that we will brush them aside as frivolous distractions, and fail to realize what they are trying to tell us. For this reason creative play requires alertness and receptivity to potential solutions that could not be deduced, but may yet be recognized. The most famous example from the field of science is perhaps Kékulé's discovery of the benzene ring. Having grappled with the problem all day without success, he took a break, poured himself a large gin and tonic and putting his feet up by the fireside, began to doze. As he did so, he saw snakes writhing in front of his eyes, one of which, as he watched, formed itself into a ring by eating its own tail. Thus it was that Kékulé saw the solution, and in presenting it to his colleagues was moved to moralize 'Gentleman, let us learn to dream!'.[24]

Einstein, too, talked about the relative importance of image and word in his creative process. 'The words or the language as they are written or spoken do not seem to play *any role* in my mechanism of thought. The physical entities which seem to serve as elements of thought are certain signs and *more or less clear images* which can be voluntarily reproduced and combined . . . this combinatory play seems to be *the* essential feature in productive thought, before there is any connection with logical construction in words or other kinds of sign which can be communicated to others. . . . In a stage where words intervene at all, they are, in my case, purely auditive, but they interfere only in a secondary stage.'[25] Or as Shakespeare makes Theseus say, in *A Mid-Summer Night's Dream*:

> The poet's eye, in a fine frenzy rolling,
> Doth glance from heaven to earth, from earth to heaven;
> And, as imagination bodies forth
> The forms of things unknown, the poet's[26] pen
> Turns them to shapes, and gives to airy nothing
> A local habitation and a name.

Despite these quotations it would be quite wrong to see reason as the villain of the piece. It is only villainous where it over-reaches itself, to tackle jobs for which it was not designed, assumes its own perfection and omnipotence, and thereby denies its limitations and rejects the need for nebulous play as a stimulus to its own developing precision. Especially in science, though also in everyday life, reason must from time to time allow itself to be stumped, and then surrender to the whispers that arise from without. Gregory Bateson, himself a remarkable advertisement for this principle, said that 'advances in scientific thought come about from a combination of loose and strict "thinking" '.[27] Poincaré paints a more exact version of the same picture by dividing the whole cycle of creative problem-solving into four stages: Preparation, Incubation, Illumination, and Verification. Preparation is a stage of reason, trying as hard as you can to figure out the answer. Incubation is what happens when you eventually admit defeat: the unconscious goes on working at it while you relax with the gin and tonic. Illumination is the conscious recognition of the relevance to the problem of a sudden inspiration or image that appears out of a clear blue sky. And Verification is the detailed checking-out, point by point, of whether the inspiration does actually work, or whether, like a lot of Good Ideas, it has in the end and with regret, to be consigned to the waste-paper basket. This last stage is important if the scientist is not to run the risk of making a fool of himself. Even Kékulé, after exhorting his colleagues to dream, went on: 'But before we publish them, let us submit our dreams to the tests of waking reason.'

One problem with defining creativity as a process is that it becomes impossible to measure: the only criteria for its presence are experiential ones. This is inconvenient for psychologists and educationalists who like the sound of 'creativity' and think there should be more of it. To help bring about more of it, they invent methods of teaching and training, but in order to know whether they are doing any good or not, they have to be able to measure a person's creativity before and after training. Thus the creative *process* becomes generalized into a hypothetical *character trait* that is assumed to generate certain *products* or *performances*. And it is only products and performances that can be measured and compared. Thus it is that this misguided logic leads to the absurdity of 'defining' a child's 'creativity' by counting the number of bizarre uses for a cardboard box which he or she can think of in three minutes. Even worse, if we try to evaluate the quality of these answers, we run up against the insoluble problem of deciding whether 'As a house for a kitten' is more 'creative' than 'As a plate.' All such judgements must reflect a host of unknown historical, social and cultural preconceptions, and therefore miss the mark.[28]

Apart from anything else 'creativity' is not a trait but a process that may occur in a certain *state*, and that state is relaxed but alert receptivity. It is almost a certainty that when a child or an adult is being subjected to any formal test, that state will not be present.[29]

CHAPTER 6

UNLEARNING TO LEARN

LONDON
I wander thro' each dirty street,
Near where the dirty Thames does flow,
And mark in every face I meet
Marks of weakness, marks of woe.

In every cry of every Man,
In every Infant's cry of fear,
In every voice, in every ban,
The mind-forg'd manacles I hear.

Truth can never be told so as to be understood, and not be believ'd.

Quite normal children, adolescents and adults (as well as neurotic ones) experience learning as a conflict between a desire to hold on to the more or less satisfactory ways of the past and a need to meet the upsetting demands of the future.

(Goodwin Watson)[1]

At a number of points in the preceding chapters I have had to say 'More of that later' and leave an end loose. Now is 'later', and in this chapter we will weave together these loose ends until they can be seen to form the very nub of the book. The nub is this: that the first unique property of human beings – the possession of language – has led, not inevitably but ubiquitously, to the appearance of a second unique characteristic, which is the belief that we are many things that we are not. Given the choice between the dictates of these beliefs and the evidence of our senses, we are prone to accept the former, deny the latter, and therefore forsake much of the learning ability that this book has described so far. It follows that adults are not, as we like to think 'grown-ups'; we are all, to a greater or lesser extent, cases of arrested development. This chapter explains how these conclusions follow from the point of view we have been exploring, and how this evolutionary error comes about. This is the Bad News. Chapter 7 contains the Good News: what we can do to unjam our learning, and what happens when we do.

6.1 The Story So Far

It will help, before we launch off into the Bad News, to recapitulate the story so far. We live with and through a theory about ourselves-in-the-world, and there is nothing that we do or see or know or feel that is not a product of that theory. Even when it seems as thin as gossamer it remains, and there is no way to rend the veil, nor to peek round it. The basic function of this theory is survival – the physical survival of the body and the survival of anything else which a person considers himself or herself to be. It works by predicting the consequences of our actions and thereby enabling us to select actions that will maximize the chances of our getting what we want or need, and minimizing the chances of our encountering whatever seems to threaten us. The theory gets better by leading us, whenever the risk is not too great, to investigate and experiment with unknown situations, and by distilling and storing information about the consequences. This is learning. When the risk is too great, we feel fear, and this is the signal to escape from the threat, to destroy it, or, if all else fails, to ignore it. This is not learning.

In addition to this experiential, inductive form of learning, and the theory it generates, we human beings possess the ability to represent parts of this theory in words – to make a map of the map. We can also develop the map of the map by understanding spoken or written language generated by others. Some of this verbal information comes to make a difference, either immediately or more gradually, to the experiential theory, and thus to what we see and do. Some of it does not. Some of this verbal information corresponds to what we have learnt for ourselves, inductively. And some of it does not. One of the puzzles we will have to face in this chapter is this: how does it come about that some things that we are told, which in many cases actually contradict the world as we experience it to be, nevertheless gain control over what we see and do? How is it possible, in psychological terms, for 'The Fall' – the loss of innocence of Adam and Eve and everybody since – to occur? And is it, as Christianity would have us believe, irreversible? Can we not rise again? Now read on. . . .

6.2 'Is it Safe?'

The job of the mind is to ensure survival, and to that end it has to keep asking, like Laurence Olivier in the film *The Marathon Man*, 'Is it safe?' If the answer is a clear 'Yes' or 'No', we know what to do: we approach or we avoid. Our survival depends on not getting it wrong, and the object of our learning is to not get it wrong more and more frequently; to be able to assign every new situation to the correct category, Safe or Dangerous, and to know how to treat it. But the 'learning problem' is that the answer to this question may *not* be clear. Instead of a 'Yes' or a 'No', you get a 'Don't know', and, if it is the latter, the next question is, 'Is it safe enough to investigate?' A confident 'Yes' leads on to the further decision, '*How* shall I learn about it?', and the learner's problem is to decide which of her learning strategies is most likely and most rapidly going to give her mastery. A confident 'No – I don't know what it is but I sure don't like the look of it' leads to further decisions about how to escape from it or avoid it. In the first case whatever-it-is is seen as a challenge to be accepted, and in the second as a mystery to be avoided. The thing may actually be Safe, but the risk of finding out is assessed as too great. Beyond a certain point 'strangeness' is treated *as* a threat because there is an increasingly good chance that, unknown though it is, it *contains* a threat. Note that what is important for a person's action is the decision that they make about a situation, not what it 'really' is. Every type of occurrence that I *assume* to be threatening has exactly the same status, exactly the same behavioural and emotional power over me, as one that I *know* to be a threat.

But here too the decision may not be clear-cut. I don't know whether this thing is safe, and I'm not at all sure either whether it is safe to explore. Yet whether I choose to explore or not may be vitally important. And herein lies the basic tension of life, the twin horns on which our learning is impaled. For on the one hand, a novel occurrence may be dangerous, and therefore it makes sense to avoid it. While on the other, if we do avoid it, we never find out whether it is truly dangerous or not. Neither approach and investigation, nor avoidance or combat is a fail-safe tactic. If I decide to investigate this strange object, I may come to understand it, master it, even be able to use it. But if it is actually an unexploded bomb, then it may blow up in my face, and my curiosity, like the cat's, will turn out to have lethal consequences. If I choose, however, to avoid it, then I don't get hurt, but I have thereby limited my competence and established a permanent no-go area for myself. The benefit of 'approach' is long-term competence and the cost of short-term insecurity. The benefit ot 'avoidance' is short-term security and the cost is long-term incompetence.

So in the domain of uncertainty, the questions are: do I approach and if so how; or do I avoid or escape, and if so how. The ability to make this decision – to know what to do when you don't know what to do – depends on having learnt a good repertoire of learning and avoidance strategies and on being able to deploy them appropriately. This, as we shall see, is not a bad definition of *intelligence*; one that applies equally, and equally productively, to animals and to people.

6.3 Dealing with Threat

We have started to use the word 'avoidance', and that requires a little explanation. Once one is actually confronted with something that is either known or believed to be a threat, it may be too late. If you ignore the warning sign that says 'Danger: Unexploded Mines' and continue walking until you feel the metal prong digging into the sole of your foot, you may already have blown it. Survival is ensured better by *avoidance*, by taking evasive action, than by trying to *escape* from danger that is already present. The trick is to learn to anticipate possible threat so that the mechanism of avoidance is turned on first. One learns to respond to *signals* of threat as well as, and preferably instead of, responding to threat itself. The signals become like 'dummy' threats, warnings that have a little whiff of danger about them, without being dangerous themselves.

When these signals are well learnt, it is as if we establish between ourselves and our threats a sort of 'demilitarized zone' (the DMZ)[2] which, while safe itself, contains alarm bells and flashing lights that tell us to turn

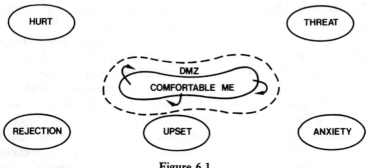

Figure 6.1

back or we might be in for a nasty shock. To the extent that this early warning system works, I can avoid all contact with those things of which I am afraid (see Figure 6.1). But to the same extent one also falls into the 'trap of Mark Twain's cat', which we will examine shortly.

6.4 Kinds of Threat

A threat is anything that is seen by a person as jeopardizing their survival. Who 'they' are, as we saw in Chapter 1 is who or whatever they consider themselves to be – their 'identity'.[3] Everything that is included, consciously or unconsciously, within my definition of myself *is* 'me'. For most people this definition consists of (a) their physical body, and (b) a load of other things that they have learnt to consider themselves as. Thus there are two kinds of threat: those that are likely to cause actual bodily harm – and those that seem to threaten the other parts of one's identity. The range of physical lacks, predators, and dangers is fairly obvious. It includes intense cold, malnutrition, tigers, muggers, and avalanches. The others – which I shall call *beliefs* – are not quite so obvious, but just as important. They need some explaining.

6.5 Beliefs

Animals and babies have no use for beliefs. They either know things, they suspect things, or they don't know things. The things they don't know they treat with caution; the things they suspect they know, or know partially, they treat with a certain amount of respect; and the things they know they interact with happily and confidently until they are let down. Monkeys do not believe in bananas, babies do not believe in milk, and I don't believe in the Queen's Elm. Our knowledge on these matters is, so to speak, 'carnal' – bodily, experiential. Yet as they grow up, all children in all cultures are told things that they accept as being so, or as being desirable or undesirable, but which are not embedded in their direct experience. Some of their theory about the world and especially about themselves has to be taken on trust, and they are required to operate as if these things were so, or ought to be so, despite either a lack of corroboration from their own experience, or worse, the presence of already formed but contradictory expectancies. Thus a child may learn that she is a slow learner, that she ought not to cry, that her parents do everything for her own good and that her Uncle Tim is uncouth and cruel and to be avoided, despite the fact that her experience may ignore or repudiate them all. Whatever we have been told that has no basis in our own experience, or whatever we discovered to be the case once, but which has no basis in *current* experience – any such piece of knowledge that nonetheless exerts some control over present-day perception, feeling, thought, or deed, I shall call a *belief*. Beliefs are beliefs not because they misrepresent the way things are but because the believer does not know, for herself, directly, whether they are accurate, yet feels constrained to act as if they were.

Now if beliefs were like most of the things we are told, we would check them out, if possible, or remain agnostic if not. If someone tells me I like spinach, or that I ought to like spinach, I can tell them they are mistaken. I don't, and I see no reason why I should. If someone tells me that the largest trout ever caught in Lake Trasimeno measured just over a metre, I can put this information on file but I won't hang for it. If a fact checks out, then I can 'identify' with it, or have an 'investment' in it, because I know not just that it is 'true', but that it is true for me. If I can't verify or falsify it in terms of my own theory, then I will not, unless I *believe* it, identify with it at all.

People include within their definitions of themselves a variety of things – their 'character', their achievements, their possessions, their capabilities, their children, and at least some of their knowledge. Thus it is that being fired from a job, having the only draft of a Ph.D. stolen, being left by your wife, the death of a child, a stock market crash or the decisive refutation of a theory on which one has staked a life's work – any of these, besides feeling shocking, may feel like a deep threat to one's own survival. When people are questioned about such traumas, they often say things like 'I felt annihilated', 'as if the bottom had dropped out of my world', 'I felt like nothing . . . completely worthless', 'as if life just wasn't worth living any more'. In fact if I feel more identified with my reputation than I do with my physical body, then the only response to the threat of my exposure as a fraud is to put a bullet through my brain. Identified more with their country than their physical safety, soldiers either win the Victoria Cross or are blown to bits. Even if we do not take such drastic action, it has recently been suggested that these traumatic dents to a person's self-concept cause them *literally* to 'die a little'.[4] Sackings, divorces, burglaries, and the like each knock a little off our life expectancy, or increase our susceptibility to heart attacks and strokes.

At times like these reality surges over the dykes of our defences. We can only build so high, and are at the mercy of freak conditions that are yet not rare enough. But of more interest to us here is the effect that our home-spun insulation has on our day-to-day existence. For beliefs, if they are to ensure their own survival, must penetrate, like viruses, into the tissues of our expectancies, and subvert them. Our mobility must be directed away from dangerous situations, and our awareness from dangerous experience. Thus while beliefs operate to prevent their own falsification – and thereby their own verification, too – nevertheless they do generate a kind of pseudo-confirmation.[5]

First, they act as a perceptual filter that only lets through compatible sensations, or seeks always to generate compatible accounts of apparently discrepant events. If I believe in God, and I believe that She is Good, then either I must ignore any evidence of suffering and injustice, or I must have up my sleeve arguments that death by starvation and errors of justice are actually manifestations of Her Goodness. In Her wisdom She sends us trials in order to test us and enhance our spiritual maturity. Or: if everyone was happy and nice, there would be no challenge in the commandment to love your neighbour. Or whatever. When we look at the world through beliefs, we cannot allow it to speak for itself, lest it speak out of turn. We paint a pretty picture of a sunny day on the inside of the blind, and keep it pulled down. Having pasted my preconceptions firmly all over you, you cannot surprise or upset me any more. The only trouble is that I am stuck with the 'you' I have created. And though it suits me well to see you sometimes as a prince and sometimes as a toad, the truth is, probably, that you are neither.

Second (and usually used in conjunction with the first), I can choose to limit the way I *act* so that the only things I can do are in accordance with the way I believe I, or things, ought to be. The trouble is, I can never quite fool myself, however much I manage to hoodwink others. If I *act* as if I were a nice, kind, generous person, I may get away with it, but I can never afford to relax enough to find out for myself whether it is true or not. Forever condemned to play the Good Guy, I must remain unaware and untrusting of any natural Goodness I may possess.

Third, there is an even more insidious way in which beliefs can fool us into accepting their rightness. If I believe my dog is vicious, I won't trust him to run around freely in case he bites someone, so I keep him chained up. Now any self-respecting animal who is chained up all the time gets pretty fed up – and becomes vicious. Whereupon I feel quite vindicated, and say 'Told you so . . . a good job I chained him up before he did any serious danage', and tighten the chain still further. I still do not know whether the dog was dangerous to start with, but he certainly is now. In just the same way, if I believe myself to be full of nastiness – anger, lust, selfishness, meanness, pride or whatever – then my attempts to control myself, to chain myself up, may produce exactly the kinds of impulses I was afraid of. The tighter the rope gets, the more I struggle and cuss – which is, of course, evidence that the rope is not yet tight enough. The only way out of this literally vicious circle is to let the dog off the lead – which, by the time one gets round to it, is a much too risky thing to do. When ordinary men and women are let slip, truly they become the 'dogs of war'. Nazi Germany showed that, as, less dramatically, does research on 'encounter groups'.[6]

Whenever we live through a belief we are in a bit of a trap. Having to act as though something were so, without knowing whether it is or not, it is difficult to avoid the deep suspicion that it just might not be. In fact it is a commonplace that the less secure one feels about a belief the more noisily and energetically one has to defend it. People do not have to go on crusades in order to persuade other people of the existence of bananas. Nor do I have to read books about them or go to a special place each week to be reminded about them. Such crutches are only needed because the obverse of all belief is *doubt*, and doubt (when it is existential and not just intellectual) is another name for the *fear* that what one needs to be true may not be true after all. Anything that I have included within my definition of myself as a matter of belief is a potential source of fear, for there is nothing more frightening than to lose my sense of identity; not even, I suspect, the moment of my physical death. Thus whatever an experience threatens a belief, the believer feels anxious.[7]

6.6 Beliefs About What?

If beliefs are ideas in whose success we have a personal investment, what does the average portfolio look like? We can for convenience (though at the expense of some accuracy) put them under five headings. First there are beliefs about the *physical world*. Second there are beliefs about the *social world* – about the nature of society and about attendant matters of politics, economics, and manners. The other three categories are all forms of belief about self. The third is to do with beliefs about *character*. The fourth concerns beliefs about *worth*. And the fifth category contains those very deep beliefs about what it actually means to be or have a self – about *personhood*.

The beliefs that I shall mention are not beliefs by virtue of their content, the domain of experience to which they refer. They are candidates for beliefs because they are commonly *believed by people*. A belief becomes a belief because of the way it is held or known or cherished by the believer. Only the believer can know what his beliefs are by noticing what possibilities and what experience he strives to avoid or deny or refute 'too much'. And only he can sense what 'too much' is; what constitutes a reasonable attempt to make life bowl along as smoothly as possible, and what constitutes the unreasonable urge to force life to jump through the hoop of his preconceptions.

For us, just as for the scoffers at Galileo, there are deep beliefs about the nature of space, time, matter, causality, and so on that are very difficult to see even *as* beliefs, let alone to question or modify. David Bohm, Professor of Theoretical Physics at London University, and one of Einstein's most eminent students, explains why. 'Though physics has changed radically in many ways, the Cartesian grid . . . has remained the one key feature that has not changed. Evidently it is not easy to change this because our notions of order are pervasive, for not only do they involve our thinking but also our sense, our feelings, our intuitions, our physical movement, our relationships with other people and with society as a whole and, indeed, every phase of our lives. It is thus difficult to "step back" from old notions of order sufficiently to be able seriously to consider new notions or order.'[8] The everyday world we inhabit is based on the Cartesian and Newtonian beliefs of stable, three-dimensional space which contains separate chunks of matter that interact in unidirectional time – that is, time that flows constantly in one direction so that 'causes' always happen before their effects. Yet the physics of relativity theory and quantum theory tells us that the 'reality' is different: that space, time, and matter are *not* separate, but are interwoven; that all 'objects' are facets of a single, unbroken field of energy that permeates the universe (so there is no such thing as 'space' between 'objects'); that even basic 'properties' of objects such as their masses reflect not essential attributes but interactions. Thus, for example, if the universe were a room, we could not rearrange the furniture without changing the shape of the room and without transmuting tables into chairs. And even if we are reasonable enough to give notional assent to these strange ideas, yet it is almost impossible to debug the programmes that construct our experience so that we see and feel ourselves to be inhabiting a relativistic world.

Not all beliefs about matter are so monumental, however. A trivial but instructive example, borrowed from Sheldon Kopp,[9] concerns the widespread belief that 'spit is dirty'. If I give you a glass of water to drink, the fact that the water mingles with saliva as you drink it doesn't trouble you at all. Yet if I ask you to spit into the water and then drink it, it feels not quite right. While acknowledging the irrationality of it, still we experience a reluctance to consume this 'sullied' water.

Next let me give some examples of possible beliefs about the social and biological worlds. To start from the bottom, people have firm but arbitrary convictions about the capabilities and merits of different species. To a Pekinese owner it may be clear that 'the little chap understands every word Mummy says, don't you Bobby?' Or, as Douglas Adams argues in *The Hitch-hiker's Guide to the Galaxy*:[10]

> It is an important and popular fact that things are not always what they seem. For instance, on the planet Earth, man has always assumed that he was more intelligent than dolphins because he had achieved so much – the wheel, New York, wars and so on – whilst all the dolphins had ever done was muck about in water having a good time. But conversely, the dolphins had always believed that they were far more intelligent than man – for precisely the same reasons.

People may passionately believe that the Prime Minister is the Saviour of the Country or 'The Lady Macbeth of the Dole Queue'; that the war in the Falklands was 'our finest hour' or 'our stupidest blunder'; that Education is a Good Thing and Britain Needs Its Universities; or that schooling is an efficient device for creating a passive work-force, and the Universities are anachronistic rest-homes for a pampered elite of intellectuals (the lecturers) and lazy, greedy and stupid young people who have been bred to have little sense of either their own limitations or their social responsibilities (the students). None of these beliefs, nor a million others like them, is open to refutation, for they are spotlights that illuminate the 'facts' from one side only, so that what is seen is what supports them.

Many beliefs surround the notion of 'childhood' and child development. 'Children are not naturally good', pronounce Cox and Boyson in the Black Papers on Education.[11] They believe that young people cannot be trusted to grow into useful and sociable adults on their own. If we do not keep them on the straight and narrow, their selfishness will submerge their sociability. Others believe the reverse,[12] that children can and should be trusted, and they too will point to a wealth of supporting evidence and argument.

People believe that certain styles of behaviour and interaction are appropriate to different ages of children – often in the face of contrary evidence. I spent six weeks in Guyana once with an American couple who had just adopted a six-year-old Guyanese girl. June's parents had been killed in a car crash and she had been living for the previous eighteen months with her uncle and aunt, helping her aunt to sell fish in the market every day, and often looking after the baby. She was an extremely tough, independent, competent little character, used to handling money, conversing with adults and going to bed late. She used adult language and swore a little. My friends, without really knowing what they were doing, set about turning her into a 'little girl' – six o'clock bedtimes, toys, ribbons in her hair, a special 'talking to a child' tone of voice, lots of encouragement to play but real or affected disapproval when she got too dirty, and so on. She was systematically disenfranchised from the adult world of responsibility and self-determination that she had been living in for the previous year.

There is a whole set of beliefs about other people through the lenses of which we magnify or diminish them. One man's 'fat' is another man's 'cuddly'. Workaholics I despise, but hard workers, now they're completely different. A common belief that causes a lot of trouble is that another person cannot be intelligent, honest, concerned and well-informed *and* hold a different opinion from me. If he has a different point of view, it must be because he is lacking in some respect. Different beliefs are activated by whether I like you or not. If I do you are 'forceful and committed', if I don't you are 'intransigent and pig-headed'. When I'm feeling good about you I admire your gentleness. When I'm feeling critical I despise your weakness. I believe that it is unmanly to cry – except perhaps when you've just won a major snooker championship or the World Cup. It's OK on telly, but we won't have any blubbering in the Public Bar, thank you very much. Eavesdrop on any gossip and you will hear a catalogue of the speaker's beliefs about what other people should do, and what gives evidence of a deficient character. Having an abortion or a nervous breakdown, being an 'easy lay', being too ambitious, having stains on your trousers, not returning books, watching too much television, being a chartered accountant, or Irish, or black, not visiting your parents often enough, being too serious, being too frivolous . . . the list of potential indictments is endless.

6.7 Characteristics, Worth, and Personhood

Some of what I know myself to be is derived from observation: it is experientially based. I know that I am five foot eleven, that I prefer chocolate to strawberry ice cream, that I enjoy detective stories and that I often find it difficult to get projects (writing a paper, painting the kitchen) properly finished. These are currently valid generalizations that I can update as and when required. But much of what people 'know' about themselves is not so accurate and not so open. We shall illustrate these under the three headings *characteristics*, *worth*, and *personhood*.

What kinds of characteristics do people mistakenly attribute to themselves? One is being a helpless victim of other people's whims and wishes – whereas in fact the 'victim' is manipulating the other's guilt in order to get what he wants. Another, which many women have been taught by their fathers and husbands, is to see themselves as much less intelligent and sensible than they (the women) are. When they dare to speak, what they say is perceptive and relevant, yet it is hedged about with a stream of apologies. 'I'm probably wrong. . . .' 'I expect I've got hold of the wrong end of the stick, as usual (with a little laugh to pretend she's joking), but. . . .'; 'David says women don't know anything about politics and he's probably right. . . .' Children come to see themselves as naughty and thoughtless who, in another family, would be seen as lively and independent. We can even grow up being mistaken about our preferences, as Abraham Maslow illustrates rather nicely:

> I particularly remember when I learned that I really hated lettuce. My father was a 'nature boy', and I had lettuce two meals a day for the whole of my early life. But one day in analysis after I had learned that I was carrying my father inside me, it dawned on me that it was my father, through *my* larynx, who was ordering salad with every meal. I can remember sitting there, realising that *I* hated lettuce and then saying, 'My god, take the damn stuff away!' I was emancipated, becoming in this small way me rather than my father. I didn't eat any more lettuce for months, until it finally settled back to what my body calls for. I have lettuce two or three times each week, which I now enjoy. But *not* twice a day.[13]

People consider themselves to be amusing despite the less than rapturous reception of their stories; to be honest despite stealing biros and stationery from the office; to be considerate despite spending hours on someone else's phone; to be plain despite the fact that everybody fancies them; to be damn sharp despite the collapse of their third company; to be physically feeble despite having just shifted that great big log off the child's leg. It should be clear from these examples, by the way, that we cannot know what is 'us' and what is belief until we are prepared to notice the facts and ditch the belief. Until a belief is seen through, it *is* 'us'.

Beliefs about personal worth or value are the 'oughts' by which we constantly judge and fail ourselves. I ought to be clear, strong, decisive, polite, understanding, and tidy. I ought not to cry, fight, shout, pick my nose, answer back, or forget things. I must fight with myself or my badness will erupt. I ought to be providing for my family: it feels as if I am diminished by being unemployed (and my wife agrees). I ought not to let little things get me down so much. I ought to go on a diet. I ought to go to the launderette more often. I ought to have Jan and Nick round for a meal. I ought not to have these macabre fantasies. And I shouldn't feel so guilty and irritable all the time. The essence of any belief of this sort is not that the quality of my life will be improved if I achieve the goal (although it might be) but that, right now, my worth as a person is in jeopardy. I am not allowed to relax and feel OK about myself until I have achieved my ideals, finished mucking out the infinite pig-sty of my own pettiness, and donned the pure white robe of perfection. We persist because of the superordinate belief that says 'If I do not feel bad about myself, I will not be motivated to try and better myself; and if I do not try to change myself, no change will happen, and I will stay just as inadequate a specimen as I am now. And that won't do.' Thus feeling bad about myself now is a necessary preliminary to eventually not feeling bad about myself. Unfortunately, clearing myself out seems to be such a major job, and progress so slow that it looks increasingly unlikely that there is going to be any rest in this life at all. So feeling bad about myself is as good as it gets. To the extent that people invest in the beliefs that the purpose of life is to get better, and that getting better requires dissatisfaction with yourself, to that extent they are trapped on an endlessly revolving exercise-wheel.

The latter belief is the exact converse of what is the case. For the most prevalent way in which people cope with the things they feel bad about is by avoiding and ignoring them, and if you avoid and ignore them, they *won't* get better. In fact unless these 'blemishes' are open to the fresh air of awareness they will not heal at all, and will eventually grow into poisonous and debilitating sores (in just the same way that the caged dog *becomes* vicious).

The final category contains beliefs about the very nature of self. What am I? Who am I, really, underneath the idiosyncrasies of character and ideology? Many people have never even thought about it, but if they did it is likely that they would agree with a list of criteria for personhood not unlike the one Bannister and Fransella offer in *Inquiring Man*:[14]

> It is argued you consider yourself a person in that:
> 1 You entertain a notion of your own separateness from others; you rely on the privacy of your own consciousness.
> 2 You entertain a notion of the integrality or completeness of your experience, so that you believe all parts of it are relatable because you are the experiencer.
> 3 You entertain a notion of your own continuity over time; you possess your own biography and live in relation to it.
> 4 You entertain a notion of the causality of your actions; you have purposes,

you intend, you accept a partial responsibility for the effects of what you do.

5 You entertain a notion of other persons by analogy with yourself; you assume a comparability of subjective experience.

In short, we believe ourselves to be separate, persistent and at least partially autonomous: our identity is localized within a particular bag of skin; it continues to exist, at some deep level unchanged, as long as the bag does; and it – I – can choose, decide, reflect and act in a way that is not wholly determined by its circumstances. It is unthinkable that 'I' should be something that has no past, no will and no fixed abode. Yet the possibility exists that the unthinkable is right and the self-evidently true is wrong. Certainly some rather eminent scholars seem to have thought so. Albert Einstein, for example, came to see that: 'A human being is a part of the whole, called by us "Universe", a part limited in time and space. He experiences himself, his thoughts and feelings, as something separated from the rest – a kind of optical delusion of his consciousness. This delusion is a kind of prison for us, restricting us to our personal desires and to affection for a few persons nearest to us. . . . Our task must be to free ourselves from this prison by widening our circle of compassion to embrace all living creatures and the whole nature in its beauty.'[15] While the no less eminent physicist Erwin Schrödinger wrote: 'The reason why our sentient, percipient and thinking ego is met nowhere within our scientific world picture is . . . because it is itself that world picture. . . . Mind is a *singulare tantum* . . . the overall number of minds is just one.'[16] Are these just the ramblings of old men in their declining years? Or might they have spotted something? The fact that they *are* on to something, and that that something is not just an intellectual nicety but a matter of supreme practical relevance to the chances of survival of an endangered species, *homo sapiens*, is what all religions, especially those from the East such as Buddhism, are at root about.[17]

6.8 The Community of Selves

If we look further into the beliefs that people hold about themselves and others, we find we can categorize them in a variety of different ways. In the last section we looked at three such categories:

Who I Believe I Am (character)
How I Believe I Ought To Be (worth/'super-ego')
What It Means To Be An 'I' (personhood)

We might just note here some of the others. For example *Character* splits into *Self-image* and *Shadow*. Self-image refers to those beliefs about myself that I hold consciously and knowingly ('I hate games'). Shadow refers to those that we have hidden away from ourselves in unconsciousness ('I hate my father').

Self-image in turn splits into *Likeable Self, Neutral Self* and *Shameful Self*. Likeable Self consists of all those beliefs about myself that I am happy to have ('I'm good at sums'). Neutral self consists of beliefs that are accepted without being either welcome or unwelcome ('I'm masculine'). Shameful self is the self 'I' struggle to improve. I am conscious of it and don't like it. This is the me that is grouchy in the mornings, forgets Mother's Day, tells lies, feels uncomfortable with people, and gets irritated for no 'good' reason. The Shameful Self consists of those beliefs about who and what and how I *am* that conflict with beliefs about who and what and how I *ought to be* – the Super-ego.

Cutting across these, character splits also into past, present, and future. As well as 'who I am now', we carry about, as a very important part of how we define ourselves, a set of beliefs about who we were, (*Historical Self*), and who we will be (*Future Self*) and who we want to be (*Ideal Self*). Note that the Ideal Self overlaps with, but is not the same as the Super-ego. The latter consists of obligations, duties and pressures; the former of aspirations, projections and ambitions. ('I feel I ought to get a job that uses my degree, but what I actually want to do is drive trucks'.)

If we change our perspective again we can look at the way these beliefs manifest themselves publicly – or not. Most of the previous categories can be cut into those bits I am happy for other people to know about (*Published Self*); those that I know about but like to keep quiet (*Private Self*); those that I would like to keep private but which (knowingly or unknowingly) tend to creep out (*Leaked Self*); those that I am happy to show to some people but not to others (*Role Self*); and those that I display, but which I construe as 'not the real me' (*Mask*).

There is much more fun to be had identifying the different parts of the community of selves, but we cannot fill in this opening sketch here.[18] We need to return to considering the *dynamics* of this tangle of beliefs, its function rather than its structure.

6.9 Self Conflicts

The self that we build up is riddled with inconsistencies and contradictions, though because we believe we ought to be consistent and rational, we try to hide as many of them as possible. A man feels attracted to a woman. What he thinks he wants to do is make love with her. But a voice says: 'You oughtn't to want "just another affair"; it's time a man of your age had grown out of this adolescent stuff.' And another voice answers: 'I don't care. I'll do what I want to.' And another one says: 'Hey, you guys, be reasonable. Maybe there's something in what Super-ego says. . . .' And another one says: 'Why can't I just stop fighting with myself?' And another says: 'I'm really fed up with all this mental chatter: shut up for a minute and get on with it.' And when they get to bed, he discovers that it wasn't sex he was after at all. He wanted a cuddle. And then he starts talking about how angry he is with his wife, and finally he discovers that the 'real him' isn't angry either: he just feels very very lost and lonely and like a puzzled five-year-old. All these selves may exist simultaneously, yet we only identify consciously with them one at a time. Instead of taking an aerial reconnaissance photo of the whole 'me', we scamper around from hill-top to hill-top, describing what we see, and then getting confused because it doesn't all fit together. I issue one statement from the top of the field looking south and another from the bottom looking north and wonder why they don't tally. They don't tally because 'I' is the whole field, not any one point of view. Thus we are subject to an endless stream of irresolvable conflicts. And, as Wittgenstein said, because our goals (in this case, consistency), are not lofty but illusory, our problems (resolving conflict) are not difficult but nonsensical.[19]

The basic function of learning *is* to resolve discrepancies: disparities between what I expected (theory) and what actually turned up (data). The problem is real and a solution is usually possible. But through identification we generate internal conflicts between parts or layers of our Self-image: head tries to fight with heart, right hand tussles with left hand, feet attempt to run away from shadow. We cannot allow ourselves to be *both* bad at maths and wanting to be an engineer; *both* wanting to be on the beach and having to go to a boring meeting; *both* anxious and angry about being anxious; *both* on my best behaviour and just having knocked a wine glass over; both answering the phone in a silly voice because Charlie said he would ring and feeling terrible because it turns out to be the Headmaster asking why your reports are a week behind everyone else's.

These internal disputes often become heated, though the heat itself is uncomfortable. The forms that anxiety takes in response to inner conflicts are called *shame, guilt,* and *embarrassment*, all variations in intensity and coloration of the repudiation of self by self.

6.10 **Individuality**

Psychology is very far from giving general explanations of why people turn out so differently. But the fact that they do reflects in large measure the definition of Self that they developed as they grew up. The beliefs to which they are committed determine the *areas* of experience to be avoided, the *extent* to which the reality of the Self in those areas has to be denied, and the *strategies* that they use for denial. We might note especially how these strategies vary in their complexity. As Alexis de Tocqueville said: 'I have always thought it rather interesting to follow the involuntary movements of fear in clever people. Fools coarsely display their cowardice in all its nakedness, but the others are able to cover it with a veil so delicate, so daintily woven with small plausible lies, that there is some pleasure to be found in contemplating this ingenious work of the human intelligence.[20] Thus some people bluster, some simper, some are alcoholic, some obese, some analyse their every move and others just throw things.

Extroverts and introverts differ in whether they are more afraid of being judged by themselves or by other people.[21] The compulsive extrovert finds it unbearable just to spend an evening alone, and doubly so if the TV isn't working. The compulsive introvert meets his monsters in a gathering where he doesn't know anybody, and where he is sure he will be exposed as dull and unattractive. Many people are intimidated by both, choosing whichever option currently seems less threatening – reluctantly turning up to the party 'for something to do' and leaving early because 'it is so boring'.

Neurotics and 'copers' differ in how firmly the lid of their defence is screwed down. The agitated person, the sufferer from nerves, is the one whose anxiety is strong enough, or whose defences are ineffective enough, for fears and conflicts to keep breaking through into awareness. The coper, on the other hand, has sewn himself up so tight that none of his guilt or grief or frustration or whatever gets through. He will seem to be, in the relevant areas, narrow, bigoted, and insensitive, and rather puzzled if anyone dares to question him. Having rendered himself untouchable, neither remembering nor sensing any challenge, he can live, captive but peaceful, within a windowless prison of his own devising. Only when someone or something bangs on the door is he forced to acknowledge that 'outside' exists, and perhaps to recall what he has given up in order to ensure his safety. At any moment in our lives we are a compendium of things that we can look calmly in the face, things that upset us, and things that are beyond our ken. Learning in the sense of growing in self-knowledge and self-acceptance means slowly transferring things from the last to the middle, and from the middle to the first category.

People vary considerably in what they enjoy doing or are prepared to do. Again each person's pattern is created jointly by the 'pull' of genuine aspiration on the one hand and the 'push' of threat on the other. A man may feel quite all right about breaking a plate while washing up, and about enjoying a good cry in the cinema, but refuse to join a game of darts for fear of making a fool of himself. A woman may be quite prepared to deliver a lecture on sex therapy to an audience of 500 distinguished clinicians, but not be able to tell her husband what's upsetting her when she gets home. Very often an experience or an experiment that just happens, unluckily, to have gone wrong when we were small, resulted in a decision to seal off that whole area for good. Thus are we shaped in the same way that a tree's development is heavily influenced by the accidents of weather and disturbance that befall the sapling.

6.11 Intelligence

Psychologists have been much interested in one particular way in which people differ. They have called it 'intelligence', or more generally 'ability'. (Bright and dull children are now euphemistically called the 'more able' and the 'less able'.) Usually it is seen as the amount of intellectual power that we have, rather like the power of different sized batteries, or the 'ability' of different sized cookers to produce meals of differing complexity. This power is said to be fixed either from birth (genetic determination) or early on in life (interaction of generic and environmental factors). And it is likely that our hypothetical potential *is* variable, and is determined in such a way. The variability that people actually display, however, is much greater than this factor suggests, and the 'ability' that they exhibit less, and often much less, than the theoretical maximum.[22] Why? Because we are not the stove but the cook, and the cook's meals depend on the size of the stove, true, but much more saliently on the cook's skill, experience, and daring. He can only use the cooker to its limit if he is completely *au fait* with it, and with the nature and possibilities of his ingredients; and if he feels confident, prepared to experiment and make the odd mistake. It also depends whether he is interested in cooking. Just so; a person's academic/intellectual 'ability' depends much more on her experience, confidence and interest than it does on any hypothetical fixed limit.[23]

A more interesting approach to 'intelligence' has to do with the ability to learn – that is, to decide (correctly) that a strange event (be it a spider or a maths problem) is safe to investigate; and to investigate it in such a way that it reveals its secrets, and therefore gives up its strangeness and becomes manageable, as quickly and efficiently as possible. A natural corollary is that it is also intelligent to refuse to engage with something that really is harmful. Intelligence inheres in having a good set of learning strategies (*and* avoidance strategies) and deploying them appropriately. Under this definition, the cause of stupidity in any normal adult is undue defensiveness or undue bravado – which in turn are caused by undue fear. Children are made to appear stupid by being taught to be afraid, especially by being taught to confuse success of action with worth of person. Intelligence tests by and large measure the degree to which the testee is intimidated by being tested, and the extent to which he is familiar and comfortable with the kind of question being asked. Studies such as those of William Labov in America show that as apprehension is reduced so 'ability' seems to rocket.[24] Why? Because anxiety, especially in the familiar forms of *worry* ('Will I fail? What will happen? What can I do?') provides a competing task, a distraction from the one in hand (writing test answers, learning to read) that captures the vital resources of attention and capacity.[25]

6.12 The Jamming of Learning Itself

Now we need to come back and conclude the story of the effect of believing on learning. First, to recap, we saw in Section 6.5 that beliefs prescribe domains of experience that are resistant to change. Some patches of our map of the world – both the maps of experience and of language and thought – are open to question, while others are not. Any experience within these latter areas that does or could controvert a belief is a threat, and must therefore be avoided. Thus are we surrounded by mental predators of our own creation. And because learning depends on attending to experience that conflicts with what is already known, learning in these domains is blocked or impeded. (It is more correct, of course, to say we have *degrees* of investment in our beliefs, and that this degree determines the force with which we resist their disconfirmation.) And so we come to threaten our own survival by refusing to keep up to date with a changing world. If the last time I stuck my head out of the window was ten years ago, I can't know now whether it is still raining or not. Or, as Mark Twain said, a cat that has once sat on a hot stove won't ever sit on one again – but it won't sit on a cold one, either. If you daren't risk getting burnt again, you can't discover whether the fire's gone out.

But things are even worse than this. There are four special beliefs that are widely held, though in varying degrees, and which have a debilitating effect *not just on the growth of certain areas, but of the whole theory, for they are beliefs that relate to the learning process itself*. They are:

1 I believe that my personal worth depends on the success of my actions. Therefore I must be *competent*.
2 I believe that my personal identity depends on being predictable to myself – that I am what I think I am. Therefore I must be *consistent*.
3 I believe that my survival and/or my sanity depends on my being able to understand, explain and predict what is happening in my world at all times. Therefore I must be in *control*.
4 I believe that it is possible and desirable to go through life without feeling bad – getting upset, anxious or guilty. Therefore I must be *comfortable*.

Now we can see the full scope of the problem, for these four 'commandments' about how I must be are the exact antitheses of the ways of being that are required of a learner.

Whenever we encounter a learning situation that is important then the struggle between hanging onto a theory that is demonstrably inadequate and plunging into the insecurity of not-knowing cannot be denied. To stand any chance of achieving an expanded competence, we have, like a snake, to slough off a familiar but constricting skin and risk the transitional nakedness and vulnerability. To take this risk requires not courage so much as a deep acknowledgement that if you do, you might die, or be hurt, or lose the gamble; if you don't, you will certainly lose because you have chosen to remain encased within a skin that becomes ever tighter and more uncomfortable. Thus it follows that only if you can risk failing, in the sense of not getting what you expect, and of allowing yourself to admit that your theory is inadequate, can you fully engage with the learning process. Learning is what happens when you take the risk of not being *competent*.

Three related risks also have to be taken if learning is to proceed unimpeded. You have to take the chance of finding out that you are not *Consistent*. If you allow yourself to experiment with previously untried ways of acting and being, you may catch yourself doing things that don't fit in with your idea of yourself. As well as your theory about the world being in jeopardy, so may your theory about yourself. You may be surprised by yourself, because in order to find out what *works*, you may have to try out things that aren't 'you'. The third risk that learning may require is that of not being in *Control*. In the gap between giving up a bit of your old theory and discovering a better bit, you have to be prepared to tolerate now-knowing and not-being-able-to-predict. You may have to flounder, thrash about, seek help, and admit you can't do it on your own, clutch at straws of advice or intuition, before the learning begins to come good, and a new, greater sense of control emerges. Finally, learning is often, as we have seen, accompanied by anxiety, so it is necessary to take the risk of not feeling *Comfortable*.

To the extent that I hold these as beliefs, therefore, *any* learning situation that threatens to make me incompetent, inconsistent, out of control, and uncomfortable appears to be a threat to me – to my survival as the person I think I am or hope I am or ought to be. When one of these triggers is pulled, learning is resisted, regardless of what the learning is actually about.

The mechanism whereby this happens is simple. Remember that in Chapter 3 we showed how a person's tendency to approach and learn from a situation increased as the degree of conflict between the demands of the situation and the current capacity of their theory increased – up to a point. At that point 'challenge' flipped over into 'threat', and the dominant survival strategies became the nonlearning ones of fight and flight. Now what happens when you suffer from the Four Cs is that *other* conflicts arise. As soon as a significant disparity between theory and experience arises,

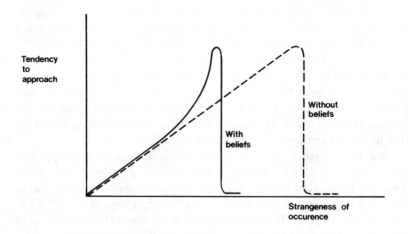

Figure 6.2

instead of just dealing with that, you now have to cope with the conflict between the effect that this disparity is having on you (e.g. making you feel uncomfortable) and your belief about how if you were half the man you were supposed to be you could handle such a situation without turning a hair. Thus you become more anxious still, and challenge becomes threat all the sooner (see Figure 6.2).

Situations of slight but manageable stress will, if they activate the Four Cs, be immediately transformed subjectively into apparent threats to survival. The upshot is that *the degree of strangeness that one can tolerate, that is, engage with and learn about, is drastically reduced and the frequency with which one resorts to escape, defence and demolition, increases*. More and more I have to deny my fallibility, my frailty, my tenuous grip on reality, my fearfulness, in order to preserve an image of myself that I do not need but cannot drop. Every time these buttons are pushed, it becomes more important for me to Be Right than to Find Out What Works. I cannot do both at once.

In this regard people compare rather unfavourably with rats.[26] Imagine a rat placed in a maze such as the one in Figure 6.3. He runs down the alleyway to the choice-point, and then down one of the arms. When he gets to the end of an arm, the experimenter picks him up and puts him back at the start again. After a few goes he discovers a lump of cheese at the end of the fourth arm. He learns that that is where the cheese is, and, being fond of cheese, he comes to choose the fourth arm every time. But after a while the experimenter moves the cheese. What does the rat do? He continues running down the fourth arm for a bit, but eventually starts exploring the other arms again – and if the cheese is there, he will find it. He may show some reluctance, even some annoyance, at having to give up his previously successful expectancy. But cheese is what he cares about, and cheese is what he will find. The human being, on the other hand, may continue to run down the fourth arm for ever, if he cannot bear to admit that he is wrong, or if he feels ashamed of being 'conned', or if he has come to *believe* that it is *right* to go down the fourth arm. 'Who cares about cheese?', he rationalizes, 'It's much prettier down here'. Or 'I don't know about any cheese. Cheese is for dopes. I tell ya – if the fourth arm was good enough for my old man, it's good enough for me.' So it is that people keep on sending their children to school, though that is not where learning is; they sit in traffic jams on sunny days getting hot and irritable and pretending they're on holiday; they keep on turning up at an office where people don't even know about cheese (or love, or laughter, or self-expression); and they keep on going home to a relationship that died ten years before. Anything rather than risk

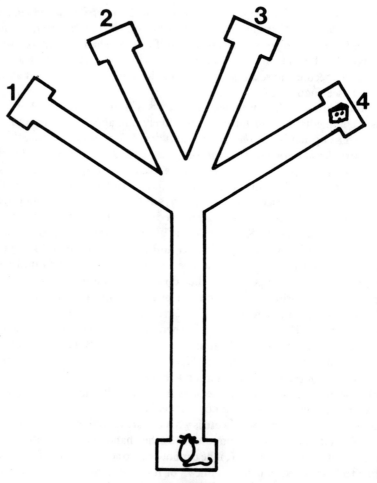

Figure 6.3

acknowledging an old failure in order to start on the road to a new success. Bertrand Russell once said that most people would die sooner than think – and most people do. By 'think' he meant not just cogitate, but actually dare to question their presuppositions about life.[27]

CHAPTER 7

DEFENCE AND GROWTH

A POISON TREE

I was angry with my friend:
I told my wrath, my wrath did end.
I was angry with my foe:
I told it not, my wrath did grow.

And I water'd it in fears,
Night & morning with my tears;
And I sunned it with smiles,
And with slow deceitful wiles.

Range him high amongst your saints, who, with all-acknowledged powers, and his own stedfast scale for every thing, can, on the call of judgment or advice, submit to transpose himself into another's situation, and to adopt his point of sight.

If the fool would persist in his folly he would become wise.

This chapter sketches a variety of strategies for living that start out life-enhancing and progress through the simply life-preserving to the absurdly life-denying. Ultimately, when even scraps of reality and vitality are too much to bear, then the only solution is to substitute a world that is entirely of one's own devising, or to quit: to turn out the too bright light of consciousness and to set in motion an unstoppable undoing of the constitution until what was 'I' becomes dust once more. This choice is the low spot of nonliving and nonlearning. That is just about as bad as it gets, and most people don't get there. However, by the way they abuse and over-use their defences, people do tend to create more trouble for themselves than they avoid, not least by cutting themselves off from the deep intimacy with other people that they were built to thrive on and enjoy. This hyper-defensiveness exists to protect things that we believe we are, or that without which we are not, many of which are obsolete or fictitious.

In the previous chapter we looked at where these beliefs come from, what fuels them, and how they cause us to shrink. We looked, in short, at the *dynamics* of self-hood and self-preservation. And we looked briefly at the *anatomy* of self – what actually *are* these beliefs? But we did not touch on the *development* and growth of personality. Having shrivelled like a seed in winter, what conditions constitute the spring in which a person can expand and bloom? The investigation of this 'relearning to learn' is pursued in the second part of this chapter.

7.1 **From Physical to Mental Defence**

When threatened, animals adopt the first-line defences of flight and fight. If these fail or are blocked, if the shock is too great, they seem able to go beyond these into a state of numbness – of being petrified. The human body possesses this ability, too, when it suffers grievous injury: we even use the same word and call it 'being in shock'. Being in shock seems to involve the disconnection of painful sensation from awareness. Instead of avoiding the cause, *in extremis* an organism is able to avoid the *experience*. The wounded soldier and the petrified rabbit show this.

It seems as if, while people are growing up, they learn to deploy this mechanism of unconsciousness much more widely, and in particular to use it as a defence against psychological threats, threats to beliefs, as well as against physical ones. Before we look at the varieties of inattention, we need perhaps to ask why this shift of defences from physical to mental ground has taken place. The first answer is that socialization (especially perhaps Western middle-class socialization) equips us with a set of beliefs about identity and worth that serve to confuse and confound our natural responses to threat. The clear picture of appropriateness and priority for cautious approach, fight and flight that I have painted becomes overlaid with a grid of learnt prohibitions. Not only are we prey to a host of new predators but the very responses to threat themselves are distorted. Children hang about in the vicinity of other children playing together, just watching, getting the measure of them, until their apprehension ebbs enough for them to make a small, exploratory overture. Through such delicate and timely forays they negotiate their friendships quickly, successfully, and with a minimum of hurt. If adults did the same thing on the beach, waiting on the fringe of a group, observing and overhearing, before deciding whether to join in, and finding a way of doing so, they would be thought rude and odd. In fact grown-ups *do* do this sort of thing, as they may have to if they are to make friends, but the protocol that surrounds it serves to make it more sneaky, more protracted and more risky (you might make a gaffe; your timidity might *show*) than it need be.

After a while children are taught that the flight syndrome – running away, crying, trembling, seeking safety, often in the form of touch and reassurance – is not the thing to do. It is no longer a response to a transitory threat, but evidence of a character deficit – being 'weak', 'babyish', 'unmanly' – of which one should be ashamed. Yet if one is not allowed to retreat, attack is not acceptable either. The fight syndrome of punching, kicking, and shouting – that too must be avoided if one is not to be called 'bad', 'nasty', 'vicious', 'selfish', 'horrid', or again, 'babyish'. Clearly such responses to threat *are* evident of immaturity. When one is young more things evoke avoidance because one's constitution is weaker, and because more is strange. In addition, the crude energy of the fight and flight reactions will become refined, so that, for example, we learn to get comfort without at the same time irritating Mum with the unwarranted volume and persistence of our demands. These developments are the inevitable outcomes of learning. But to teach children to despise and hide their uncertainty, fear, or aggression, rather than to modify and eventually outgrow it is not to promote but to cripple their development.

The second reason why we resort to mental flight is this. If the threat is a physical one, and if I cannot do anything to defend against it, then it might eventually make some sense to 'switch off'. Tied firmly to the tracks with the train approaching, and nothing further to be done, why not turn off the screaming and struggling and replace them with happier memories? But if the threat is something *within* me, if it is a fantasy, if I do not perceive it but project it, then actual flight is always useless. If the thing under the bed is my imagination, if the predator is illusory, then real fight and real flight are just a waste of energy. Only an imaginary solution is possible. Thus we are left pretending that something that isn't there isn't there.

There is a story of a shabby old man on a bus, who from time to time slipped pieces of bread into a large paper bag. The man next to him, intrigued, asked what he was doing, to which the old drunk replied he was feeding his mongoose. 'Why do you carry a mongoose?' the man asked, to which the drunk replied that he needed it to keep away the snakes. 'But there aren't any snakes around here' pointed out the traveller. 'I know,' said the old man, 'but I drink a lot, and when I get really drunk, I imagine that I am surrounded by snakes.' 'Don't be stupid. You don't need a real mongoose to deal with imaginary snakes.' 'Don't worry,' said the old drunk, 'the mongoose is imaginary as well.'

What is a person made critical of her sporadic need for avoidance to do? The only possibility left is for her to conceal it at all costs from the others who have judged and defined her, and preferably also from herself. If we are not allowed or not able to avoid or neutralize the threat itself, the best we can do is to ignore it and hope it will go away. The problem with this, the Big Con that stands in opposition to the small pros, is that (as we have seen before) ignorance is a strategy that by its very nature prevents us from seeing whether 'it' has gone away or not. Here I am, my head still buried in the sand, not knowing that the predator I am trying to forget has been extinct for the last ten years.

Though it is of dubious value and creates problems of its own, ignorance is a favourite strategy of modern man. *Selective inattention* to that which threatens to upset us is a common way of trying to deal with mental predators. 'The Unconscious' is not, as Freud conceptualized it, a store, a dungeon where we keep all our horrors under lock and key. It is rather a process – a deliberate, learnt, culturally sanctioned method for coping (albeit ineffectually) with threats.[1] Whether it be an external threat like the mounting resentment in a repressed subculture (as occurred in Zimbabwe or Kenya), or an internal one like the uprising of a feeling such as fear or rage, the option exists for us to 'go unconscious' about it. If we blot it out totally, we can call the mechanism *denial*. If we blot out only selected parts of the experience, then we end up with *distortion*. And the strategy of voluntary ignorance works most successfully if, having purged our consciousness of that which is upsetting us, we can at the same time plug the gap so created with alternative, soothing contents – what we shall call *distractions*.

In the next section we shall look at different forms of denial, distortion and distraction.

7.2 Defences

Before going on to look at some of the defensive ploys that people have learnt to use, a reminder is in order. In reading this discussion it is possible to imagine a moralistic voice as well as a descriptive one. That voice is not there. Defensiveness is not wrong. It is a useful and valuable attribute, for people as it is for animals, if used appropriately and flexibly. Our defences exist to be wound up and down like sluice gates, to staunch temporary floods of fear and uncertainty. But they become problematic and counter-productive when they get stuck in position, when they turn into rigid dams, so that they become habits, or when they are misused to staunch trickles as well as floods. Then they prevent us from being sensitive to a much wider range of experience, and our tolerance for stress, and our learning ability become permanently inhibited. The purpose of the present discussion is only to point out the nature of defensiveness, its consequences, and the manifold ways in which it manifests itself. 'Defensive' is not being used here as a pejorative term, though it often is in everyday arguments. 'You're just being defensive', is a very effective accusation: an act of aggression that usually serves to make people more defensive still. If the reader recognizes himself or herself in the ensuing catalogue, there is no need to feel judged at the same time.[2]

Physical avoidance. The first and perhaps simplest kind of strategy is to avoid situations in which threat might arise. Understandably one may learn to *avoid situations which are known to contain threat*. If I know that I feel edgy and uncomfortable on my own, then I may organize my social life so that I never am on my own – or at least when I am alone I am always either drunk or asleep. Having failed an important examination, I avoid for a while the friends who are likely to ask me about it, so that I do not have to face their heavy-handed commiseration or undergo another post-mortem. Rather than stay in a relationship where real conflicts are proving painful to explore, I pack my bags and leave. Thinking that you dislike me, I pretend I have not seen you on the bus, bury my nose busily in my newspaper, and get off sooner than I had intended.

Someone with an even lower tolerance for upset may decide to *avoid situations which are unpredictable*, because an unexpected threat may suddenly appear. One person may not go to parties because he feels lonely. Another chooses not to go because he *might* feel lonely. Most people are apprehensive about taking LSD for fear of what might happen. Some people will always refuse a second sherry for the same reason. Perhaps the most debilitating example of this refusal to take risks is the person who is afraid to make friends with anyone, lest they find out his guilty secrets and reject him. 'Nothing venture, nothing lose' is his motto, and he does not see the force of its more common variant.

Alongside this may go the strategy of deliberately constructing and *inhabiting an environment that is completely predictable*. Older people, particularly, tend to do this. They may live a life that runs on tracks, with shopping on Thursdays, bridge on Fridays, a place for everything and everything in its place. Minimal uncertainties like not knowing where to park, or finding a strange dog in the garden provoke consternation out of all proportion. People who work in inherently unpredictable or stressful contexts, like hospitals or schools, may seek security in small islands of ritual and routine.[3] To find someone else sitting in *my* chair, or using *my* mug, may feel like the last straw.

Bodily avoidance. Instead of trying to eliminate an Antecedent that would lead to an uncomfortable Consequence, it may be possible to inhibit the Behaviour that links the two. While this strategy may or may not prevent us feeling uncomfortable, it will, if successful, stop other people seeing that we are uncomfortable. In particular, there are things we can learn to do to take the motion out of e-motion. Strong emotion is usually associated with physical movement. If we let ourselves, we shake with rage, tremble with fear and so on, just as a baby does. When he is upset, he exhibits his feelings throughout his body, from the tips of his fingers to the tips of his toes. But he may well be taught that such an exhibition is unacceptable. And if he cannot stop the explosive of his feelings being primed (through the involuntary release of adrenaline and so on) perhaps he can at least stop it going off.

How can we avoid making an exhibition of ourselves? One strategy depends on noticing that emotion requires exertion, which uses up energy, which usually leads us to breath harder in order to replace the energy. If I inhibit my breathing instead, sustained exertion becomes very difficult. Thus one way of suppressing my emotional displays is to stop breathing. And this is indeed a common defensive strategy in adults as well as children. Often when people feel anxious, their breathing becomes shallower and shallower until they are practically asphyxiating themselves. Before children have 'tuned' this strategy properly, they may overdo it and literally hold their breath until they turn a funny colour. Adults who have not quite got it right may go into what is called an 'anxiety attack', in which their breathing tightens up so much that they begin to panic and struggle for more air. The genuine anxiety aroused causes them to tighten up still further, and they find themselves in a very vicious circle indeed.

The second strategy relies on the realization that a part of the body that is tensed cannot move. Thus if I want to stop my arms moving I tense my arms and shoulders. If I want to stop my legs moving I tense my pelvis, hips and thighs. If I want to stop my mouth trembling I adopt a 'stiff upper lip' or a fixed smile. And so on. It is no accident that we describe people who are trying to control their feelings as 'tense', 'wound up', 'uptight', or 'highly strung'. As with other defences these strategies make useful servants but bad masters. For if they become ingrained, forming what Wilhelm Reich called our 'body armour', they may cause more problems than they solve.[4] Many of the so-called psychosomatic disorders have been, or may be attributed to such chronic tensions: lower back pain, stiff necks and shoulders, headaches and migraines, asthma and other respiratory disorders, hypertension (obviously!), insomnia and persistent tiredness, cramps, accident proneness and clumsiness, constipation, various digestive disorders such as ulcers and colitis, and a variety of others.[5]

Anaesthetics. In addition to not letting on to others, we sometimes need to turn down our own awareness of what is going on inside, and to help us do that we can call on a range of commercially available chemicals. People drink to forget the past, we say, but they also drink in order to ignore an uncomfortable present, whether it be socially awkward or just plain lonely. The physiological effects of alcohol are complex, depending on the amount consumed, the state of the stomach, the social situation, and so on. But a general and ubiquitous correlate of drinking is the temporary inhibition of social taboos. When the inhibitions are themselves inhibited the voice gets louder, the jokes sillier and the sexual advances less diplomatic. It is perhaps as well that in a country with such complicated protocol as Japan, one is considered neither responsible nor accountable for actions and indiscretions performed while drunk. Smoking may well work as a defence by providing a distraction, but it is not an anaesthetic. It actually mimics, and therefore exacerbates, some of the symptoms of anxiety. Cannabis in its various forms is not a very good chemical defence either. Its effects are even more variable than those of alcohol. While it too often acts as a social disinhibitor, the most that one can say, according to a recent text-book, is that it 'brings out what is latent in thought and emotion'[6] – and that is exactly what the person on the defensive is trying to avoid. The hallucinogens like LSD magnify this tendency for defences to be swamped rather than reinforced.

The anaesthetic drugs are primarily the analgesics, sedatives, painkillers, tranquillizers, barbiturates and the opiates, especially heroin. From the doctor one can buy anaesthesia in the form of Nembutal and Seconal,

Librium and Valium, Thorazine and Largactil. On the streets you can find heroin, which will give you a strong chemical blast of euphoria, peace, contentment, and a lovely sense of security. But the security offered is that of death, not life; of increasing passivity, insensitivity, and dependence. It is like leprosy but rotting bit by bit the emotions and the self-respect, until only the body is left, too lethargic and too inept to look after itself. Opiate addiction is a nasty and protracted form of 'chemi-kaze'.

Physical pain-killers such as aspirin, paracetamol and dystalgesic offer useful ways of ignoring what the body is trying to tell us. When we try to defend against fear by winding up the muscles, the first thing they will do is inform us of the abuse through an ache or a pain. Chemicals allow us to suppress these signals, and so to deepen and extend the abuse. It is like having a loudspeaker from the baby's bedroom installed in the living-room, so you can hear when the baby cries – and then responding to its distress by turning down the volume.

Psychological avoidance. These abuses of pharmacology and physiology are adjuncts to the core set of procedures for altering the content of awareness – the mechanisms of denial, distortion, and distraction – that we have introduced already.

Denial, the total blocking-out from awareness of threatening events, is rare if the events in question are current ones, but more common if they are past. People sometimes react to bad news by refusing to acknowledge its existence. They fiddle away while Rome burns or the Titanic sinks. Told that their son has been caught torturing little boys, or that their baby is handicapped, or that their husband has been killed, people may react: 'There must be some mistake.' In such dire cases, a temporary denial of reality may provide a vital breathing-space.

The total *repression* of memories, as Freud called it, is something that many people use. While much of psychoanalysis is over-fanciful, the fact of people's ability to recover buried memories of painful experiences is undeniable, as is the therapeutic value of such recovery. On a more mundane level, it is often the things we forget to do that are the things we don't want to do – the things that, for one reason or another, we 'push to the back of our minds'.

When it comes to censoring our current experience, it is much easier and more effective to cut the offending portions, rather than to ban the whole film. And when we selectively excise parts of a percept or a record, we inevitably create *distortions*. Of these there are many variations, depending on what we delete. If we cut out feelings, then we create experience that is safe but flat. People who go in for this in a big way may come to complain of *emotional isolation* or *deadening of affect*, of having squeezed out the fun, the love and the spontaneity along with the anxiety. It is almost certainly this general loss of vitality that brings more people to therapy these days, than any other cause.[7] The wall that was built to keep out foes and poisons is found to isolate us from friends and from nourishment as well.

One interesting class of distortions is characterized by *disowning* the experience. At first sight this seems fruitless. What does it gain me to allow an experience, bad feelings and all, but to deny that this experience is a product of my own theory? How does it help to see myself not as the author but the victim? What am I avoiding by so doing? Cast in this latter form, the answer is more obvious; I am avoiding having to *learn* about this nasty experience, having to engage with it and explore it. And this kind of learning is indeed threatening. If I see myself as the helpless victim of a painful situation, the pay-off is that I can drop the even more painful responsibility for doing something about it. I can swap planning the escape and digging the tunnel for resignation and the pseudo-satisfaction of complaint, fantasy, and self-righteousness.

This sense of victimization is a good example of the illusory helplessness that the Existentialist philosophers call Bad Faith. Bryan Magee in his novel *Facing Death*[8] quotes the following description (from an unnamed source):

> Bad Faith consists in pretending to ourselves and to others that things could not be otherwise – that we are bound to our way of life and that we could not escape it even if we wanted to. Most appeals to duty, most suggestions that one could not have done otherwise, even most of our strong beliefs (such as the belief that we *must* return hospitality, or get up in the morning, or be polite) are instances of Bad Faith, since in fact we *choose* to do all these things, and we *need* not do them.

And the pay-off every time is that we can give up being responsible and stop struggling with novelty, ambiguity, and indecision.

What ploys do we use to bring about this self-imposed con trick? How do we engineer it? One way is to *awfulize* the situation – a crude neologism, but a graphic one.[9] If we can convince ourselves (and preferably others too) that things are not just inconvenient and uncomfortable but *terrible*, then we can rightly argue that nobody could have coped with such overwhelming odds. Having conjured the storm in the teacup we can resign gracefully and with self-image intact. To throw in my hand prematurely is cowardly. But if I am convinced that you have the fourth king in your hand, then it is not just reasonable but sensible to 'fold'. Feelings here will be magnified and dramatized, rather than suppressed, in order to support the desired sense of powerlessness. Coming out of a bad lesson, you cry 'I'll *die* if I have to go back in there', and really believe that it *is* as bad as all that. And your colleagues, given to using the same strategy themselves, agree: 'They're animals, aren't they? Nobody could control 4Z.'

A variant of awfulizing is *regression*. To create the desired effect I can either magnify the height of the wave, or minimize my own apparent size: the latter is effectively achieved by acting as if I am younger, less competent, and therefore less responsible, than I actually am. 'Sorry!' I spit, with the aggrieved scowl of a six-year-old; 'I didn't *mean* to.' And if you buy the act, how can you go on being angry with the innocent clumsiness of a child? People under stress, constantly guilty of misperception and forgetfulness, like teachers, resort to regression frequently. Staff-rooms reverberate to the whines ('How was I supposed to know?', 'Why *should* I?', 'It's not fair', 'She's always picking on me') and tantrums ('Bloody stupid board-rubber!', 'I *hate* that woman!') of the primary school playground. People tell small, spiteful lies ('Sorry, Nigel, I haven't seen it all day'), sulk, and pretend not to hear, just like a child in a paddy. Both awfulizing and regression have a useful side-effect which is easily discovered. Other people around you do not like displays of temper or withdrawal, it makes them feel uncomfortable, and they will pay you to stop – by doing what you want. Behaving in ways that other people find upsetting is therefore a very good way of controlling them. 'I will cheer up if you are extra specially nice to me, make the dinner and walk the dog.' This form of manipulation is also a regressed one: it is learnt very early on in a child's life. On his potty, perhaps, an infant will discover that others will do things for him in order to get him to do something for them. There is not room here to go into all the refinements of this strategy that people work out as they grow up. Many of them are described in an entertaining and evocative way by Eric Berne in his *Games People Play* and other books.[10] They are largely based on the creation and manipulation of guilt. If you believe that you are (at least in part) responsible for the way I feel, then when I feel bad, you feel guilty, and to expunge your guilt you do what you can to make me feel better. Having caught you, I can then play with you, like a cat with a mouse. I become a bitch and you a fawn. But if I refuse the premise that you are a victim, then the game falls flat. Try as you might, despite all the threats and tears and histrionics, I am free to treat you as a grown-up. How infuriating!

A strategy that often goes along with regression and awfulizing is *blaming*:

if it's not *my* responsibility, then it must be *yours*, or *theirs*. Having found a reasonable explanation for why I feel bad that has nothing to do with my competence, I can drop the lingering suspicion that it's my 'fault'. It is part of the way we are brought up (see Section 8.10) that when I do something badly, I should feel bad about myself. It has become very difficult for us simply and realistically to acknowledge responsibility in the matter without at the same time feeling judged and condemned. Having accepted the reality and relevance of blame, the best I can do is to hang it on somebody else. We rarely stop to see that the whole game is as dysfunctional as it is unedifying.

The third class of defences are the distractions. The holes left by denial and distortion are much less noticeable if they can be stopped up with some sort of anodyne cement. The two major forms of distraction are created by *doing* things and by *thinking* things. The doing distractions which we will look at first, are *business*, *displacement*, and *sublimation*. Business, or busyness, works well for people who tend to be threatened by disquieting thoughts or feelings in quiet moments. The defence is: never have a quiet moment. Forestall them, avoid them, fill them up with the compulsive creation of harmless inputs – chattering, arguing, playing games, reading books, watching TV, smoking, fidgeting, repapering the hall, going to cookery classes, stalking the next lover, working late at the office. Only as I lie down to sleep do the predators of emptiness and fear that I have kept at bay all day begin to bay at me – and I can dope them even then with a whisky or a Seconal. People who have relied heavily on keeping busy are those most at risk from enforced inactivity, for they may not have very effective *internal* sources of distraction. The devil makes work for idle hands, but only if the hands are used to being constantly employed. For no other animal than man would solitary confinement be an effective torture, for, unlike us, they would not have their predators incarcerated with them.

Displacement is a special purpose strategy for distracting ourselves not so much from a feeling, such as anger, but from the natural consequences of expressing that feeling unguardedly. Resentful with the boss, and angry with the large workman who spilt my drink in the bar, I can displace the feelings by going home and picking a fight with my wife, shouting at the children and kicking the cat. The anger does not belong to them, and no effective communication will result, but if I can bluster enough I can let off steam and ignore my own cowardice. If all works well, I will never find out, consciously, who I am *really* mad at. Nor will I see that the defence is really against engaging with an opponent who has the power to inflict actual bodily (or 'career-ily') harm. The final form of defence by action, sublimation, is a classic Freudian one, and is, not surprisingly therefore, more difficult to spot. Whereas displacement involves shouting at one person instead of another who is too threatening, sublimation involves substituting one *activity* for another that is related but taboo. Freud argued that all creative activity is a sublimation of blocked sexual activity. Perhaps. But it is rather more plausible to see sublimation at work in *particular* cases such as the intense loving of a pet in the absence of a partner, the devotion to 'good works' of a childless couple, or the pursuits of such sports as boxing or rugby by aggressive young men.

Distractions that are generated internally serve equally to occupy consciousness with a relatively painless content so that other, more threatening, voices cannot be heard. In fact it could be argued (see my *Wholly Human*) that 'the stream of consciousness' consists very largely, in Western adults, of such self-generated psychological pacifiers. A favourite ploy, particularly amongst the educated middle-classes, is *rationalization* – the protracted attempt to come up with a story about why and how come something unpleasant or unfortunate came about. While there is, of course, much merit in finding out where one went wrong, people will sometimes indulge in the exercise of reason at the expense of actually paying attention to what happened. As Jung once remarked, we are like a householder who hears a noise downstairs in the night – and immediately rushes up to the attic to search for the intruder. A young teacher, coming out of a bad lesson, may immediately indulge in a court of inquiry, creating within himself prosecution, defence, and judge. The only participants who are missing are the witnesses. The only data that the inquiry has to work on is that the lesson was 'a disaster'. All the rest is rhetoric, analogy, and a merciless scrutiny of the defendant's past record. It is no wonder that such an impoverished diagnosis usually leads to a crude and ineffectual cure such as 'I must prepare better', 'I need to be firmer . . . that's it!' or 'I'll never do it. I might as well drop out now.'

Rationalization, when it is hogged by defending counsel, becomes *justification*. Anyone who will listen is subjected to a pitiful tale, the gist of which is It's Not My Fault. They always give student teachers the worst classes *and* it's Friday afternoon *and* the World Cup was on telly *and* the technician hadn't given me the right equipment *and* it was raining *and* mixed-ability teaching is impossible anyway *and* they didn't prepare me properly in college . . . so It's Not My Fault . . . right? Somebody once said that the difference between a Good Teacher and a Bad Teacher lay in how they reacted to upsets. They can both come up with twenty good ideas and for both of them only three turn out to work in practice. The Good Teacher says 'Oh, Well', and starts work on the next twenty good ideas. The Bad Teacher drags the seventeen failures around after her, endlessly chewing them over and building up a case to refer either to prosecution or defence or both. Obsessed with her self-image she loses valuable time for experimenting and finding out what works. Thus the longer she spends defending herself, the longer that self remains open to attack – because it is not getting any more competent. Having punished the wrong kid, you can either defend and say 'Well, he had it coming to him anyway, the little bugger', or you can notice more carefully the way they set you up and how impetuous you get when you are uncertain.

Alternatively, you can escape from a threatening present not into thinking *about* it, but into the past or the future – into *reminiscence* and *fantasy*. Henri Charriére, the author of *Papillon*,[11] describes graphically how he survived two years of solitary confinement in a small dark cell in a prison in French Guiana by using these strategies, totally immersing himself, sometimes for hours on end, in reliving events from his childhood, in fantasies of revenge, and in vivid day-dreams. And to a lesser extent nearly everyone indulges from time to time in chewing over the past ('I wonder if she still remembers . . .') rewriting history ('Now what I should have said was . . .'), planning ('Next time he says that, I'll . . .') and wool-gathering ('Wouldn't it be lovely if . . .'). Again these activities are often entertaining and sometimes issue in genuine insights and clear intentions. But if we look closely at *when* we are most absorbed in this sort of activity, we may find that their primary function is palliative. As a teacher of mine once said: 'Before we are wise. After we are wise. In between, we are very often otherwise.'

Defence against character. So far we have talked about defences that are mostly intermittent, that is, they are activated by and designed to cope with certain kinds of event. Some more deep-seated defence-mechanisms, however, have been developed to avoid the conscious recognition of *character traits* that we have learnt to attribute to ourselves. Some of the things that a person may have come to write into his definition of himself are attitudes or characteristics that are in conflict with other beliefs about himself. In childhood he may have accepted both the beliefs that his worth as a human being, his lovableness, depends on his being kind and considerate *and* that he is, in fact, a selfish little boy. To acknowledge both is extremely painful, for it involves admitting that he is, at least sometimes, unlovable. And just as a painful conflict between experience and belief can be handled by selective inattention, so can the conflict between two beliefs. *Projection*, for example, enables one to perceive the existence of an unlovable trait, but to attribute it not to oneself but to others.[12] It is they who are dirty, lazy, mean, selfish, careless, over-sexed, unfunny, aggressive, devious, boring, and untrustworthy. Not me! The things that we despise and repudiate most strongly in others – these may be things that we have most difficulty seeing as our own. Yet how expert we are at diagnosing other people's shortcomings. 'Why beholdest thou the mote that is in thy brother's eye, but considerest not the beam that is in thine own eye? Or how wilt thou say to thy brother, let me pull out the mote out of thine eye: and behold a beam is in thine own eye. Thou hypocrite, first cast out the beam out of thine own eye: and then shalt thou see clearly to cast out the mote out of thy brother's eye.' Or thou may even discover that his vision is fine, the mote having been just a reflection of thy own beam. The more subtle we are, the more we choose people to be the objects of our projections who *do* have the projected characteristic, thus making the projection more 'reasonable' and more difficult to spot. I project my meanness onto really mean people. But at a pinch we can always pick on an innocent bystander. 'And as for you . . . I don't know what you're looking so smug about . . . you're no paragon of virtue . . .'

We might mention three other strategies in this category. If someone has a deep belief, about some aspect of sexuality, let us say, that is in conflict with the beliefs of their community or friends, then they can avoid the clash by absorbing their values. This may be done consciously, as when a teenage girl goes along with her friends' casual and cynical attitude to sex, while secretly keeping to the belief that 'proper sex' is something very special to be saved for a long-term partner. Most young people draw a clear-cut but ultimately arbitrary boundary between what constitutes 'casual' and 'serious' sex, but even within a crowd of youngsters who profess a common attitude, their location of this boundary may vary enormously. It is not uncommon these days, for instance, for sexual intercourse to be casual, while a kiss – a *real* one – is serious. Often, with time, the attitude that was adopted consciously becomes assimilated into a person's automatic habits and accepted self-image. As Kurt Vonnegut said, 'We are what we pretend to be – so take care what you pretend to be.'[13] And thus a conflict between self and other becomes, through *introjection*, a conflict within a self.

We can compound the fracture within a self-image by means of *compensation* and *reaction formation*. We can ignore a feature or a trait of character that we think is bad by exaggerating something else. 'Who cares if I'm no good at running: I bet I can play the guitar better than you.' This is called compensation. Or we can come to espouse consciously a belief that is the exact opposite of what we believe to be true underneath. Typical of this reaction formation is the brash, cocky, super-confident, bully-boy, with his 'I'm the greatest' attitude – an attitude that masks an underlying, deep acceptance of what parents and teachers have been telling him for years: that he's just good for nothing.

7.3 Going Crazy

Each of these methods of defence, if it becomes too successful – too powerful, too rigid, too compulsive – can take over, and when it becomes master rather than servant, dam rather than sluice-gate, it leads to neurosis and ultimately to the total incapacitation of real psychotic craziness and/or serious physical disability. Before we take a quick flip through the catalogue of madness it is worth making explicit our underlying assumption: that even these very weird forms of behaviour and experience are (or were) chosen by the person who now 'suffers from' them because they seemed to have survival value. That is, they are not *caught* or *inherited* like a physical disease, nor are they *forced* on one by pathogenic circumstances. Certainly an individual may be predisposed by his constitution and by his history to go crazy in one way rather than another. (Mental 'illnesses' even have clearly discernible fashions, like the length of skirts. Hysteria, for instance, which was very popular in Freud's Vienna, is now quite rare.) But psychosis, I shall assume, can always be seen as the unintended consequence of an extreme attempt to defend one's self against what appears to be extreme threat. In particular, if the circumstances of one's life are such that there is no *reasonable* way of resisting attacks, then only unreasonable solutions can be tried.[14]

The first type of defence we looked at was physical avoidance – keeping away from situations that are known to be dangerous, or, for the more fearful, are not known to be safe. The *reductio ad absurdum* of this is the avoidance of any situation that is not completely controllable and predict-able – and this state is *agoraphobia*. This word, by the way, derives from the Greek, *agora*, meaning an assembly or a meeting-place, and not from the Latin for a field. Thus it refers not to a fear of open spaces as such but, much more commonly, to the fear of the unpredictable social encounters that one meets as soon as one steps outside the front door. From the agoraphobic's point of view the fear is real, and the self-imposed isolation with which he responds would be a perfectly reasonably strategy if it did not at the same time make his life unworkable. Agoraphobia is a good example of a 'rational' response to an 'irrational' perception that fails because of its unlooked-for but crippling side-effects. Once a person adopts such a life-strategy he is trapped between the threat he is trying to escape and the horror he has inflicted on himself. It is like someone with a terror of mice trying to haul himself out of their way with a rope that is secured round his own neck. Or perhaps the hallmark of the insane strategy is that it has the same good intention and the same disastrous effect as struggling in quicksand.

The second way of allaying anxiety is to fill your safe environment with predictable actions, habits and rituals. One good way of ensuring that the next thing that happens is safe is to do it yourself. Yet when such rituals become too embedded, one feels taken over by *compulsions* and *obsessions* – the social life after which one apparently hankers is ruined by the recurrent need to wash one's hands or to check that one's fly is done up. Again the fine line between a haven and a gaol, between security and imprisonment, is transgressed.

Abuses of the body in order to control the awareness or display of emotion, by either muscular or pharmacological means, leads eventually, as we have seen already, to an increasing paralysis of mind or body – perhaps even to the total paralysis of *catatonia*.

What happens when we tamper too successfully with the contents of awareness? If we are denying or repressing whole chunks of experience, we are creating for ourselves a state of 'sensory deprivation'. It is literally as if the amount of input we are receiving had been attenuated. Now when people are actually deprived of stimulation, it has been found that the mind will fill the vacuum itself; it will create *hallucinations*.[15] And so it is with the self-imposed deprivation of denial. For a person who, in pre-psychotic days, had been partial to the mind-games of reworking the past and inventing the future, the building materials of hallucination are readily available.

The road of distorting experience by deleting its emotional and motivational components leads eventually into the flat, barren, infinitely pointless terrain of *depression*. Life becomes meaningless and empty because you have too successfully purged it of everything that is interesting and significant. If, however, you erase the sense of your own responsibility, then you are left feeling victimized and ultimately *paranoid*. Your own hostility, projected, creates a world that is out to get you.

Those given to rationalization, to telling themselves stories, run the risk of becoming compulsive talkers, the creators of long and earnest tales that are devoid of feeling, sense, and purpose. And finally the strategies of awfulizing and regression may develop into the violent and infantile irresponsibility of *mania* – a wild and inappropriate release of pent-up rage or sadness or sexuality.

Sometimes these pet ploys turn on their masters and mistresses not singly but in packs. Often thought-disorder, hallucination and paranoia hunt together. When they do, their victim is said to 'suffer from *schizophrenia*'. Or a sudden attack of physical symptoms like trembling and sweating, together with tears or screams, and a panicky feeling of going out of control, we call a *nervous breakdown*.

Ultimately only one state is guaranteed free of stress, and that is death. People are sometimes so bound up in barbs and chains of their own creation that the absurd logic of suicide becomes attractive. You don't even get the satisfaction of finding out whether they are feeling as sorry and as guilty as you hoped.

7.4 The Risks of Recovery

And now, having hit the bottom, so to speak, we are in a position to bounce back up, and look at the processes and methods involved in giving up defensiveness, thereby beginning to expand the ability to learn itself. For the rest of this chapter we shall be concerned with learning as the development of personality, not in the sense of coming to *know* more, or even to be able to *do* more, but of allowing oneself to *be* more, of coming to relax into oneself, to see through illusory threats, to reevaluate freshly for oneself what one's priorities in life are; what really matters. We are talking about reorientation, not acquisition; stopping and really looking at the scenery rather than belting on to the next mountain top. We are talking about a process of giving up ideas that have been seen to be alien or phoney; and this is a very different kind of learning, this shedding, from those that we have considered up to now. We shall also be looking at the recipes and rewards for knowing thyself. But before we open this study of what Carl Rogers[16] calls 'significant learning', we need perhaps to be reminded of one thing: that learning to submit one's deep beliefs about oneself to the test of experience always feels, and sometimes is, a very risky business. Learning is, by definition, risky. The kind of learning that involves possible change to the content of *identity* is all the more risky because there is a chance not just

of objective failure but of subjective annihilation. This point is well caught
by Val Blomfield in her poem *The Abyss*.

> The terrain's very tricky here, you know.
> You go for miles, untroubled, till you find
> You feel a sense of danger and you see
> With one false move that you could stumble in
>
> To that great, dreadful, yawning hole, you know,
> Just gaping wide in dismal emptiness
> And it could suck you down and down inside
> Just falling, falling, with no hope at all.
>
> I'd say it's even worse than death, you know,
> With such a drop and with that lurching fall
> I call it the abyss and spend my time
> Devising ways to keep me from its threat.
>
> I'm always very busy here, you know.
> I work till I'm exhausted and I drop
> Because that leaves me with no time to think
> About that place of emptiness and gloom.
>
> I only walk on this one track, you know,
> And try to keep my eyes upon the ground
> The scenery can tempt me from my path
> And make me stray into the danger zone.
>
> It's very safe upon this track, you know,
> And many people follow with closed eyes
> Then they pretend the abyss isn't there
> And that can help them to contain the fear.
>
> I've other ways to deal with it, you know.
> These flowers that you see have special seeds
> I eat them and it helps me to forget,
> With blissful, swirling feelings in my head.
>
> I'd say that I am happy then, you know,
> But I can't quite convince myself it's true
> Because I find the abyss is still there
> When my good dream is gone and I awake.
>
> I met this woman walking here, you know,
> At first I thought her mad, but I'm not sure.
> She told me she was scared of the abyss
> Until she had this very strange idea
>
> That you could jump right in – and live, you know,
> And even face that dreadful, endless drop
> And come out safely at the other end
> Where you would find a better place than this.

The woman talked about that land, you know,
The one you'd get to if you risked that jump.
You'd feel the earth there firm beneath your feet
And know your inner rhythm and the world's.

There's free and open country there, you know,
Though that could lead to danger too, of course.
But she believed you'd find that you could cope
If you had faced the abyss and survived.

So, in a way, she tempted me, you know,
To jump into the abyss and be free
And find my own good country and my truth
And be in touch with my reality.

But I'm so scared of that long fall, you know,
I would not care to take the chance myself,
Although that woman really made me think
About the land where I could find some rest.

But then it is a most grave risk, you know,
And I don't feel I can be so strong,
Although my life is weary here and strained
I think I'll try the jump another day.

And I'll keep on in my old way, you know,
And I'll stay busy and keep on my track.
I'll close my eyes and eat my flower dreams
And hope I'll rid myself of this dull ache.

Clients come to therapy believing that who they are is fixed, and that this fixed self is being attacked by nasty circumstances, nasty habits or nasty feelings. They believe that the feelings *are* nasty, and that the solution will be to have them go away. What they discover is that they are resisting the feelings because they lie outside the boundary that they have drawn around their selves, and that it is none other than this resistance that creates the nastiness. The solution is not to amputate the painful limb, but to broaden the sense of self so that hurt, fear, grief, guilt, anger, shame, and lust are allowed to become part of 'me'. If I restrict the drama of my life to 'The Goodies', it will constantly be subverted and interrupted by the cat-calls of the Baddies. By refusing to write them a part in the play I ensure that they have an influence out of all proportion to their importance. When I allow them on stage it turns out they are content with a small role, and, when not taken too seriously, they even add spice to the drama.

The process of growth is one of allowing an increasing part of my experience to be me, part of the family. That does not mean I have to like it all. It is not required that I think everything about me is wonderful. I can even wish that some of the members of my family would go away and leave me alone. But I do not as a result have to throw rocks at them or pretend that I'm out whenever they turn up. We can rub along, as most communities do.

There is a real, though temporary, risk of recovery and that is that it often does get worse before it gets better. It is now possible to understand why. Any domain of experience from which I have consistently and effectively withdrawn awareness does not develop, because if it is not attended to it cannot be learnt about. Thus while the rest of me moves on, becoming more skilful and sophisticated in its dealings with the world, and more integrated, more coherent in itself, the bits I ignore remain marooned, unintegrated, and immature. So when, aged forty, I begin to reexperience my anger, say, what I find is the crude, blind, overwhelming temper of a two-year-old. As I slowly open up to it, I find myself getting angry at the same things and in the same way as I did when I was two. It has a lot of catching up to do before the ridiculous consuming tantrums of a baby can be transmuted, through learning, into a solid, grown-up sense of when my real needs are being trampled on, or when something or someone genuinely dear to me needs defending, and of how to go about it in an economical and effective way. Thus when such characters are first invited onto the stage they do, for a while, tend to hog the limelight and strut up and down in a boorish and egocentric fashion, showing off their 'power', just like an infant. But it doesn't take long before they get fed up with it, and want to belong. The risk is that the audience of significant others will get fed up and walk out first – so it is important to assess their temper before you display your own. If they love you, and are not harbouring a complementary infant who will get upset by yours, then they will probably wait for you. A therapist is an onlooker who you pay to sit there. But with others the risk is real.

7.5 Relearning to Learn

To recover the ability to learn well all that is necessary is to unpick the knot that we have been tracing in this and the previous chapter. Learning, we have argued, is an activity that is inseparable from life: it does not have to be created or tried for, but simply to be allowed. Allowing it means not starving it of its vital raw material – awareness, and in particular, feeding it with the experience of any disparity between what one expected, or wanted, or needed to happen, and what did happen. Openness to experience, noticing what's so, is all that is required. Awareness is a sufficient condition for learning. 'Observation is alchemical':[17] to allow your theory to be touched by open observations is to initiate a process the end result of which is the transmutation of the old theory into a better one.

The solution is easily stated; carrying it through is more difficult. The knot is a tricky one, and difficult to untie because our experience – the data itself – is heavily contaminated by the theory; and because it is dangerous. If the theory says X is a threat, X *is* a threat, until and unless I experience it not to be. And the only way I can experience it not to be is to open myself to the possibility that it *will* eat me, swamp me, reject me, or kill me. For these reasons significant learning is exactly how everyone experiences it; slow and painful.

However, there are a number of ways into the problem. One way is to understand, intellectually, what is going on. That is what I hope is going on now. Another is to become increasingly aware of the *costs* of over-defending. If I begin to see what I have given up and to experience the lack of intimacy, vitality, spontaneity, playfulness, richness in my life – then the scales may begin to tip, not because I am trying to open but because I am giving up being closed. Another way is to be lucky enough to find a person with whom you can be safe *and* be yourself; someone who manifestly, and time after time, doesn't bop you on the head when you stick your head out of the shell. Being in love is a very satisfactory situation because at the same time as it is getting safer outside, it is getting hotter inside, so the urge to 'come out of your shell' is increasing. Another way is to keep asking yourself 'Is it safe?', and refusing to take the habitual 'No' for an answer unless you are sure. Still another way is just to practise being more open, more receptive to experience when there is no obvious threat around; just to let the stream of consciousness flow by as it wants to and notice what it consists of. This is meditation. And the final way is to winkle out and begin to experiment with those deep beliefs that are responsible for jamming up the learning mechanism itself. These are the beliefs that can make learning frightening regardless of the domain of experience under investigation – because one is frightened of the *experience* of learning itself. These beliefs are the four Cs. We will look at them first.

7.6 Learning to Suffer

The learning experiences we tend to resist are feeling uncomfortable, feeling out of control, feeling inconsistent, not sure of who we are, and feeling incompetent. The first thing to work on is increasing our tolerance for 'suffering' (i.e. for feeling anxiety, fear, uncertainty, confusion, etc.). It is not nice to be upset but it is not wrong either, and sometimes it is appropriate and useful. And indeed one of the first discoveries to be made is that most of the suffering is created by the effort to resist the initial suffering. It is not fear that hurts so much as the fear of the fear; not the confusion but the shame about the guilt about the frustration about being confused. As Khalil Gibran says so clearly in *The Prophet*:

> Your Pain is the breaking of the shell that encloses your understanding. Even as the stone of the fruit must break, so that its heart may stand in the sun, so must you know pain. And could you keep your heart in wonder at the daily miracles of your life, your pain would not feel less wondrous than your joy.[18]

The process of personal growth, therefore, is not one of becoming more and more immune to upsets, but the reverse: one starts by becoming increasingly 'mune'. To someone who has not yet realized that there is no way 'out' but 'through', this sounds like masochism at best, and more likely complete craziness. They cannot see that when pain is unavoidable, it is much less painful to submit than to resist. Hermann Hesse recorded this discovery, in uncharacteristically dramatic prose, in his diary in 1918:

> Suffering only hurts because you fear it. Suffering only hurts because you complain about it. It pursues you only because you flee from it. You must not flee, you must not complain, you must not fear. You must love. You know all this yourself, you know quite well, deep within you, that there is a single magic, a single power, a single salvation, and a single happiness, and that is called loving. Well then, love your suffering. Do not resist it, do not flee from it. . . . It is only your aversion that hurts, nothing else.[19]

It is important to be clear that we are talking about adopting an open attitude to psychological pain *that is actually present*, and not pretending that it isn't. We are not talking about a life-style that involves seeking or creating upsets: that would be absurd. What is required is 'the courage to change those things that can be changed; the serenity to accept those things that cannot; and the wisdom to tell the difference.'[20] The cumulative reasoning of the previous two chapters leads us inexorably to this counter-intuitive conclusion: that the only way to overcome the predators of rejection, ridicule, and unpopularity, self-criticism and self-hate, failure, uncertainty, and confusion, is to stand your ground and look them squarely in the face. And when one dares to do so, it is they who lower their eyes, tuck their tails between their legs and slink away. 'The first necessity is that we should have the courage to face life, and encounter all that is most perilous in the world. When this is possible, meditation (i.e. awareness) itself becomes the means by which we accept and welcome the demons that arise from the unconscious . . . The more a man learns whole-heartedly to confront the world that threatens him with isolation, the more are the depths of the Ground of Being revealed and the possibilities of new life Becoming opened.'[21]

Badly burned after a car crash, you may hide for the rest of your life, sure that no one could love a monster, or you may go out and about and discover that the initial pain of being stared at is tolerable, and that quite a few people actually, honestly enjoy your company. Left by your husband after twenty years you may conclude that relationships just aren't worth it, and implode into a lonely and resentful old age. Or you can get your hair done, leave the kids next door, and see if you can find someone else. Many people come to the conclusion that the basic equation of life is:

$$\text{Love} = \text{Pain}^{22} \tag{1}$$

It isn't. The basic equation that applies universally, looks similar, but is really very different, is:

$$\text{Love} = \text{Pain (sometimes)} \tag{2}$$

The difference is that if (1) applies, the game definitely isn't worth playing. If (2) applies, it just may be – not least because the third equation

$$\text{No love} = \text{Pain} \tag{3}$$

does seem to apply, if we allow ourselves to feel it. And if we don't, then constant defensiveness is required. Openness to experience reveals that it is worth feeling bad from time to time because the alternative is worse.

It is almost impossible for a person on her own to discover these truths, for the experiences on which they are based are disallowed by the processes through which she meets her familiar world. They cannot, as should by now be clear, be set aside by an effort of will. But if by chance or design she finds herself in a different environment in which these processes do not work, and in which she can allow herself to experience their not working, then, gradually, unlearning can begin, and she can begin to be amazed and amused by all the nonexistent bogymen that have been inhabiting, and inhibiting, her life. Situations of this sort we can call *therapeutic*, and we now need to identify what their salient characteristics are. What are the circumstances that facilitate relearning to learn and encourage openness to experience?

7.7 **Therapeutic Contexts**

This section is about therapeutic *contexts* that involve other people. The following section is about therapeutic *ploys* that one person can use to help another. And Section 7.9 is about therapeutic *activities* that an individual can do on his own. Here we ask: what are the characteristics of a therapeutic relationship?

At the outset, it needs saying that therapeutic relationships appear in a variety of guises – not just in a one-to-one hour's meeting between a paid, professional 'therapist' and an unhappy 'client'. Such relationships occur in groups, between friends (especially lovers), in the confessional, the changing-room, and the disco. People labelled 'psychotherapists' do not have a monopoly in the business of helping other people to wake up from bad dreams. Far from it. Indeed one of the giants of modern therapy and counselling, Carl Rogers, believes that untrained lay people, especially those with experience of people in distress, like nurses, clergymen, and mothers, are better at it than half-trained, self-conscious, trying-too-hard, on-their-dignity, theoretically sophisticated professionals.[23] Just as coarse fishing is all the more effective as a meditation for not being seen as such, so a chat across the garden fence benefits from not being labelled 'therapeutic'. Nonetheless, despite the variety of disguises, we now know quite a bit about what are the active ingredients of the therapeutic relationship, and, by the same token, what is irrelevant or counter-productive.

Three things that therapy is not about are *advice-giving, collusion*, and *finding causes*. As Jung said sixty years ago, advice-giving is about as typical of therapy as bandaging is of surgery. It has a place, but it is not of the essence. When people feel upset, they often do not know what to do, and, believing that that is the problem, they ask other people to tell them. That this is *not* the problem is revealed by the ambivalence or obstructiveness with which the advice is often greeted. 'That's all very well for you. You haven't got children/a mortgage/such an awful mother/a wooden leg. . . .' The problem is that when people are upset, they defend. Defending means denying, distorting, or distracting yourself from the situation, that is, being more or less insensitive to what's going on and how you feel about it. And doing this you rob yourself of the information that you need in order to decide what to do. A doctor who couldn't bear to see spots, to hear the sound of coughing, or to use a stethoscope, would be equally inept in his diagnosis and indecisive in his prescription. Thus in our haste to solve the 'problem' and alleviate the suffering, we blunder about not knowing what the 'problem' really is. When people stop rushing about and actually pay attention to where they are, often the correct course of action becomes clear 'of itself'. Here I am making all these complicated plans, and I haven't yet asked myself the only question that matters: do I still love you?

Neither is therapy about collusion, because colluding means that I reinforce your belief that you are right and the rest of the world is wrong – and that means I am siding with the attempt to shore up your old theory rather than the effort to find a better one. 'The man who, being really on the way, falls upon hard times in the world will not, as a consequence, turn to that friend who offers him refuge and comfort and encourages his old self to survive. Rather, he will seek out someone who will faithfully and inexorably help him to risk himself, so that he may endure the suffering and pass courageously through it, thus making of it a "raft that leads to the far shore".'[24]

Contrary to popular opinion, therapy is not about working out how come you're in this mess. It is not about finding out who did it to you and why. Freud thought it was, but Jung and every major therapist since have known better. 'Freud emphasizes the aetiology of the case and assumes that once the causes are brought into consciousness the neurosis will be cured. But mere consciousness of the causes does not help any more than detailed knowledge of the causes of war help to raise the value of the French franc', said Jung.[25] The desperate need to *understand* unhappiness is, like the unhappiness itself, a symptom of the chafing of the 'mind-forg'd manacles'. It does not constitute the key.

The three conditions that help people to take the 'growth choice' rather than the 'fear choice', as Maslow called it,[26] to begin to reinterpret threats as challenges, were described by Carl Rogers over thirty years ago.[27] According to him if the 'therapist' (whether identified as such or not) is *congruent*; if he exhibits *unconditional positive regard* for the 'client'; if he is *empathic*; and if the client perceives these qualities and is prepared to change, then change will occur in the direction of more open, full, trusting experiencing of himself, and consequent insight into the tacit assumptions and beliefs that had been hanging him up. This insight, if truly experiential and not just intellectual, allows the client to relax into himself, and the 'problem' that moments before had seemed so dense, disperses like mist.

Congruence means authenticity. It means that the therapist is being himself. It means he is 'all of a piece', not being blocked or defended, not feigning more interest or understanding than he has. He is clean, clear, and therefore trustworthy. The client does not have to worry about whether the therapist is trying to impress or has any other hidden agenda: here is at least one human being with whom he knows where he stands. Congruence is the most basic of the three qualities. If either unconditional positive regard or empathy have to be affected, if they will only come at the expense of genuineness, then they are counterfeit, and they lose their therapeutic force.

Unconditional positive regard, an ugly phrase, is also called 'nonpossessive warmth', 'prizing' or even just 'acceptance'. It means, in Rogers' own words, 'an absolute respect for the dignity and integrity of the client.'[28] It means viewing the client, genuinely, as a fully paid-up and valuable human being, regardless of how he views himself or of how other significant people have viewed him. Unconditional positive regard is unconditional because the client does not have to do or know or be anything in order to get it. He has it already. Whereas previously positive regard, whether from parents, peers or teachers, has been highly conditional: 'I would love you, but . . .', 'I won't love you, unless . . .', 'I might love you, if. . . .' The fears, doubts and prohibitions that he has picked up from them can be slowly unpicked with the help of such a friend.

The third condition, empathy, Rogers describes thus. Being empathic, he says:

> means entering the private perceptual world of the other and becoming thoroughly at home in it. It involves being sensitive, moment to moment, to the changing felt meanings which flow in this other person, to the fear or rage or tenderness or confusion or whatever, that he/she is experiencing. It means temporarily living in his/her life, moving about in it delicately without making judgements, sensing meanings of which he/she is scarcely aware, but not trying to uncover feelings of which the person is totally unaware, since this would be too threatening. It includes communicating your sensing of his/her world as you look with fresh and unfrightened eyes at elements of which the individual is fearful. It means frequently checking with him/her as to the accuracy of your sensings, and being guided by the responses you receive. You are a confident companion to the person in his/her inner world. By pointing to the possible meanings in the flow of his/her experiencing you help the person to . . . experience the meanings more fully, and to move forward in the experiencing.
>
> To be with another in this way means that for the time being you lay aside the views and values you hold for yourself in order to enter another's world without prejudice.[29]

In short, there is nothing too magical about the process. It is just like helping a young child to explore an object that he is scared of, such as a big dog. You don't drag him kicking and screaming until they are nose to nose.

That will very probably result in a life-long dog-phobia. You don't mock him for being afraid. You may know that the dog is just a great big softy, but you also know that the child doesn't know that, and you respect his timidity. You don't threaten to send him to his room without tea unless he goes and strokes it This Minute. You don't give him a little lecture on the psychology of learning. And you don't send him to a psychiatrist. You go and stroke the dog yourself, so that the child can see that it doesn't bite you, and that you aren't afraid of it. And you hold one of his hands as he gingerly stretches out the other. That is precisely what a good therapist does.

Aside from the 'problem', as the client understands it, the whole business of seeking and receiving this kind of help raises certain beliefs and fears. It is *weak* of me to have to ask for help. I *ought* to be able to sort it out on my own. Only *crazy* people need therapy. He'll probably think it's *silly* of me to be so upset by such a *trivial* thing. It's *wrong* to have to *pay* someone to listen to me. He'll be *bored*, I expect: it's boring to talk about yourself. Anyway it's *dangerous* to spend too much time contemplating your navel. And so on. These are a good example of a little nest of beliefs that act to inhibit a person's learning – in this case by preventing them from soliciting other people's assistance. And in return for running this nasty gauntlet of self-mockery, the client confidently expects to be rewarded with someone who will wave his wand and make it all better.

Instead she finds herself in a situation that raises, rather than allays, her anxiety. The classical therapist makes no attempt to put her at her ease, does not congratulate her on having come nor agree wholeheartedly about how bad it is. The very unconditional-ness of the therapist's acceptance is at first experienced as a problem. Brought up to win people over, it is disconcerting to discover that her usual tricks – being charming, witty, flirtatious, sub-missive, appealing, bossy, or whatever – don't work. She gets upset as she discovers that *nothing* seems to work, before she realizes that, incredibly, she already has, and cannot lose, what she is after. At this stage it is not surprising that she usually falls in love with the therapist. The phenomenon is called *transference*. However, if she thinks this is Paradise she is probably wrong. Far from having finished she has only just started, because she has been given not perfection but only permission to be and to explore herself. And this, as they say, is where the story really starts. For the therapist's job is not to agree that the weather is awful, nor to read to her from the travel brochures, but to provoke her into making the journey to sunnier climes and greener fields herself. And to do that he has first to get the client to give up her psychological paralysis and rediscover the use of her own legs. And if the paralysis is born of despair, so the first thing to do is to let her see that it is possible and worthwhile to walk, and to give up giving up.

This is the essence of the therapeutic relationship. Having achieved it, therapists of different persuasions will tend to use different goads and crutches to help the traveller on her way.

7.8 Therapeutic Ploys

There are a vast variety of these now, all designed to nudge, kick, or support a client on his way. Without the context of trust, understanding, and example, however, they will not work. With it, they can be very effective. All I can do is mention some of them here.

Psychoanalysts use *projection, association*, and *dreams*. The real Freudian effaces himself as completely as possible, thus providing a blank-ish screen onto which the client can project his monsters. The therapist becomes the overbearing father, the sly mother or the cruel husband, and by daring to give free rein to his miserable fantasies, by blowing them up big enough, the client, even with his poor vision, will eventually see them for what they are – and with irreverent glee, stick pins in them and blow them up in quite another sense.

The technique of free association is very cunning. It is part of the effectiveness of 'going unconscious' about things that upset us that we can go unconscious about what it was that *threatened* to upset us, about what heralded it. Thus we conceal the whole business. In free association – which is not 'free' of course, but reflects his knowledge and preoccupations – the client reels off a string of ideas until, sooner or later, he 'goes blank'. He now has hold of an 'end' – the last idea before unconsciousness descended – which he can fiddle with and tug in order to try to bring to light whatever murky object it is attached to. Thus by locating the 'buoys', one identifies the points where it is interesting to dive. And every so often an evil-looking (but probably harmless) sea-slug or a squid can be brought to the surface and examined, first with caution or even revulsion and then, if all goes well, with confidence and perhaps, sometimes, a sort of affection. Even the occasional sting ray is out of its element on the surface, in the light, and loses its danger. Unseen terrors mostly derive their terror from being unseen.

Dreams work in the same way. They too provide a collection of flotsam that indicate where something interesting might be sunk. Freud encouraged people to go diving with their reason and their logic, and often tried to do it for them. But, as we saw in Chapter 5, the creatures of the 'experiential plane' cannot readily be caught in a net of words and logic. Better to drop in the occasional depth charge or some scraps of meat and then sit quietly and see what floats to the surface.

What we are trying to do is bring to light those aspects of the self we have hidden by picking up their trails. Their signs can be detected, like oil from a damaged submarine, by the therapist in his helicopter, and relayed to Base. Other areas where leakage is likely to occur are *gesture* and *intonation*, which are used by Gestalt therapists, and the products of what Jungians call *active imagination* such as poems and pictures. Anything that the client produces spontaneously and intuitively may contain a little bit of his unconscious 'fixed' within it, and he can examine it under the light to see what meaning it contains.

These are introspective techniques. More dynamic ones are used to encourage people to see that they are more than they usually allow themselves to be – and that when they permit this 'more' to express itself, the sky does not cave in. In particular, relearning to learn can be facilitated by encouraging people to overthrow the tyranny of the four Cs, and to be less competent, less consistent, less cool, and less controlled than usual. These sorts of techniques are often used in groups, where, for example, people are invited to drop the cool, controlled adult image for a while and to become more childish. Twirling each other round and round, laughing hysterically; pretending to be a farmyard of chickens; holding conversations in meaningless babble; going on a fantasy journey through a giant strawberry; deliberately making a fool of yourself in front of the group . . . people who haven't tried it, or who cannot let go of their grown-up image will label these activities 'pointless', 'stupid', and 'self-indulgent'. Yet most people who try it experience, often to their surprise, a wonderful feeling of release, of relaxation, of camaraderie with each other, of gratitude at the opportunity to drop, just for a while, the burden of being 'responsible', of being bound by the four Cs, and not to be scolded for it. And the point, a serious and therapeutic one despite the playfulness of the means, is to see that being grown-up is OK but so is being not grown-up: that we have perhaps become a little too identified with being reasonable, and thereby disowned the part of us that is less reasonable, but more alive, and more fun. And to see also that we do not need the excuse of having children or getting drunk in order to indulge our wider selves in this harmless way.

In a similar, though more serious vein, people who are most out of touch with their feelings may choose to be provoked into catharsis by more confronting methods. If the bear will not come out of its own free will to join the fun and games, it may need to be prodded with a sharp stick. It is not surprising that the most confronting and cathartic kind of therapy, called Synanon, was developed for use with heroin addicts: a desperate attempt to extract signs of life from almost dead people. When the heart has all but stopped beating, one way to try to start it is to thump it hard, or give it a big electric shock. So it is with the metaphorical heart, too. However, not just any thump, anywhere, will do: too soft and it won't work; too hard and you'll kill the patient; wrong place and you'll crack his ribs. You need a trained doctor and a good therapist for this sort of work. Beware of quacks and charlatans.[30]

The final family of techniques that I want to mention here rely on Kurt Vonnegut's insight that 'we are what we pretend to be'. Just what I exhibit about myself depends on what I believe myself to be, so my self-image must incorporate and reflect what I see myself doing. It is difficult to keep denying that I am what I manifestly do. Thus one way to try to break open a calcified self-image is to get someone to *act* consistently in a new way. Though it starts out as pretence, 'phoney', soon the client has to expand her beliefs about herself to acknowledge that she is at least the sort of person who *can* act like somebody different. And this is the thin end of a wedge that can lead to more thoroughgoing reappraisals of herself. This is precisely what George Kelly's *fixed-role therapy* does. The client is asked to create and then act out, a character who she finds plausible and sympathetic but different from herself. Having used the rock of one character who she isn't to break up the rock of the character she thought she was, the little shoots of who she really is can begin to grow up through the cracks.

7.9 Meditation as a Therapeutic Activity

There are many misapprehensions about meditation. It is not the mindless repetition of certain words or sounds. It is not withdrawal from everyday life. It is not about cultivating either serenity or fatalism, nor about sitting in a funny posture. It is not about having visions or gaining special powers, nor about learning esoteric knowledge. It is not about changing your thought, action, or personality at all. It is about learning to become more receptive and attentive to whatsoever you are.[31] It is the cultivation of what different teachers have called *mindfulness*, *self-remembering*, *choiceless awareness*, or *witnessing*. It is the deliberate sharpening and broadening of the instrument that is essential for all learning, however profound or trivial: attention.

Some forms of meditation use certain conditions, like sitting upright in a quiet room, that seem to facilitate the development of mindfulness. Some start out by training the meditator to concentrate on a specific thought or image or sound or bodily sensation. But neither posture nor concentration is essential. What is essential is receptivity, openness to the current experience, whatever it may be.

You cannot observe the stream of consciousness if you are in the stream: you need to sit quietly on the bank. The best position for a train-spotter is not on a train but in the station. Thus to watch one's own experience one needs to be outside it, other than in; a *witness* to it. And to feel oneself other than a particular thought or feeling one can not believe oneself to be it: one has to *disidentify* with it. And disidentification, giving up one's investment in being what one isn't, and in not being what one is, is the heart of significant learning and personal growth. It follows that being attentive to experience is not a preliminary to growth: it is symptomatic of it. They are one and the same thing. You cannot become more attentive without disidentifying and you cannot disidentify without becoming more attentive. This is important, though it is a bit slippery to get hold of, and may take a little while to grasp. It is the reason why, as we said earlier, 'observation is alchemical'. Nothing else is required: no good resolutions, efforts of will or plans of campaign. And this of course is very hard to take for an 'I' that sees its very foundation as residing in deciding, planning, willing, and doing. It is second nature to believe that things ought to be different and to try to shift them. So it is much less easy than it sounds just to let them be as they are, without any judgement or interference. And just to let the judgements and impulses to interfere to be as *they* are without trying to improve them.

Of the four Cs, meditation leads us to examine the one that is most central to our sense of self: control. Is it possible to give up the idea that 'I' decide and determine and will and enact? And what would happen if 'I' did give up control of thought, feeling, or action? Would I go crazy and run amok? If I let myself off the lead, would I ever be able to catch myself again? Because one believes or fears it to be so dangerous, various forms of meditation have been developed that enable one to experiment with the sense of control in limited ways. The pure contemplation of whatever happens, called in Buddhism *vipassana* and in Zen *shikan-taza*, is primarily an experiment in relinquishing control of thought. A meditation such as Bhagwan Shree Rajneesh's *dynamic meditation* requires a surrendering to feeling. And practices such as the famous *whirling* of the Sufi dervishes enables one to experience kinds of bodily movement as 'doing themselves' without any effort or control. While meditations such as the latter two are designed to test specific beliefs about self, and are therefore more specialized, witnessing is a knack that will facilitate anybody's attempt to become more observant, and so a better learner.

7.10 Good Learners

When people have relearnt to learn, what happens? Are there any general observations one can make about such folk, or do they go shooting off in different directions? In terms of their interests and habits they do become more diverse than the average group of people. In terms of *process*, however – the way they live their lives, deal with other people, respond to uncertainty and so on – certain trends have been noted and described by both Carl Rogers and Abraham Maslow. Rogers,[32] for example, lists some of the changes that occur in successful psychotherapy as the following:

> The person comes to see himself differently. He accepts himself and his feelings more fully. He becomes more self-confident and self-directing. He becomes more flexible, less rigid in his perceptions. He adopts more realistic goals for himself. He behaves in a more mature fashion. . . . He becomes more acceptant of others. He becomes more open to the evidence, both to what is going on outside of himself and to what is going on inside of himself. He changes in his basic personality characteristics, in constructive ways.

Rogers' description is based on the observation and evaluation of people 'getting better' in therapy. Maslow's description of 'self-actualizing' people, in contrast, derives from the study of individuals who were widely agreed to be a bit special.[33] He found them to be efficient perceivers, able to detect phoneyness and illusion; to prefer to face unpleasant facts than to avoid them; to be acceptant of themselves and others; to have good, close, loving relationships with at least one or two other people; to be able to identify with and feel for other people whoever or whatever they were; to delight in experience, to 'appreciate again and again, freshly and naively . . . a sunset, a flower, a baby, a person'; to be spontaneous, simple and natural; to have a good sense of humour, to be independent and creative thinkers; and to enjoy challenging and investigating assumptions and beliefs, whether personal, political or cultural.[34]

CHAPTER 8

GROWING UP

INFANT JOY	INFANT SORROW
'I have no name,	My mother groan'd! my father wept.
'I am but two days old.'	Into the dangerous world I leapt:
What shall I call thee?	Helpless, naked, piping loud:
'I happy am,	Like a fiend hid in a cloud.
'Joy is my name.'	
Sweet joy befall thee!	Struggling in my father's hands,
	Striving against my swadling bands,
Pretty joy!	Bound and weary I thought best,
Sweet joy but two days old,	To sulk upon my mother's breast.
Sweet joy I call thee:	
Thou dost smile,	
I sing the while,	
Sweet joy befall thee!	

No bird soars too high, if he soars with his own wings.

To the as-yet-unborn, to all innocent wisps of undifferentiated nothingness: Watch out for life. I have caught life. I have come down with life. I was a wisp of undifferentiated nothingness, and then a little peephole opened quite suddenly. Light and sound poured in. Voices began to describe me and my surroundings. Nothing they said could be appealed. They said I was a boy named Rudolph Waltz, and that was that. They said the year was 1932, and that was that. They said I was in Midland City, Ohio, and that was that.

They never shut up. Year after year they piled detail upon detail. They do it still. You know what they say now? They say the year is 1982, and that I am fifty years old.

Blah blah blah.

(Kurt Vonnegut: *Deadeye Dick*[1])

Up to this point we have been looking at the processes through which human beings endeavour to ensure their survival: the ways they distinguish between challenge and threat, and the strategies they have for responding to each. We have looked at what constitute threats to self, and ways of avoiding them; and also at learning opportunities and methods for trying to find out what to do when we don't know what to do. The principal question to which this chapter is addressed is: how do these strategies and decision-making processes develop? How does it come about that we learn to tune, experiment, and play; to remember, understand, and repeat things; to build bridges in thought and action; to repress and project and rationalize? We shall be concerned with *what* people learn as they grow up, particular skills, knowledge, and beliefs that they pick up. But more importantly, we shall continue our investigation of *how* they learn by looking at how they learn to learn. How do we develop the particular repertoire of learning amplifiers (and suppressors) that we do?

8.1 Views of Developments

Before we pursue this view of development, we should locate it in the context of other, complementary, views. The first, which we shall need to draw on, is of *development as the unfolding of a genetic programme*. This is sometimes called *maturation* to distinguish it from the more psychological perspectives. Given that certain minimal environmental conditions are fulfilled – adequate food, liquid, air, stimulation, and so on – then physical development unfolds in a way that is largely independent of the particular nature of the stimuli and nutrients received. Limbs, organs, facial features, and nervous system tend to turn out much the same. If the infant were a computer we might say that maturation is concerned with the development of the *hardware*.

The second view sees *development as the accumulation of knowledge and ability*. This approach, which is the predominant one in psychology, concerns itself with the increase with increasing age of what people can know and do. This is the tradition that Jean Piaget initiated.[2] Its goal is to uncover the general features of the developmental sequence. Is there a fixed order in which knowledge and skill have to be acquired? Are there abilities that cannot be acquired before a certain developmental 'stage' has been reached? If the child were a computer, development in this sense is concerned with uncovering the *software* he possesses at different ages. *What* does he know, and *when* does he acquire it?

The third view, the one that locates the study of growing up within the general psychological perspective of this book (as expressed in Chapters 1 and 2), is of *development as the elimination of survival errors*. A human baby is born too early to be able to look after his own survival. He cannot flee, he cannot fight, and he cannot feed himself. His physiology is immature, and it will take years to develop sufficiently to allow fast running, effective combat and the digestion of oysters. But even this physical capacity is useless without knowing what is dangerous, what is safe, and what is good to eat. It is no use trying to boil a rock or running in terror from a cheese roll. Development is centrally about finding out what relevance things have to one's own survival, what to do about them and how to reduce the frequency of the occasions on which one gets it wrong. It is important to keep this view in mind if we are to see development as purposeful. Development is at root about increasing the probability of survival, and becoming more able to survive on one's own.

And issuing from this is the last view, the one I want to emphasize here, of *development as the acquisition of learning amplifiers*. We want to find out *how* the child comes to know what he does. What are the processes whereby he becomes more purposeful and more sophisticated about finding things out? The focus is not so much on what he knows how to do, but on the changes that occur in the way he reacts when he doesn't know what to do. This approach to development is only just beginning to emerge, and much of what I shall have to say will be speculative. If the child were a computer we would call this approach the study of *programming*, and particularly of *self-programming*; of how the computer comes to write its own software.

8.2 The Basic Learning Ability

If we are to look at development as the accumulation of learning amplifiers we need to know what exactly is there to be amplified (or suppressed, of course). To understand the telescope and the microscope as vision-amplifiers, it is necessary to have some understanding of the unamplified organ of vision, the eye. The telephone, the weighing-machine and the fork-lift truck would be of no use to us unless we possessed *natural* abilities to hear, to feel, and to move. And so it is with learning: some learning ability, some basic capacity to be modified by experience, must be inherent in the nervous system. We shall consider what this might be. And we shall have to consider what it is that is modified by learning, in neurological terms, and also in terms of the basic response-abilities, sense-abilities and needs with which the human infant is endowed, together with any wired-in connections between these – the 'reflexes'. When we know how it is that a nervous system with certain functional and structural characteristics, exposed to certain kinds of stimulation, turns into an adult that knows and believes all that it does, and learns and defends in all the ways it can, then we shall have told the complete story of development. But that might take another week or two.

The early development of the baby's nervous system is fascinating and complicated.[3] For present purposes all we need to know is that the new-born's brain is functionally like a formal garden with a lot of new little plants and seedlings in it. The general form of development is fixed by the position of the paths and flowerbeds: in the brain this 'framework' is laid down by the 'macroneurons'. But within these limits the bushy, branching 'inter-neurons' continue to grow in profusion, and it is the way they come to link up and intertwine that forms the basis of learning. It is the nature of this tangle that is influenced and shaped by the 'elements' of experience.[4]

The problem with this simple 'garden' model is that the brain is not 'quiet'. Unlike branches and twigs, neurons are constantly creating impulses themselves. They are spontaneously active, 'firing' every so often like a very slow automatic machine-gun. A 'stimulus' does not *create* a pattern of activity in the CNS (the Central Nervous System); it adds into and modifies a very complex, preexisting pattern. So we cannot trace the path from Stimulus to Response along a single, neat channel. The effect of a stimulus is more like the effect on the water of one child jumping into an already crowded swimming pool.[5] Thus learning *is* about changing struc-tural connections within the brain, but the functional effect of that is to facilitate or impede the spontaneous occurrence or flow of activity at par-ticular points. Learning modifies the pattern and timing of activity within the CNS, and makes the pattern of firing of one neuron or group of neurons contingent on the state of activity of another neuron or group of neurons.

How this happens is not yet fully explained. But what the basic learning mechanism does seems clear. Donald Hebb, one of the earliest, and still most influential researchers in this area, summed up what happens like this: '. . . a growth process accompanying synaptic activity makes the synapse more readily traversed. . . . When an axon of cell A is near enough to excite a cell B, and repeatedly or persistently takes part in firing it, some growth process or metabolic change takes place in one or both cells such that A's efficiency, as one of the cells firing B, increases.'[6] Or to put it another way, cells that 'glow' together, grow together. The spontaneous firing of B becomes modified so that it slowly comes under the control of A. A becomes a governor for B, being able to speed it up, turn it down, or change its pattern of firing. This, of course, will affect C, and so on.

8.3 Registering Regularities

How does this mechanism come to pick out and store not just experiences but *regularities*? For this is what the child needs in order to be able to anticipate and control his world. From the moment of birth (and probably before) the infant's neural learning mechanism is working. That is to say, the total pattern of activation in the brain in every moment is etched in. All the simultaneously active neurons 'grow together' a little bit, so that they form an interconnected circuit or channel round which the activation is more likely to flow next time. But the channel that is dug for each instantaneous pattern is a very shallow one. The channel that is created to represent a total multi-media snapshot of a moment of 'now' we might call a *memory*. It is the record of an event.[7]

Such a trace is established each and every moment, so clearly there are going to be quite a lot of these weak memories very soon, each leaving its own faint track across the landscape of the brain. And no track, no route will ever be repeated completely. But *parts* of memories – the parts called Daddy, Angela, 'feel of cot', but most especially Mummy's voice, Mummy's face, and Mummy's breast – will be repeated, and their tracks, being traversed again and again, will begin to be worn away, and to become more prominent, like a sheep track on a hill-side. But the track is not a linear one, running from A to B, or even round in a circle. It is more like a growing-together of every feature on the path with every other feature directly, so that they begin to form a cluster of interwoven features – sensory, behavioural, motivational and emotional – that tend to fire off together. They tend to 'recruit' each other, so that when a few of them are activated, the whole package is likely to light up.[8] We have met these clusters before, in Chapter 3, and there we used the metaphor of *dunes*. This process of gradual erosion is how the dune-scape arises and develops. As a result of constant coactivation, a common, deeply worn set of channels emerge that represent Mummy, linking together the smell and sight and feel of her breast, the taste of milk, the sound of her voice, the cut of her hair, the colour of her eyes and the warmth of her body. And inextricably entwined with these 'perceptual features', the clues that lead him to believe that he is in the presence of Mummy-hood, are developing specifications of what to do with her, and what happens. Antecedent, Behaviour, and Consequence begin to intermingle. (You may wish to refer back to Section 3.2 at this point.)

The process I have described is what we earlier (Section 3.5) called *tuning*. It thus emerges that tuning is the basic, biologically given, learning mechanism. Tuning is implicit in the nature of the nervous system. We could define a nervous system as that which tunes. Tuning is what is amplified, speeded, and facilitated by the other learning strategies.

One modification needs to be introduced to this discussion of the pick-up of patterns before we conclude it. Are the patterns and regularities that we pick up simply determined by the patterns that occur in our experience? No. As we discussed at the beginning of this section and in Chapter 3, the patterns that we are particularly interested in are those that *matter*, those that affect us, those that are relevant to our survival. Thus those patterns that contain components that are to do with the satisfaction of need, the avoidance of threat or the removal of pain are treated preferentially. Those are the ones, out of the infinite number that Nature contains, that we need to know about and retain. There are a variety of ways of handling this theoretically. Let us suppose here that *patterns that are relevant to survival are dug deeper every time they occur than those that are not.*[9] If this is so, then they will tend to emerge more quickly than the others, and they will come very rapidly to dominate the landscape.

8.4 The Newborn Baby

How can we describe the baby, perhaps a day or two old, in terms of what he can sense, what he can do, what his needs are, and what connections, whether innate or acquired during birth itself, exist already between the domains of sensation, action and need?[10] What is the raw material of the baby's experience that the learning mechanism we have just described will get to work on and refine?

(a) *Sense-abilities*   The newborn baby's perception is crude but working. He can focus his eyes on objects about eight inches from his face. He can discriminate between certain sounds and will turn his head towards a sound. He can tell the difference between the smell of his own mother's milk and that of another mother. He can detect and react to an object that is actually, or appears to be, approaching him. It is not easy to do experiments with newborn babies: they tend to doze off and topple over, and the responses you can use to detect their ability to discriminate are as crude as their discriminations. However, vision in particular has been closely investigated recently, and it turns out that the newborn's visual perception is more sophisticated than had previously been thought.

(b) *Feel-abilities* From the word go a baby is, necessarily, sensitive to signals which arise from within his own body, as well as those that he will learn to attribute to 'the outside world'. These are his needs – to be more accurate, what Murray calls (see Chapter 2) the viscerogenic needs. These needs are conditions that must be fulfilled for survival to continue. Clearly if a baby is insensitive to a need he will not respond to the absence of a survival condition, and unless someone else can spot it and rectify it for him, he will die. The infant needs include food, air, liquid, light, warmth, touch, a certain intermediate range of stimulation, and the freedom to move somewhat, to defecate and to urinate.

(c) *Response-abilities* Throughout his life a baby will be refining the repertoire of actions he is born with, learning to modify in time, manner, and place the execution of his fundamental set of verbs. They include moving eyes, opening and closing eyes, turning head, opening and closing mouth, chewing and swallowing, dribbling and spitting, blowing and sucking, cooing, babbling, crying and screaming, wrinkling nose and sniffing, tensing the muscles of shoulders, chest, midriff and hips, urinating and defecating. He can walk with his arms supported, though he will temporarily lose this ability for most of his first year. At first most of these acts are reflex or aimless. Gradually he will discover what can be *achieved* by variants of each. And as he does so, he will discover, too, the effectiveness of not doing them, especially when other people want him to.

(d) *Reflexes* Various basic associations between sensation and movement seem to be given at birth. A baby will track with his head and eyes the path of a slowly moving object. He will turn his head in response to sound. He will remove a blob of some irritant from his face with his hand, and from one leg with the other. He will respond to a touch on his cheek by turning, seeking with open mouth, and sucking. He will close his eyes in response to a puff of air or a bright light. He will close his fist round a finger. He will respond appropriately to the sensation of a full bladder or a full bowel.

(e) *Learning at birth* For many people, if not all, it is no exaggeration to say that birth – especially the modern, supine hospital birth – is as near as we get to death until death itself. Birth is the archetypal threat to survival. And if experiences relevant to survival are recorded right from the start, perhaps birth too leaves an indelible mark. Ejected from his warm, dark, wet, safe, five-star haven, subjected to inconceivable and interminable pressure and physical discomfort, dumped (in most hospitals) into an intensely bright, intensely noisy, intensely cold atmosphere and, literally cut off from his ever ready supply of oxygen and nutrition, he must swallow a mouthful of dry air, unstick his soft, wet lungs, and breath. It is not at all fanciful to see this as a painful and frightening time, and to suppose that the association of pain and fear with harsh stimuli on the one hand, and with crying and squirming on the other, is thereby established, and that it remains a profound though inarticulate memory throughout life. Bright lights, loud noises, isolation and strangeness, meaninglessness and unfamiliarity become potent associates of threat and fear; while dim light, soft, familiar and repetitive sounds (like a heartbeat), warmth and physical contact become the concomitants of safety. No wonder that we curl up under the covers when we feel miserable.

(f) *Habituation*   The reflex of turning head and eyes towards a new occurrence, the so-called 'orienting response', is given at birth. The presence of *learning* at birth is signalled by the gradual reduction of this response to a repeated occurrence. The same sound repeated over and over elicits less and less reaction from the newborn baby: he 'habituates' to it. And this habituation is not just a turning down of awareness, because a small change will be sufficient for him to pay attention again. Habituation is actually the outward and visible sign of neural learning: as the baby's nervous system binds together the features of the stimulus, so less and less attention is required in order to identify each occurrence as another example of the developing package. In electrical terms, as the 'resistance' of the circuit gets less, so a smaller injection of 'current' is sufficient to light up the bulb. Attention is freed to learn about something else. As we saw before in Chapters 3 and 7, awareness and learning are two sides of the same coin. What one is aware of is, *ipso facto*, what one is learning about; and the current object of learning is the current object of awareness.

8.5 The Development of Expectancies

During the first two years of life a child is learning what the game is and what the ground-rules are. She lays an unshakeable foundation of knowledge about the physical world, about relationships, and about herself. And it all boils down to survival. For if her First Great Learning is that Life Hurts, the second, that follows immediately, is that Satisfaction is No Longer Guaranteed. Things can go wrong: threats to survival are real, recurrent, and unavoidable. This would be traumatic were it not for the dawning of the third great learning: What I Do Makes a Difference. One of the patterns that the child begins to pick up is the coincidence between the way things turn out and what she happens to be doing at the time. It is not hard for her to spot that her well-being is linked to the presence of her Mum, and that Mum's presence in times of trouble is related to her cries. She does not yet know that her sphere of influence is limited, nor, in most cases, what precisely is required. But once she has an inkling of the association between her actions and her survival, she is ready to join the game. The game is to discover the extent and the nature of her control. And the currency with which the game is played is expectancies – the three-way links between what's going on out there, what's required in here, and what I'm up to. She knows she has a say in the matter: now all she needs to know is the language of command.

To have fully mastered the nature of expectancies and how to acquire them takes about two years. This is the major preoccupation of the first phase of a child's life, what Piaget called the *sensori-motor period*. Much needs to be worked out before full expectancies are established. (Expressions such as 'worked out', 'realized', 'problem-solving', and so on, when used in the context of young children, refer to organismic, biological activities that are very unlikely to be either conscious, verbal or deliberate. We are still talking about the CNS 'doing its thing'.) First the child has to discover what her repertoire of senses is: she has to find out what 'vision', 'touch', and so on are. She probably does this on the basis of their connection with simple types of movement. 'Vision' is what alters when she moves her eyes. 'Sound' is what alters when she moves her head with her eyes shut. 'Smell' is what alters when she sniffs. 'Taste' is what alters when she sucks or swallows. And 'Touch' is what alters when she wriggles.

Then she has to discover subdivisions within these senses. She learns to distinguish sensations that alter only when she moves her eyes ('still objects') from those that alter even when her eyes are fixed ('moving objects'). Gradually she refines these crude divisions and identifies more and more subtle features of her sensation. Human beings, to take a very important case in point, vary in their *distance* (which she learns is predicted by retinal size), their colour (pigmentation, clothes, make-up), their orientation, the pitch of their voices, and many other features – but they can be reliably identified by the presence of eyes, nose and mouth in a certain spatial relationship. Small wonder that babies latch on to these features very early on. Eyes in particular make ideal stimuli: they shine, they are patterned, they move and they often appear at the right distance for her to see them clearly.

At the same time, the child develops connections *between* the senses, and between perceptual and behavioural parts of his system. A baby only weeks old, for example, has learnt to expect both sound and vision of her Dad to come from the same place. Seeing him to her right through a window, and hearing him to her left from a loudspeaker she gets upset. There are no *general* rules for relating sight and sound to each other: the child has to discover, ultimately, the thousands of conjunctions that occur in her world – of people, animals, cars, machinery, wind, water, and telephones. There are three important sets of rules that she needs to discover early on, however. They are the *limb-proprioception, eye–hand*, and *ear–voice* co-ordinations. The child's sixth sense comprises the information from joint and pressure receptors within her own limbs, that tell her where the different bits of her body are, and how they are moving. This sense is called proprioception. Clearly there is a highly reliable mapping, which the child has to discover, between the motor commands that issue from her brain – what she tells her limbs to do – and the proprioceptive stimulation that results. If her actions are to be successful, in reaching for and grasping small toys, for example, she cannot issue the same instruction to her hand on every occasion, for its starting position will always be different. Thus it is vital that the child be able to coordinate what her body 'feels like' now, and what it *would* feel like if it were in the desired position, and generate the appropriate movement to turn one into the other. Although this integration is quite complex, it is easy to learn in principle, because the correlations are very stable and predictable. If the same motor command is executed from starting position A on a number of occasions, the consequent position B will always be the same. There is almost no 'noise' in the system. The same is true for the related eye–hand system. A repeated instruction to a hand to move from A to B will also produce a quite consistent change in the visual world: that is to say, the child can *see* the hand move from A to B.

An equally clean set of correspondences between hearing and vocalization are there to be discovered. Not only can the child learn that she can produce changes in her own experience (by babbling, crying, cooing, etc.); she discovers that she can precisely control what sound she is to hear by controlling the vocalization that she produces. The child's play with this system – her experimentation with its range and limits – comes before she sees that it has anything to do with speech. Up to the age of about six months her babbling and cooing 'research' is unrestrained by the sounds of the language which the adults around her are producing. Beyond that age, though, she begins to register that there is some connection between what she can do with her mouth and what adults spend a lot of time doing with theirs, and her researches gradually concentrate on the problem of detecting and reproducing the sound-patterns that the grown-ups are making.

These early stages of learning are preparations for the emergence of full-fledged expectancies. On the one hand she is learning what states of the internal and external world reliably follow one another – what Antecedent–Consequence relations she can count on. On the other hand she is playing with her own Behaviour and with the sensory Consequences that she is capable of producing. As yet though, she has not put these two learnings together and realized that she is capable of intervening in the Antecedent to Consequent flow of events so as to create certain Consequences that are to her advantage and exclude others that are not. In terms of Piaget's six-fold division of the sensori-motor period of development, the child has now moved from reflex action through the acquisition of primary circular reactions (registering the internal proprioceptive consequences of action) to secondary circular reactions, where she can register and reproduce the external consequences of her movements.

The next stage, the coordination of secondary reactions, is the crucial one. Now the child discovers that she can link together internal and external consequences through the medium of her own actions, so that she is capable of using her behaviour to produce what she needs. And furthermore she realizes that the success of this enterprise depends on fitting these actions to the prevailing external circumstances. Her acts begin to become both intentional and appropriate. She can modulate the loudness of a cry to take account of whether her mother is in her field of view or not. She can distinguish between mother and father, and, through learning their idiosyncrasies, can control them better. She can differentiate between objects that stay the same over a period of absence (so-called 'object permanence') and those – like people – which may change from occasion to occasion, and therefore demand more attentive perception and more selective responding.[11]

So far all these discoveries have been made using nothing other than the basic mechanism of tuning. Patterns that recur are gradually stamped into the brain's circuitry, and those patterns that matter to the learner emerge more quickly and more sharply than those that don't. During her second year, however, certain expectancies are formed that refer to learning itself. That is to say, their Antecedents are certain kinds of *Learning Situation* and their Consequences are *More Efficient, Successful, Comfortable, Speedy Learning*. The Behaviours that link the two are the learning strategies or amplifiers to which we now turn.

8.6 The Discovery of Learning Strategies

A learning strategy is a way of speeding up learning while cutting down risk. Sometimes it would take ages to retune an action that has been found wanting. And sometimes the 'observed consequence' is not only different from the 'expected consequence', but painful too, so that a *gradual* discovery of how to avoid it might only follow a lengthy period of not avoiding it.[12] If somebody steals my wallet from my jacket pocket, I want to change my habits quickly, now, to try to stop it happening again. I want to avoid trial and error if possible, and come up with a guess, preferably an educated one, that has a good chance of working first time. So I do not shift the wallet to *any* other pocket, but to the anticipated safety of an inside, button-up pocket. The better my guesses the quicker I learn, and the quicker I learn the faster does the scope of my competence develop. A good set of instruments for dealing with situations that you don't know how to deal with is the most important component of the developing child's tool-kit. Nothing is more vital than to learn how to amplify the basic learning ability that God gave you. The parable of the talents applies especially to the talent for discovery. Unfortunately there is not space enough to do more than mention some of the learning strategies that we have identified, and how they might arise.[13]

Tuning, as we have said, is the strategy that is built into the brain. It is the process whereby experiences, and especially successful experiences, come to modify the neural hardware, and thereby to gain control over our spontaneous thought and action. *The learning amplifiers are designed to generate, as candidates for tuning, actions that are successful, or that are good enough to be allowed to be gradually refined.*

Investigation is perhaps the earliest strategy to be used as such. It covers a variety of activities that have been discovered to increase the amount of information available from a situation that is partially unknown but non-threatening. These activities include: moving closer to the object or occurrence; grasping it and bringing it closer to you; feeling rather than just touching; sniffing rather than just smelling; listening rather than just hearing; and putting it in your mouth (a very early one, this). Each of these will be first discovered by floundering (see below) with particular objects, and then discovered, through attempts to tune them, to apply widely to the pick-up of information from any interesting source. The pay-off for using these investigative techniques is the increase in data, and it does not take much to learn that knowledge is control: the more you know about something, the better chance you have of getting out of its way, neutralizing it or bending it to your own ends.

Prodding. Investigating involves paying closer attention to something. It is essentially receptive. Often more data can be collected by prodding it, like a cat with a beetle, and noticing how it reacts. The purpose of the prod is not to find out whether prodding is a suitable way of relating to it, so it is different from experimenting. The purpose is to get the beetle or the toy or the TV set to reveal itself. Students of chemistry are taught a number of simple tests that are worth applying to any strange substance. Does it dissolve in water or acid? What happens when you heat it? Does it colour a flame? Students of life rapidly discover an equivalent set of tests. What happens when I push it? Shout at it? Wave at it? Chew it? Throw it? When I prod it does it squeak, or run, or curl up into a ball, or do nothing? These techniques are first discovered as the child attempts to explore the repercussions of floundering. Different *types* of flounder are seen to be good at getting things to give away important information about themselves: whether they are alive, whether they move, whether they bite and whether you can eat them.

Floundering is not a very good learning strategy, but better than none. In fact it starts life, probably, as a general response to threat, a very early attempt to fight or flee, for in its crudest form it involves simply thrashing about, literally floundering like a fish in a net. For many unknown situations this reaction is quite useless: you cannot discover how to solve a chess problem, nor how to tie a shoelace by flailing your limbs, however vigorously or protractedly you do it. But occasionally it works, if you want to get the blanket off when you are too hot, say, or (especially) if you want to draw attention to yourself. A few such experiences may convince you that if you are really stuck for something to try, floundering may just about be better than nothing. Animals, being less sophisticated than us, tend to use floundering more. Thorndike's classic experiment, you remember, showed cats in a box floundering until they happened to hit the latch that opened the door. They, like us, then began to transfer from floundering to tuning: once an approximate solution is found we can investigate more closely just those features that are relevant, and refine our actions accordingly.

Note, however, that floundering + investigation + tuning may leave you with a refined response that contains unnecessary features – what Thorndike called in his cats 'superstitious behaviour'. If you started out by spinning round three times and yelling 'Geronimo!' before pulling the latch, and every time, after you've done the war-dance and pulled the latch, the door opens, there is no reason for you to drop it. It appears to work. Thus this learning sequence is designed to discover features that are necessary to produce a desired consequence, but not to discover and drop features that have become part of the habit, but which are actually not relevant. For that, a more advanced strategy such as *experimenting* or *playing* is required (see below).

Imitating is a better strategy for generating possible solutions when you don't know what to do, and it is one that parents are very keen to teach children. They tend to reward with praise or affection any imitation of their own behaviour or values because it makes them feel good and powerful, and it is the earliest and easiest channel of communication between parent and child. They feel in touch. Interestingly, the imitation game that develops within the first few months of life is based on the parent's self-deception. Katie blows a raspberry, enjoys it, and before she can do it again, Dad blows one. So when she does the second one that she was going to do anyway, Dad is delighted, and attributes the roles of model and imitator, mistakenly, to himself and his daughter. But after a few of these illusory communications, Katie begins to pick up the pattern:

A: Dad does something
B: I do something similar
C: I get hugged and kissed.

(Note that for the game to work properly, Katie has to have some idea of what 'similar' means. She needs to have learnt some rough set of correspondences between her own body and actions and other people's.)[14] At this stage, imitation is a technique for creating affection; it is not yet seen as a *learning* strategy. But as the game develops, so the child will notice that, as well as getting Dad's affection as a consequence – what Bandura and

Walters in their *Social Learning and Personality Development*[15] call 'vicarious reinforcement' – their action sometimes produces the same 'natural consequence' as Dad's. If I try to copy his digging, not only is he pleased but I make a hole in the earth. My act creates what his act creates. Thus the hidden potential of imitation emerges, and its status shifts. It is now a useful source of clues about how to achieve a desired consequence: if I don't know what to do, watch someone else. Imitation becomes a true learning amplifier. As with floundering, and *bridging*, which we look at next, however, imitating does not guarantee success. The action that is imitated still has to be tried out as an experiment, and assessed, refined or rejected on the basis of first-hand experience of how it works. The conjunction of Antecedent, Behaviour, and Consequence must occur if the 'experiential plane' is to be affected.

Bridging is the next strategy that the child discovers for generating behavioural experiments. It is the technique of fitting together expectancies that he already possesses, but none of which is itself adequate for *this* problem, in order to create a tentative 'bridge' between problem and solution. This is the most rudimentary form of problem-solving, and its acquisition constitutes the sixth and final stage of Piaget's sensori-motor period. A simple example of this concerns the child's ability to find his way about his home, after he has begun to crawl. He may know from his own experience how to get from X to Y, and from Y to Z, but without ever having crawled from X to Z. On finding himself at X one day, and wishing to be at Z, he may, instead of howling for his mother, review the expectancies he possesses that have X as their antecedent and, to start with independently, those that have 'arrived at Z' as their consequence. When X-Y and Y-Z are active soon after each other, they can become associated via the common activation of Y, and Y can therefore become a bridge for the functional connection of X and Z. Note that, put this way, we still do not have to attribute to the child any conscious or rational control of his own 'thought processes'. The combination of originally separate expectancies emerges from the developing sophistication of the CNS itself, reflecting a generalization of the processes that are inherent within it. It is certainly an ability that the young human being shares with other organisms.

Off-duty learning: practising. The strategies reviewed so far are designed to generate educated guesses about what might work. The strategies of practising and playing are designed to expedite the tuning of habits that have been already adopted, but which do not yet work perfectly. A baby has got 'the basic idea' about crawling or cup-holding or saying 'Mama' or piling bricks up, but he hasn't quite 'got it'. There remains a risk that it will let him down – that he or the tower will topple over, or that the juice will be spilt. He won't get what he wants, or avoid the threat. What to do?

Some expensive radios have *two* knobs for tuning, a gross one and a fine one. The gross one enables you to get quickly to the vicinity of the station you want – to do a quick scan of the dial. Once there you can switch to the fine tuner in order to get it 'spot on'. What the child discovers, again through trial and error, is that he is equipped with the same dual system. The rough tuner is what is used when the consequence matters: his object is to find something quickly that will work well enough. Floundering, imitating, and bridging are components of the rough tuner. When we have to learn while trying to gain a consequence that actually, in that moment, matters, we might say we are 'on-duty'. And on-duty learning, as we said in Section 8.3, cuts a relatively deep channel in the brain. Patterns that are experienced in the absence of a strong need, we said, leave a trace, but a weaker one. What the child discovers is that he can use this off-duty, low-risk, weak-effect, kind of learning as his fine tuner. He can take an expectancy that is in the process of being refined and run it *when the need for its consequence is not present*, off the job, and the information so gained is effective in very slowly honing the expectancy.[16] This is called *practising*. It is the attempt to replicate as precisely as possible an action that has been found to be successful, but which is not yet specified clearly enough in the expectancy to be perfectly reproducible. Practising means binding in to the specification features that are known to be relevant or necessary.

Off-duty learning: playing. Playing is the off-duty complement to practising. It is the attempt to discover and drop from the action-specification features that are not necessary. While such 'superstitious' features may seem harmless, they will inevitably take up time and energy. To drop them may not improve the effectiveness of an action directly, but they will improve its *economy*, and, in a tight corner, when one is back on the job, that may be of help.

Playing village cricket, the height of a batsman's back-lift as he prepares to play a shot may not matter. Facing the fastest of bowlers you may be glad that all your time in the nets has helped you lift the bat six inches less, and thereby given you an extra split second to judge the stroke. Playing in the sense I am defining it here means trying out slight variations on the expectancy, in order to reassess the value of its different components.

Doing this inevitably raises the risk of failure, of cutting out or interfering with elements that are actually vital, and so 'losing it' for a moment; but the *cost* of failure is small because the current need for the consequence is weak. Because each little experiment will be conducted only once if it fails, the risk of undermining your existing expertise is small. Only if performance is maintained or even improved, will the experiment be repeated, and the modification that was on trial be retained and consolidated.

A baby learns to amplify his learning through practice and play, through actively experimenting with the limits and details of his expectancies, during the early part of his second year. For Piaget, I think, the discovery of the fine tuner and how to use it occurs in the fifth sensori-motor period – which he calls the stage of *tertiary circular reactions*. Exactly how these discoveries come about, however, I don't yet understand. Much remains to be discovered about how these and the other learning strategies arise, and about such questions as which are universal and which are encouraged or prohibited by different cultures.

8.7 Learning Language

Contrary to popular, or at least Chomskean, opinion in the 1960s, children learn language by using exactly the same mechanisms and strategies as they use to learn everything else.[17] Language is a strange and very complicated set of *objects*, with its own special secrets, just like a mah-jong set, or a railway system, or insects. Language is also a complex and versatile set of *actions*, like playing cricket or teaching fourth-year General Science, or making friends. It is simultaneously a part of the world that affects us, and a very important collection of habits for affecting the world back. Children have to crack the code of the language they hear and learn how to produce the code themselves. Before that though, they have to find out what a 'code' is: how it is that the sounds a person makes are fundamentally different from the sounds that a dog, or a plastic spoon, or the central heating system makes. In fact the true ability to use and understand language involves the putting together of a variety of different insights and skills that are first learned separately. Language is quite a difficult jigsaw puzzle to learn how to put together. Here are some of the components.

(a)*Eye–voice coordination*   We have discussed this in Section 8.5. The child during his first 'preverbal' year is learning to correlate what he does with his mouth with what comes in through his ears. Babies babble a lot on their own, perhaps because, when there are no other sounds, the correspondences are 'cleaner'.

(b) *'My voice' – 'Your voice' coordination*   Through observation, and through imitation-games, the child comes to associate certain sounds that he makes himself with certain sounds that other people make. He has to discover the 'phonemes', the basic vocabulary of sounds that his language will consist of, and to be able to recognize them as equivalent despite being spoken by people (himself included) with very different voice qualities.

(c) *Concepts*   Before he can learn to talk, a child has to have something to talk about. While his earliest speech-like sounds will be empty of meaning, his first true words and little sentences must be parasitic on his own, already well developed, system of expectancies. They will be, as we said in Chapter 4, like flags planted in the dunes. You can't plant a flag in mid air.

(d) *Sound as control*   He will observe, without at first knowing how it works, that human sounds are special, powerful stimuli for other human beings. Things happen when he cries, and when he babbles people attend to him. And he sees that people pay attention to each other, and are affected, when *they* 'cry' and 'babble'. Frustrated with people constantly misunderstanding what his own cries mean, it would be surprising if he wasn't on the look-out for a better signalling system, and, if he hadn't begun to realize that language was it. 'Only connect' is all very well – but *how*?

(e) *Pointing*   In order to learn that a sound is associated with an object or an event, they have to be present at the same time. But there is so much going on in the child's world that he has no way of knowing which thing his mother is talking about. For the connection to be made, he has to be *attending* to both sound and object together. He has to learn about pointing. First of all he will learn the association between word and object by having the latter (cup, shoe, Daddy, Teddy) put in front of him, at the crucial moment. The two 'circuits' begin to become connected within his brain, just as the sound and vision of dog or clock or Mummy have already done. For these first associations, the sound becomes a *feature* of the object, of the same kind as the clock's tick and the dog's bark. Or of almost the same kind, we might say, because while clock and tick, Rover and bark come from the same place, cup and 'cup' do not, or not quite.

Using these well learnt associations, mother teaches the child the signals of pointing.[18] First she stops thrusting the cup in front of the child and just holds it. Then she just touches it with the end of a finger. Then she extends arm and finger in the direction of the cup, but without touching it. And finally, and most subtly, she just *looks* in the direction of what she is naming. Complicated though it is, babies learn that the thing (perhaps unknown, this time) that Mummy is talking about is to be found somewhere along her line of sight. Looking along this imaginary line, the common focus is established. And finally the child comes to look for and attend to objects whose names he knows simply when he hears its characteristic 'sound'.

Gently he is led to discover that words are not just attributes of things but are themselves used for pointing. They are the most elegant of this increasingly refined repertoire of pointers. It is now not such a long jump from here to the final insight that is necessary to crack the code of *naming*: what is being pointed to is not the shoe itself, but the concept of 'my shoe' within his own conceptual system. He is able to understand, with just a little more help, what 'Where's your shoe?' or 'Daddy's gone', can mean, when there is no shoe and no Daddy in sight.

(f) *'Reading music'*   At the same time as his vocabulary is beginning to develop, the child is coming to recognize the characteristic stress patterns and intonations of the language and its users around him. As well as discovering the words, he has to learn the music. Before understanding the words that are spoken, the child, like a pet, can clearly tell the difference between approval and disapproval. Mummy's voice sounds quite different when she is cuddling him lovingly, from when she has just discovered that he has spilt his orange juice again. The way she speaks signals the way she feels.

And he goes on to make more subtle discriminations between a warning, a reprimand, a command, an attention-drawer, and a question. Every 'tune' is learnt through its association with a type of event. As he hears more people talking, so he can separate what is idiosyncratic to his parents from what is characteristic of the local dialect, and eventually, from what is general to the language. The existence of these linguistic tunes is demonstrated by putting the wrong words to them – saying 'You're a lovely little baby, aren't you, darling?' in a stern, forbidding voice; or by imitating an accent like Glaswegian or Italian without using real words at all. It's easily done.

(g) *Grammar*   After vocabulary is established, the child begins to register syntax: he records the fact that consistently different states of affairs are reliably predicted by consistent differences in the *order* in which he hears words that he knows. '. . . Tom hit', is a sequence that seems to happen when he (Tom, the child) is bashing something, as a comment on it. While '. . . hit Tom. . . .' happens when something has bashed *him*. This apparently minimal difference between the verbal Antecedents, he realizes, is symptomatic of significantly different kinds of nonverbal consequence. Grammatical conventions typically refer to *relationships* between concepts. Since they are less perceptually immediate to both adult and child, it follows that they should be detected later on by the child, and should cause more theoretical difficulty to the adult. Chomsky's assertions, for instance, that the child required some special genetic predisposition to learn language reflected his own inability to understand what it was in the child's nonlinguistic experience that syntactical rules referred to. What they refer to is the *roles* that the concepts happen to be taking in the event that is being described, roles like *actor, action, object, instrument, location*, and so on, that we discussed in Chapter 3.

The rules for assigning the roles and relationships to the words in a sentence are very complicated and they take years to discover. Children go on learning new grammatical constructions into their teens, just as they will continue to learn new words throughout their lives. An early rule to be tried out, for example, is that: 'The first Noun–Verb–Noun sequence in a sentence represents the roles Actor–Action–Object'. This works well enough for 'Tom is drinking his juice', and 'Daddy is washing the car', but it will let him down with passives ('The car is being washed by Daddy', 'The match was watched by millions') and other more complicated constructions, such as 'It's the yellow car that Bill's driving', or 'While washing the car Daddy was stung by a wasp'.[19]

(h) *Production*   Lagging somewhat behind his ability to decode language is the child's developing capacity to create the code himself: to *produce* utterances, and to *use* them effectively. In some ways learning to talk is the reverse of learning to understand; instead of decoding sound into meaning he has to encode meaning into sound.

He starts with some pattern of activation in the experiential plane that he wants to communicate, and his task is to convert it into a string of flags that he can wave, like semaphore, at someone else. They will then recreate, within *their* experiential plane, the same pattern. That is the goal. When he is listening he does not have to decode everything. He can take short cuts, like not actually hearing the end of a predictable sentence but filling it in for himself. But when talking he can't take so many short cuts. (In talk we do use some short cuts like 'you know' and 'whatsisname', but when we write even these have to go.) He has to be explicit.

Allied to this there are three further problems. One is that the pattern that the child wants to communicate will very often not fit exactly, with the repertoire of flags and grammatical rules that he possesses. He wants to tell us about an 'igloo' pattern, but all he has are large rectangular blocks, which he has to try to stack together, as best he can, to give us a rough idea.

The second problem is that the 'dune-scape' is shifting and developing at the same time as the 'flag-scape' is coming into being. Thus the correspondence between the two levels is changing. He plants a flag at the top of a dune, but the next time he goes back to it the dune has shifted, so the flag is no longer at the summit. Especially during the second year, when so much basic nonverbal learning is still going on, this causes extra problems.

Third, as we saw in Chapter 4, the verbal plane begins to acquire its own conventions and connections that do not and cannot have any experiential underpinnings. Sometimes the child is forced to use verbal forms that cut across what he is trying to say simply because there are no others. He will find himself later, for example, carried swiftly by the 'logic' of an argument from a position he feels to be true to one that he has no wish to occupy at all. Yet if it 'follows', he is not allowed to disagree.

(i) *Use*   Finally, the child has to convert into action his developing understanding of what language is for. He discovers that he can increase his control over other people (up to a point) by learning how to produce *commands* and *instructions*. While his earlier 'Milk!' was open to misinterpretation, now 'Want milk!', or eventually 'I would like some more milk, please', are much more precise. He can draw people's attention to what he is aware of by making *statements*. And most importantly he can use other people as sources of information by asking *questions*. 'Asking' is found to be a potent though often infuriating, learning amplifier. If you want to know the time, ask a policeman. If you don't know what a word means, ask Mummy. If you don't know how to fasten your buttons, ask someone to show you.

8.8 Learning to Reason

When a child 'runs' an expectancy, the expectancy creates action and it creates experience. She perceives a situation in a certain way, this triggers a real action which produces a real consequence, and she perceives the action and the consequence as they happen. At about the age of two or so, she discovers a wonderful ability. She can 'decouple' the production of actual movements from the production of the *experience* of movement. She can reduce the intensity of the energy she uses, so that the expectancy runs inside her brain. But there is not enough power available to produce discernible movement in her muscles.

It is possible to witness a comparable process later on as she learns to read – first 'out loud', and then, gradually, 'under her breath', until you can barely see her lips moving. Why is this ability to run expectancies covertly so useful? Because it enables her to expand enormously the scope for off-duty learning. She can play and practise, bridge and imitate, and even flounder in her mind's eye, without ever having to run the risk of being hurt or frustrated 'for real'. The more extravagant her mental experimenting, of course, the more likely is the real world to deviate from the way she has imagined it. But nevertheless this strategy, what people used to call 'vicarious trial-and-error', is rapidly discovered to be very useful indeed. As far as her motor skills are concerned, play and practice in imagination (or *fantasy*) are the most valuable and trustworthy strategies. Sports coaches, as we saw in Chapter 3, are only just beginning to discover that fantasy remains a valuable (though largely unexploited) asset for improving skills in adulthood.

Having acquired a reasonable beginner's kit of words and grammar, the child, into her third year now, discovers as a matter of course that her ability to produce language can, like her other skills, be activated covertly. She can refine her utterances until they are only audible to the mind's ear.[20] And once she has perfected this she is ready to develop the learning amplifiers called *thinking* and *reasoning*.

The child realizes that, just as she can build experimental bridges out of expectancies, so can she construct them from *propositions* – verbal knowledge. She does not yet know that this internal, linguistic bridge-building has a special rule-system of its own (called *logic*), but she has got the idea.

Piaget's work on what he called the *preoperational* stage, the second of his four major periods of development, highlights the kinds of bridges that children do and don't construct, between the ages of about two and seven. Actually, one of the current criticisms of Piaget's work is that he paid too much attention to the answers to problems that children *didn't* give, and was too ready to infer from their apparent failure that they *couldn't* solve the problem – that they lacked a critical ability. This attitude stems from a point of view which says that children do or don't have particular abilities at particular ages, and that if they do they will manifest them whenever and wherever they are relevant. That attitude is different from, and less accurate than, the present one, which, in essence, says that *relevance has to be learnt*, as well as ability. Recent experiments have shown that children *do* possess many of the abilities that Piaget denied them, but what they haven't learnt yet is that the ability being tested is relevant to the problem with which they are confronted.

One example of this concerns the basic method of bridge-building called *transitive inference*, which means getting from A to C by realizing you can go through B. The traditional problem is of the form 'If John is taller than Terry, and Bill is shorter than Terry, who's the tallest?' Children of six or seven years old don't get this right, and Piaget concluded that they lacked the ability to make these sort of inferences. Now this would be strange if it were true, because in other areas children have been building bridges since they were two. And it turns out that their difficulty is not with the inference as such, but in hooking up their inference-making, bridge-building capacity to a problem about which they have no factual knowledge. Who are John, Terry and Bill? Where do they live? How old are they? What do they eat for tea? Are they nice? Nobody knows. They are mere ciphers, and a six-year-old needs something more substantial than a name to hang on to. So what happens if you replace Terry with 'you'? 'I've got two friends, John and Bill', you say, 'and John's taller than you, but Bill's shorter than you. Who's the tallest?' No problem. Even four- and five-year-olds do pretty well with just this minimal change.[21] When children shift to the next stage, that of *concrete operations* at about eight or nine years old, they do not suddenly become able to build bridges of this sort. What they have finally realized is that the *logic* of A>B, B>C; therefore A>C applies absolutely, regardless of what A, B, and C happen to be. The inference ability is triggered not by the content of the problem any longer but solely by its form.

Many other elegant demonstrations of the same general point are reported by Margaret Donaldson in her excellent book *Children's Minds*.[22] She also describes the last of Piaget's stages of development, the *formal operational* period, which is not attained before eleven or twelve years old, and often much later. This is the stage of adult, abstract, logical reasoning, where the learner has fully pared away from the rules of logic and reason the 'incidental' features of content and context through which they were originally acquired. He can solve algebraic equations, unconcerned about who or what X stands for, and can reason about hypothetical entities in his chemistry and physics lessons.

At this stage man-the-scientist has become man-the-conscious, deliberate, articulate, logical scientist. But it is not an ability that everybody needs. It has been found that the survival of some African tribes is not noticeably jeopardized by the fact that they *never* achieve formal operational thought. Though they fail Piaget's 'conservation test' (by insisting that a tall thin container holds more than a short fat one of the same volume), they do not fail to conserve their limited water supply. For them, as for children, the ability to arrive at a workable solution is of greater value than the abilities to construct a logical conclusion and to explain and defend it.[23]

8.9 Learning to Remember

To recall the past is a natural, though fallible, ability. When an earlier record is reactivated, we have the experience of reliving, recognizing or recollecting. But there are occasions, the growing child discovers, when his recall lets him down. He is told to remember to write his thank-you letters and forgets. He is sent to the shop to get three things but when he gets there he can only remember two. It slips his mind to give his teacher the note from his mother.

Knowing that lists of things are difficult to remember, what strategies are available to help him? The first and best, which he will learn by observation, is to write them down. As he begins to read so he will easily discover that writing is a very useful adjunct to memory. Instead of having to remember the story or the list, he now only has to remember where he left the book or the piece of paper.

Some memory-enhancing strategies seem to be discovered spontaneously by children through their own experimentation, while others are not used unless taught. Tricks like tying a knot in your handkerchief, or mnemonics like one-is-a-bun, the orator's walk (see Section 4.8) or Richard of York Gave Battle in Vain (for the colours of the rainbow) seem to be taught. They are passed on through instruction. Whereas strategies like *repeating* things over and over, or organizing a list into sub-groups of similar things (called *clustering*) seem to appear spontaneously between the ages of about five and ten.[24] This is fairly late, it appears, but there is good reason for it. First children have to meet situations where this kind of natural limitation to memory is revealed. The under-fives are not usually sent to the shops, or entrusted with messages because their overall memory ability and general competence is still too low. It is only as their general incompetence lessens that these particular, lasting difficulties are left exposed. Second, a child has to realize that his memory is lacking, and that others expect him to do better. Without this experience or disappointment he will not see his lapses as a problem to be solved. Third, he has to develop or possess already a suitable strategy. Fourth, he has to realize its helpfulness. Finally, he has to experiment successfully with it. This developmental sequence is illustrated by children's performance at remembering lists. Their awareness that there is a problem increases steadily from about four to nine years old. Their awareness that repeating things over and over helps increases a little later, and their actual *use* of repetition, later still. Before the use of repetition has become automatic, however, there is a period when they can and will use it if instructed, but do not avail themselves of it spontaneously.

8.10 The Development of Character

Now let us turn from intellectual and behavioural to social aspects of development: how do the child's personality, his emotions, his defences, and his interpersonal style come about?

The story of a child's social development is one of a developing attachment to a very few special people, followed by an expansion, and eventually a shift, of the circle he cares about and whose good opinion he values. Up to six months the baby is learning that the objects called people are of paramount significance to him, and he is finding out how to spot them. Drawn initially to their warmth, smell, and food-dispensing properties, by six months, he recognizes them by sight and sound, and seeks and prefers humanlike stimuli.

A month or two later he begins to prefer particular individuals, and sometimes, in reaction, shows for a while a marked apprehension of those whom he doesn't recognize.[25] Even at this tender age, by the way, boys and girls are being treated differently, for example girls being held less, but talked to more, than boys.

Though his primary attachment is to his mother, or whoever looks after him most, he has established a 'pecking order' between other familiar people. If Mum is not available in a time of upset, Dad or an elder brother or sister will usually do. Though if the upset is severe, then Mum may be the only consolation. During his third year, the child begins to loosen these special attachments, beginning to include others who he will later call 'friends', as well as 'family'. The way in which attachment expresses itself also changes. Previously expressed in very physical ways – clinging, hugging, crying when the special person leaves – he now learns to be more sophisticated and less obvious in his display of affection. He talks to, and looks at, the people he likes.

In some societies the child will be discouraged from using touch until it reappears in adolescence as a signal not just of affection but of sexual attraction. After a gap of ten years, it is all right to hold hands again. From those to whom he is attached, his 'esteem-arena', the child seeks *attention* and *approval*. He learnt soon after birth that these two components of other people's reactions to him are highly relevant to his survival. Life runs smoothly with these ingredients and rather roughly without them. He will continue to see them as important, and to seek them from those he loves, throughout his life, particularly at times when he feels vulnerable. Contact, being 'in touch' with others, whether physically or emotionally, is the balm that he will continue to need for his wounds, and rejection the salt that he will do an awful lot to avoid.

He thus gives enormous power to those whose approval, affection, acceptance, and attention he believes he needs, and they are, for the most part, only too happy to have it. For it is the instrument which they can use, whether with care or indifference, to carve out the child's character. (We started to discuss this earlier, in Chapter 6).

Keeping their ultimate sanction in the background as much as possible, parents and teachers set to work to influence his habits, his aspirations and his self-image 'for the best'. They can do this in two ways. First they can organize the child's world so that it contains certain contingencies, certain patterns of action and consequence. He will come to learn that breakfast is served at 8 am, that his potty lives down by the bath, and that spilling food, poking the cat and trying to climb up to the clock will all be met with a slap or a sharp word, and he learns these in exactly the same way as he learns about the properties of gravity and the taste of chips. He is being *trained*, as a dog-owner or a lion-tamer trains his animals; some of this training is vital. It pays not to lean out of the window or run across the road, even if you don't yet understand why.

Some training is socially useful, like not swearing in front of Granny. And most of it is derived from the parents' beliefs about how children *ought* to behave. 'Keep your elbows off the table', 'Don't play with your food', and 'How dare you speak to your mother like that?' While one man's virtue is another man's irrelevance, and nobody agrees about the training children need, even learning some rather silly habits is no problem to the child. It is all part of his finding out about how his world works and what the limits are. Training does, however, become pathological when punishment is too severe, or unrelenting (see Section 3.8).

Part of a child's developing theory about the world is his developing sense of himself – his Self-Image. He knows that the world is thus-and-so; he knows that parts of it hurt; and he knows that, of those parts, there are some that he can counteract or avoid and there are others that he cannot yet cope with. He knows his competence and his limitations. He also knows his 'style' – how he reacts to events, what he likes and what he doesn't, whether he sleeps on his front or his back, and so on. This picture is an accurate and flexible one: it is no more than a way of categorizing his current quota of expectations according to their success.

As soon as children can understand a bit of language, however, their parents have a second way of influencing them. They can tell their children about themselves and in particular they can tell them about their short-comings. They learn the categories 'good boy/good girl' and 'bad boy/bad girl', and they have to try to work out what these labels refer to. This is not easy, because they do not match up with *any* distinction that children can make about themselves. 'Good' and 'bad' refer to ideas, which are often rather vague, that the parents hold about what little boys and girls should be, and these may be very different from what their sons and daughters actually are. They will quickly discover that Good/Bad does *not* correspond to the distinction which they can make between Successful and Unsuccess-ful actions – those that are growth and survival-promoting and those that aren't. For they are told that some of their Successful acts are Bad (like say, having a tantrum or masturbating), while some Unsuccessful ones (like failing to avoid going to school, or being praised for an unsuccessful attempt – 'You're a good girl for trying') are called Good. Furthermore they are told not just that the actions are good or bad but that they – the actor – is good or bad. It becomes a matter of identity as well as performance. Parts of me are bad, parts are good, and quite a lot ought to be better. 'Bad' means 'those parts of you that we, your parents, like less and accept less.' Hence the Catch-22 of childhood: first you learn that to survive you need to be approved of, and then you discover that some of the things your parents don't approve of feel very strongly survival-positive, while some of the things they like seem life-denying, and crazy. What is to be done? You must *identify* with their picture of you and their values and dis-identify with those bits of your real self that don't fit. You disown them, and from this first fallacious fissure arises the other divisions between Me/Not Me, and Con-scious/Unconscious, that we studied in Chapter 6.[26] You end up spending a lot of time and energy pretending to yourself as well as to Mum and Dad that these bits aren't there, in ways that we studied in Chapter 7. In Chapter 6 we also looked at the precise way in which some of these defensive strategies are learnt. The ideas about yourself that you accept without evidence because you dare not do otherwise, are the prototypical *beliefs*. It will not be until adulthood, if ever, that you will again become aware of just how much of this distorted image is not 'the real me'.

8.11 Adolescence

If the first identity crisis is accepting that he is not himself, the next one is the transition from childhood to being grown-up. For the second and possibly the last time in his life, the question 'Who am I?' will be seen to have no clear answer. I am no longer a child, for I am being asked to tidy my own room and do the washing-up. I am not an adult because I go to school and have to be in by eleven. My mind and body are suffused with sex, yet to act on my impulses is full of risk and guilt. As Peter Sellers said: 'Too old for Mother Goose and too young for Lolita.' I hanker after freedom and responsibility, yet fear it too, and want at times to be taken care of, cuddled and told what to do. I profess the cocky bravado that my friends seem to have, yet inside I know it to be phoney. In the middle of all this conflict and uncertainty, what is the real me and what is just pretence? Which of these new suits will I eventually own, and which of my favourite old sweaters will I have to chuck out?

Between the ages of two and three the child lets go of his mother a little and opens himself up to other relationships. Now, at twelve or thirteen, he again feels the need to expand and shift the circle who matter to him. Over the next few years he will find himself drawn to people who he is sure his parents wouldn't like, and using language and expressing opinions that are at odds with theirs. He will meet the opportunities to smoke, drink, take drugs and have sex and will have to decide what to do, knowing that he can no longer please all of the people all of the time. Whatever he does, someone, if they knew, would disapprove. No wonder that he is drawn towards secrecy and tempted to lie, or that adolescence is a time of inner fantasy and play. Because real (i.e. overt) experimentation so often carries a risk of rejection, it is safer to try and work some of it out in imagination. In the privacy of your own mind you can play at being Debbie Harry or Boy George, and see what it feels like without being laughed at.

The adolescent's problem is not that he is rejecting either his parents' culture or his friends' culture, but that they reject each other. They seem to be immiscible, like oil and water. He wants to embrace them both, and he knows that it may well not work. For this to happen, both he and his parents have to be prepared to shift ground, to negotiate a new way of being a family. If both sides know that their love and need for each other is more important than their values and their points of view, then it is very likely to work. But if either party is too identified with its beliefs, then they will refuse to enter into this negotiation, talks will break down, and there will be trouble. Adolescence is a phenomenon of parenthood as much as of growing-up. Learning is required by all concerned: the young person is changing shape, and there is no way that the family will fit snugly together again unless his parents and brothers and sisters are prepared to change their shape too. If they refuse to shift, and defend their existing positions, then both pressure points and holes will begin to appear. Metamorphosis is always tricky, but it is really dangerous if people keep trying to push the butterfly back into its cocoon.

The job of the adolescent is therefore to discover ways of being – life-style, job-style, speech-style, music-style, hair-style – that are satisfying to him and acceptable to those around him. He has to conduct experiments with different styles, trying them on to see how they fit, and he has also to make some exploratory stabs to see what the limits are. He needs to 'go too far' a few times, in order to get some idea of the kinds of experiments that might work. So a certain amount of conflict is useful and healthy as the young person tests how flexible his parents are going to be.

The second characteristic of adolescence, as well as this testing-out, is its fickleness. As he tries on his styles, sometimes deliberately choosing outrageous ones, and looking at his reflection in the eyes of his friends and his parents, he seems to shift his ground in a confusing and apparently capricious way. Both characteristics are inevitable concomitants of the learning process: they are certainly not causes for concern in themselves. The appropriate parental responses tell the learner accurately about how his act is going down, how they feel about who he is being today, but without censoring him for trying it out and without making a 'problem' out of his need to experiment. However, sometimes parents and teachers forget what is going on, perceive their children's transient rejection as a real threat, and come back with all guns blazing. Negotiation changes into confrontation in which both parties are now more concerned to preserve a point of view than to have the family unit work again.

Various consequences can follow. Before diplomatic relations are broken off entirely, the young person's natural impulse may be to experiment more wildly, in an increasingly desperate attempt to break out of the childhood mould in which he is trapped. If his preliminary, reasonable requests for more money or more freedom are met with bland indifference or hostility, perhaps banging on the table will make them take him seriously. It might. It might equally convince his parents that they were right to be firm in the first place or that he has already rejected them. It may be the parents who give up first, and conclude that a working arrangement is impossible: or it may be the adolescent who, finding it all too frustrating, or too anxiety-provoking, packs his bags and leaves – physically, psychologically or both. Once either side gives up, all goodwill evaporates and all sense that they are actually both after the same thing goes. It may never reappear.

A final consequence is that the adolescent may get stuck with a style that doesn't really work. If his parents assume that his extreme views are as deeply held as their own, he may come to believe them, and actually adopt as his battleground a position at which he had only intended to stay the night. And having fought for it . . . well, it must be valuable, it must be 'me' . . . mustn't it?

Whether the adolescent's transition is an easy one, or a time of great 'storm and stress', as people have called it, therefore depends on the disparity between the young person's developing habits and values and his parents', and on the amount of goodwill and common sense or common purpose with which the negotiations are conducted. It is rarely, but not rarely enough, that the only identity the young person is left to take is criminal or insane – Bad or Mad. Unsatisfactory though these are, the need to have an answer to the question 'Who and What am I?' may be so strong that anything is better than nothing. Parents may unwittingly collude with these labels; for by accepting them, painful though it is, they themselves are let off the hook of having to change.[27]

CHAPTER 9

TEACHING

THE GARDEN OF LOVE
I went to the Garden of Love,
and saw what I never have seen:
A Chapel was built in the midst,
Where I used to play on the green.

And the gates of this Chapel were shut,
And 'Thou shalt not' writ over the door;
So I turn'd to the Garden of Love
That so many sweet flowers bore;

And I saw it was filled with graves,
And tomb-stones where flowers should be;
And Priests in black gowns were walking their rounds,
And binding with briars my joys & desires.

The wisest of the Ancients consider'd what is not too Explicit as the fittest for
Instruction, because it rouzes the faculties to act.

The tygers of wrath are wiser than the horses of instruction.

Teaching is what one person does to try to help another to learn. When two
or more are gathered together and the intention of at least one of them is that
the others shall, as a result of their meeting, come to do more, know more,
or be more, then what that one does in order to realize his intention, is called
teaching. This is the definition I shall adopt in this chapter. Clearly it covers
a multitude of sins, virtues and activities. It may or may not be appropriate,
desirable, solicited, successful, damaging or even perceived. It includes
demonstrating skills, giving friendly advice, explaining things, training

animals, dictating homework, trying to understand the learner's problem, giving driving lessons, punishing children 'for their own good', giving speeches at party conferences, and making pupils repeat their 'times tables'. I will review some of the considerations that affect *any* teaching activity, and that any teachers should have an explicit or preferably an intuitive understanding of. Then we will look at some particular types of teaching to see what their effects are, when they are appropriate, and how they work best. Finally we will look specifically at teaching in school, and the range of special opportunities, extra duties, and frustrating limitations that school teachers encounter. It will emerge, not as a matter of rhetoric but as the conclusion of this book, that school, like a well-known disinfectant, kills a large percentage of all known germs of intelligence. It will emerge, too, that the implications and prescriptions that seem to follow from my diagnosis, I also find congenial. I shall not attempt to hide the fact, in this final chapter, that my psychological conclusions and my personal values coincide.

9.1 What All Teachers Ought to Know

If teachers do not understand what learning is, and how it happens, they are as likely to hinder as to help. Unless their intervention is timely and their exhortations appropriate to the learner, they will be unhelpful. They will upset her, undermine her confidence, distract her from what she is doing, and impede the development of her own learning strategies. Teaching *is* a subversive activity,[1] but it is often the learner, not the system, that is subverted. Here are some things that teachers need to know in order to avoid making learning more difficult.

1   *You can take a horse to the fountain of knowledge but you cannot make him drink from it*

Teaching does not produce learning, any more than horticulture produces plants. Learning and growth are things that happen, and cannot be forced. They can be helped to happen more readily and more economically. But they cannot be *made* to happen. A gardener cannot 'make' a graft take, a heart surgeon cannot 'make' a body accept the transplant, and a teacher cannot 'make' a learner assimiliate new knowledge and skill. Teaching is not like carpentry, where the carpenter can create the joint he wants, subject only to the limitations of his skill and ingenuity. He is working with dead material, so connections have to be produced, products *assembled*. But the surgeon, the gardener and the teacher are working with live material and connections in the living world are *grown* organically, not assembled mechanically. To put the cutting in the ground is not enough: it has to grow roots, and so does knowledge.[2]

If teachers do not understand that teaching is grafting, and that grafting is a slow and subtle business which requires much concern for the nature of the plant and which cannot be made to happen by force, then it will be 'hard graft' indeed, full of wasted effort and misplaced blame. 'Damn trees', they will fume. 'I keep shoving the twig in as hard as I can and it keeps dying. Last week they seemed to understand and this week it's gone again. Lazy trees! Stupid trees! Naughty trees!' And, because the teachers' mistaken understanding makes them angry, it is they who act stupidly by kicking the trees and shouting at them. This is the first and greatest insight into teaching. And the second is similar, namely this:

2   *People learn best what they most urgently need and want to know*[3]

Nothing is learnt that is not connected, however remotely, with the satisfaction of need or want and the avoidance of threat. Learning is the improvement of our theory about the world, and the only yardstick of improvement, the only 'motivation', is the quality and security of our survival. Learning is the search for an answer to a question that matters. Thrown in at the deep end, the question 'How to swim?' becomes urgent. Pupils who have been labelled 'less able' (or just plain thick) by their school may have vast stores of knowledge about cars, or skill at sport, acquired with great ease under the influence of such motives. But the answers that school kindly provides them to questions that do not concern them will not stick at all. The most likely reason, after all, that the horse will not drink is that he isn't thirsty.

An un-thirsty horse can be motivated to drink, however, if you hit him until he does. Now he has an urgent question: 'How to avoid the whip?' And if the answer is 'Drink', he will learn to drink. You can teach someone something that they don't want to know, in other words, by hooking the learning up to a reward that they do want, or a threat that they will seek to avoid. Whether this works, and for how long, depends on the shifting balance between the learner's needs. The threat of detention, for example, may not be sufficient to outweigh the need to impress his friends. That which is to be learnt gets used as a pawn in the battle between conflicting needs.

To use these goads may 'work'. But the beaten horse feels doubly uncomfortable, distended by the liquid and frightened by the whip, and he will not love either you or the fountain any the more for the experience.

This applies, it is important to know, when you offer a reward, as well as when you threaten a punishment. The learner may work for the reward, if he wants it, but he is still unlikely to be interested in either you or the learning as anything other than a means to an end. The doing or the knowing that he is acquiring will be pursued only for as long as, and to the extent that, they produce the reward.[4] Cutting corners, copying other people's homework and bluffing your way through become sensible things to do, because proficiency is not the point. Many pupils in school learn to 'get by' because getting by is what they need and want to do – whether that means winning teacher's approval, or just avoiding detention. Learning French and Physics are secondary, and it is appropriate for the majority of adolescents that Secondary Schools are so called, for they are full of secondary activities. Some children need and want to pass exams, and for them this primary goal requires more 'learning'. And some need to want to be good at swimming, or at Chemistry, or at Leadership. Only for these few is the learning both the means *and* the end.

3 *When people feel threatened they stop learning*

Teachers have to be sensitive to the difference between challenge and threat. When people feel challenged they can be prodded and pushed. Their learning can be encouraged and stimulated. Often there comes a moment, though, when it becomes too much, and they 'switch off' in one way or another. 'Switching off' means defending, for example, by going unconscious; and defending is not learning. Prodding and pushing are now the last thing that a person wants. Once they have 'gone blank', whether it is about reading or sums or how to hold the racket, previous attempts to 'stretch' them are counter-productive, creating a thicker and thicker fog of confusion, anxiety and hostility, and self-doubt. When you say 'Come on . . . you remember what that word is, don't you?' the fact that they don't is experienced as another nail in the coffin of their dislike of the subject matter and distrust of themselves as learners. Though from the outside it appears unjustified, defending is *always* appropriate, being the natural response to a perceived threat.[5] If teachers do not spot the shift, and they keep on pushing when a learner is threatened, the learner can very quickly be turned off the teacher, the subject, the context (for example, school), learning in general, and eventually himself. Frightened horses have other things on their minds than drinking.

4   *Teachers need to know the learners' signals of threat*

It follows that, if teachers are not to make this mistake, they must know the signals that the learner uses to signify that he has had enough. One may say he feels bored, another may start playing truant, and a third may suddenly sweep the half-finished jigsaw puzzle off the table. Learners develop very different responses to such situations and they need to be decoded. Usually when a learner has had enough the appropriate reaction by the teacher is to leave him alone for a bit. If he is not too upset all he needs is time to cool off. He does not need a post-mortem on how come he finds maths so difficult, or soccer so threatening. The majority of long-term learning difficulties are created by teachers themselves who have persuaded learners that they have 'learning difficulties' – thereby adding to the uncomfortable weight of having failed the guilty burden of being 'not good enough' – a flawed person. Parents mostly have the time and inclination to learn their children's signals. Secondary school teachers, while they may or may not have the inclination, almost certainly do not have the time to get to know any of their students well enough. They are, therefore, unaware of how often and for how many students their teaching is threatening.[6]

Being constantly exposed to things that you cannot understand (like Maths) or required to attempt actions that you cannot do (like gym) is itself threatening for many people: unable to run away, every moment is fraught with the danger of being exposed, yet again, as incompetent. And this in its turn threatens to bring the public humiliation that we would do almost anything to avoid.

5   *People cannot learn what they are not ready for*

As we have seen, certain ideas and skills presuppose others, and if the skills are missing it is impossible to grasp and digest the more complicated ideas.[7] It's no use having a thirty foot ladder if the first eight feet of rungs are missing. The important question for teachers is: who knows best what the learner is ready for? Once you've acknowledged the necessity not to force people to study what they cannot grasp, there are possible ways to proceed. One is for the teacher to try to diagnose the learner's current state of competence, infer from that what he is ready to learn (i.e. what he is capable of learning; not necessarily what he wants to learn), and present it to him.

Educationalists currently favour this course, and are busy devising diagnostic tests of 'cognitive level' and structuring curricula according to their 'cognitive difficulty'.[8] Robert Gagné, for example, says that: 'One important implication of the identification of learning conditions is that these conditions must be carefully planned *before* the learning situation is entered into by the student'.[9] This method is expensive, crude and generally ineffective. The alternative is to have a rough, intuitive shot at what the next thing to teach might be, and *modify it according to the learner's response*. Let him tell you whether it feels right or not. This is the simple and trustworthy method whereby new parents learn to play with (i.e. teach) their babies successfully. If you are sensitive to how your teaching is going down, you will very quickly find the right level. A learner's readiness to learn from what you are presenting is indicated clearly by his interest. If he feels challenged, then he's ready. This in turn makes the teaching challenging and fun. When your Enid Blyton is rejected as 'kid's stuff', or your attempt to introduce 'the Classics' produces squirming and a flood of unrelated questions, like 'What's for tea?', then you know you've got it wrong.

The first approach separates motivation and ability: it attempts to discover the latter without regard to the former. The whole philosophy of this book is contrary to this: it says that what one needs to know is what one is ready to know, and readiness is therefore signalled by need or want or interest. This signal is occasionally mistaken: every so often we find we are 'out of our depth', or have 'bitten off more than we can chew'. But on the whole it is reliable. Learning is essentially a growth, not an accumulation, and it must always spring from and return to what is known.

6   *Learners may lend their control to a teacher but they cannot give it away*

When someone chooses to be taught, she is saying to the teacher: 'I want some knowledge, ability or quality that you have, and I am temporarily going to hand over to you the responsibility for deciding what, when, where, how, how often, and in what sequence I study it, because I trust that by doing so I shall learn better.' This is the nature of the teaching–learning contract, when voluntarily entered into by the learner. Remember the quotation from Jerry Bruner in Chapter 5: 'Instruction is a provisional state that has as its object to make the learner . . . self sufficient'.[10] If teachers do not see that the power they are given is only on loan, and that they are hired to increase the learner's autonomy as well as her competence, they are liable to get an inflated idea of their own importance, and to resist the fact that teaching is an activity whose goal is to make the teacher redundant. Since most school teachers are hired not by the learner but by an intermediate agency, it becomes harder still to see that students and their families have only lent their power of self-determination and that they can, like an investor, withdraw their capital if it is generating neither growth nor interest.

Another way of saying this is that, in general, it is the learner's right and responsibility to decide what her 'end' is, and it is the teacher's right and responsibility, if the learner chooses to be taught, to decide on the best means of attaining that end. When I decide to have golf lessons, or driving lessons, or to study a book on psychology, or to become an apprentice stone-mason, or to become a disciple of a guru, this is what happens. I submit to you because I guess that the best learning-amplifier in this case is to be taught by you.

Just like other learning strategies, *being taught* is a technique for creating learning opportunities, and getting the most out of them. An experienced flaw or hole in my theory about the world determines *what* I need and want to know about. My accumulated learning strategies determine *how* I go about finding out about it. It follows that teaching is all to do with facilitating learning, and nothing to do with deciding what the object of learning shall be – or only to the extent that the teacher may set minor goals (like playing scales) which she knows are helpful or necessary to achieving the major goal (playing the piano) that the learner has set for herself. When one person takes it on herself to decide what another needs or ought to know, that is something different. It is *indoctrination* if the object is knowledge or belief, and *conditioning* if it is habits and manners. Indoctrination and conditioning are attempts to teach things whose values and appropriateness have been determined by the teacher, and which may therefore not be rejected by the learner. The indoctrinator/conditioner drives a wedge between need and want. Your own appetite is no longer to be taken as a trustworthy guide to your hunger and your diet. Somebody else Knows Best.

There are circumstances in which any parent or teacher or society thinks that they do Know Best, and that a child will ultimately benefit from being moulded. In certain basic cases, such as a baby's wish to investigate things that are physically dangerous, everyone would agree that her frustration is justified. In all other cases the justification is arguable. What is not open to question, however, is the effect that conditioning and indoctrination have in dividing the child against herself. As we saw in the last chapter, to be told that something for which you have no energy is Good, while things you like are Bad is to be fractured. You become split between a centre that discriminates between Challenge and Threat. Pleasant and Unpleasant,

Successful and Unsuccessful, and another, often antagonistic one, that is based on a conditioned and indoctrinated sense of Right and Wrong, Good and Bad. Thus to be subjected to experiences – especially learning experiences – that are said to be Right but feel Nasty is to be systematically estranged from your own natural sense of what is right *for you*. The more such experiences one suffers, the more confused one becomes. Indoctrination and conditioning – choosing what someone else should become – are, therefore, sometimes necessary, sometimes justifiable, but never fail to leave unwanted chips and dents in the learner's developing identity. For many children, being at school becomes an endless nightmare (screenplay by Kafka; direction by Orson Welles) of being told that what feels wrong is right and what feels right is wrong.[11]

7   *Whatever you are teaching, you are teaching 'yourself'*

That is to say, the learner is learning *about* you as well as *from* you. Whether you intend it or not, you are a potential model of an adult and of a teacher, and if you are teaching children, it is likely that they will be as interested in you as in the subject matter. Children will learn, through observation and imitation, from who you are as well as from what you are saying and doing. You are on display. Your pupils' manners will be influenced by your manner – for good or ill. Albert Einstein once said, 'The only rational method of educating is to be an example.' And he added, 'If you can't help it, be a warning example.'[12]

Teachers model what it is to be a teacher – teaching style. The fact that pupils have picked up a very clear, though unconscious, model of teaching is indicated by student teachers when they start their teaching practice. Their first intuitive guess at how to teach reflects the way they were taught. Yet it is doubtful that any of them consciously intended to absorb those values and habits. Very often they don't even *like* the teacher that they discover lurking inside them, and often that model is inappropriate to the new situation. This off-the-peg teaching habit has to be unpicked, rewoven and remodelled into a more hard-wearing and comfortable style. This does not apply only to school teachers. Being a driving instructor is different from being a preacher; being a university lecturer in high-energy physics is different from training new recruits in the army, or from trying to interest a group of day-release apprentice butchers (called Meat One) in the subtleties of *Lord of the Flies*.[13] If you try to rehearse an orchestra the same way you are trying to train your daughter to keep her elbows off the table, it won't work.

Teachers may provide a good model of a learner – or they may not. Good learners take their time, don't mind asking questions, aren't afraid of saying 'I don't know' or of being wrong, can change their minds and enjoy finding out.[14] If a teacher does not model these attitudes, and thereby show that it is safe for the learner to learn, then all his preparations and exhortations will be undermined.

And as well as all these mannerisms of the teacher *qua* teacher, he is also a model of a grown-up person. A school teacher's accent, hair-style, clothes, and vocabulary, the car he drives and his political views – everything about him is of intense interest to his pupils because it is a possible piece in the developing jigsaw puzzle of adulthood. How I feel about his attitudes, how they fit in with the rest of me, how my friends feel about them, are all important bits of data in my search for a suitable grown-up self.

8   *Even water takes time to digest*

When you show someone how to do something, or explain an idea to them, what you are doing is suggesting a solution to them. Your demonstration, instruction, or explanation, if it is to 'take' has to be assimilated by the learner into her existing scheme of things. She has to chew it over and, if necessary, modify it a little, or 'put it into her own words'. This may happen in seconds, or it may take weeks or years, but it is a process that takes time. However 'right' you know you are, however much you know that the learner could save herself trouble by taking what you say for granted, she needs to make it her own. Teaching is not like programming a computer. It is not just a matter of sliding a floppy disc into someone else's brain. In learning, *digestion* must always come between *ingestion* and *constitution*. If a teacher does not realize this she may be inclined to get impatient. This issue we discussed earlier (in Section 5.4) on Instruction, in which I pointed out that the impatient gardener who pulls on the seedlings to make them grow faster, is more likely to pull them up than accelerate their growth.

9   *'Teaching' is always part of the learning context*

Remember that learning is, at root, the creating of an association between all simultaneous or consecutively active bits of your mind-theory. That means that what you learn will be tied to its context. To put it more concretely, if somebody learns something by being taught, 'being taught' becomes part of the context for what is learnt. In the most extreme case the concepts or abilities simply will not be reactivated unless the teacher and the class-room are present. In all other situations their relevance is not perceived. And these 'other situations' may include just those occasions when the knowledge is supposed to be available. Despite having been taught in college that shouting at a class doesn't work, a student teacher, faced with 4B, finds himself shouting. Despite having been taught in school that electricity is dangerous, a 14-year-old may still stick his penknife into a socket, not believing that he can really get hurt. Despite having done 'compound interest' in Maths, and passed the tests, it remains a puzzle that the Building Society interest gets bigger every time.

It is one of the jobs of a teacher to vary the nonessential features of the learning context so that they do not gain control of what is learnt. And, equally, she can help by drawing attention to those features that *are* relevant. If the learners are studying for exams, it helps to give them exam-like tests. If they are rehearsing a play, it helps to rehearse on stage, and to have at least one 'dress rehearsal'. If you will have to perform under pressure, practise under pressure.

People sometimes say they have forgotten everything they learnt at school. And it is true that some of it seems to be lost for ever. But some is not lost, but only buried in the archives, filed under 'School', a classification that nobody asks for any more. 'School' is the trigger, but the circumstances rarely arise to pull it. Take people back after twenty years to their old school, sit them down at their old desks, and you will, both of you, be amazed at the warehouse of memories that is unlocked. A teacher who wants to teach for real-life competence must be aware of this 'contextualization' problem.

9.2 The Teacher's Needs

When the learner feels safe with the teacher he is free to open himself and commit his energies to the job of learning. There are various personal qualities that the teacher may exhibit that diminish the safety of the relationship. If the teacher is disappointed or critical when the learner fails, it becomes more difficult to try. In addition, if the teacher has an investment in the learner's success, he will not be able to tolerate his failure without censure. And, if the teacher has an investment in the learner's failure, then he will not be able to tolerate or permit his success. If the teacher does not have a sympathetic ear, then he will not be able to help unstick the learner when he gets stuck. He needs to be able to sense where the learner has got to before he decides whether it is a short-cut, a detour or a blind alley. Let us look at these three new considerations in a little more detail.

Sometimes it happens that a teacher, who may be a parent or may not, becomes identified with the learner's success. Aiming perhaps for the university place that Dad was denied by the War, his child finds himself handicapped by the weight of two loads of ambition. Or a piano teacher, accustomed to a string of mediocre, half-hearted students, suddenly seizes on the new pupil with real talent and commitment and terrifies him with the intensity of her enthusiasm and demands. Seeing him capable of much, she imagines him capable of anything. The teacher, identified with the goal, but unable to achieve it herself projects her desire into the learner, and insists that he win for both of them. The intensified fear of failure inhibits the chances of success. It is better to have a teacher who wants you to win, but who does not need you to.

Equally dangerous is a teacher who needs you to fail, for he will encourage you with one hand and restrain you with the other. He may do this for various reasons. He may be afraid that your learning will liberate you from him. Perhaps your studies will eventually get you the job that you want, and you will become financially independent. Perhaps your Women's Group will give you too much insight. Perhaps all your learning will lead you away from your 'roots'. In this case the learner's success creates a change in her circumstances or her attitude which might threaten a relationship that somebody else needs. This somebody else may be the teacher, but is often likely to be a person close to the learner who is not the teacher as such, but whose support or permission is necessary for the learning to happen.

The second reason for a teacher to resist the success of his student is that he needs someone to teach. It is not that he needs *this* learner, but he needs *a* learner. And if he lets you go, there may not be a replacement. The need may be financial. If I earn my living as a freelance driving instructor, and business is poor, I may be able to persuade myself and my pupils that they really ought to stay on and do the 'advanced course'. Alternatively, the need might be emotional: the teacher is on a power-trip and he needs to have students so that he can, in comparison, feel important – knowledgeable, competent and powerful. School teachers may be of this sort: people like Crocker Harris in *The Browning Version* who feel so bad about themselves that their only source of self-respect is to feel more powerful than children. However, school teachers are not so likely to resist success because there is a constant stream of new chicks to replace those who have learnt to fly. A better example is bad therapists who, by defining success as reaching the horizon, manage to keep their students (or 'patients') enthralled for years. Psychoanalysts are especially prone to create this form of self-serving enslavement.

The third quality that a teacher needs to have, at least for many forms of learning, is the readiness and ability to help learners overcome the blocks and difficulties they encounter. These blocks are sometimes intellectual, sometimes physical, sometimes emotional, and often a mixture. The teacher needs to be able to find out, whether by careful observation or by careful listening, what's going wrong. He has, in other words, to be prepared to learn about the learner. Except in the case of the simplest drills, teaching always involves a combination of starting the learner off in a certain direction, with a lecture or a demonstration, say, and then correcting the learner's efforts to do it for himself. The classic 'lesson', whether tennis or calculus, involves first an *input* (a demonstration or a talk) and then practice (hitting backhands or doing examples) *with feedback*. If teaching is all soliloquy and no conversation, it misses its mark. To be a good diagnostician the teacher had to be a good learner. He needs *empathy*, the definition of which by Carl Rogers in Section 7.7 is worth rereading at this point.

9.3 The Teacher's Strategies

Now let us look at some of the particular ways in which a teacher can operate. What techniques can she adopt in order to try to speed or smooth a learner's development? The background conditions we have just looked at are mostly ways in which the teacher can help the learner to learn as freely as possible. But there are, in addition, ways in which a teacher can accelerate the learning process.

Just as the learning strategies are attempts to amplify a single, basic learning ability, so teaching strategies are attempts to amplify the learning strategies. *Being taught is not so much a new learning strategy as a strategy for finding and implementing other learning strategies more quickly and more successfully*. Thus the skill of a teacher is to get the learner to plug in the right strategy for the job. And the techniques she uses must be parasitic on the learning skills and sensitivities that the learner brings. Let us see, then, how the strategies of teaching and learning hook up. We can divide them into the four domains of learning to do more, learning to know more, learning to be more, and finally learning to *learn* more.

Learning to do more is the realm of the modification of expectancies, and it relies on *tuning*, amplified by *investigating*, *prodding*, *floundering*, *imitating*, *bridge-building*, *playing*, and *practising*. The aim of these strategies, and therefore the teacher's aim, too, is the rapid discovery of a type of action that will, in a certain type of situation, reliably bring about (or avoid) a significant consequence. What is likely to make the discovery slow and difficult is if the Antecedent situation contains a complex pattern of relevant features to be dissected out of an even more complex background of irrelevant features; if the Behaviour is a complex skill, involving a long sequence of precise actions (like solving Rubik's Cube); if the shift in the Consequence is significant, but hard to detect; or if the learner has no existing basis of expectations on which to build. For a three-year-old, even learning to tell visually which shoe goes on which foot isn't easy. The perceptual feature that signals an important consequence (getting them the right way round) takes some spotting.

How can a teacher help? First he can act as an *orchestrator* of events, not leaving them to take their uninterrupted course, but creating situations that are simplified and exemplary, or designing sequences of experience that occur in a helpful order. We can use the model of a successful *apprenticeship* again to illustrate this. The master begins by giving the apprentice only simple jobs to do, like planing a straight edge, filing a cylinder down to a prescribed diameter, or painting only bamboo stalks in black. Gradually he is given more involved situations to learn from so that his set of skills and his intuitions are refined and developed. While the process may seem slow and tedious to the learner, the master knows that there is no other way to achieve mastery. (The master may be wrong of course. He may force the learner to do it this way simply because it's *always* been done this way, and he has not, from his own position of competence, ever experimented with other ways. His way will work, but it may contain what we called 'superstitions' elements that are actually quite unnecessary).

Without being able to draw a clear line between them, we might distinguish orchestration from *training*. As orchestrator, the teacher sets up a helpful environment and leaves the learner to find out what to do. The apprentice is given the file and a piece of tin, knows that his goal is to produce a perfect six inch square, and is left to find out how best to do it. As trainer, however, a teacher takes a more active part in determining what precisely is learnt by manipulating the outcome of each experiment. He orchestrates the *consequences of action* through reward and punishment, as well as, or instead of, setting the Antecedent conditions within which learning is to take place. If the learner is an animal, the trainer, or an instrument of his devising, delivers or withholds tit-bits that tell the animal how it is doing. If the learner is human, the trainer may use verbal signals to tell him whether he is getting 'warmer' or 'colder'. Such feedback is especially useful when approximations to the right action don't work. If the action has to be spot-on for the desired consequence to follow, the unaided learner might never discover it.[15] The natural consequences of his experiments, unless perfect, do not tell him how his learning is progressing. A trainer can fill the gap.

Used together, the judicious orchestration of both antecedents and consequences, in a sequence and at a rate that are appropriate to the learner, form a powerful way of teaching older children and adults, too. In the clinical sphere, phobias and other incapacitating defences can be alleviated through 'Behavioural Therapy', while the same techniques applied in an educational setting, to cope with disruptive pupils, for example, are called 'Behaviour Modification'.

A great deal of behavioural teaching involves not tampering with the world but simply *pointing* to relevant bits of context or consequences. There may be so much going on that the learner does not notice the small features that are crucial, and it helps to have his attention drawn to them. Pointing acts as an amplifier of *investigating*. To spot the googly, you have to pay close attention to the bowler's hand as he releases the ball, and you may learn faster if you are told what to watch for. Sports coaching has traditionally revolved around instructing and demonstrating (see below). But recent, highly successful innovations, such as the 'Inner Game' approach of Timothy Gallwey,[16] rely heavily on just keeping the learner's attention focused on and open to the relevant aspects of his practice. Do not *try* to hit the right shot, they say. Just hit whatever shot comes naturally and notice what happens.

In this way the learning strategies are provided with an enriched supply of raw experience to work on. And if they are allowed to assimilate this experience at their own rate (i.e. without undue pressure) effective learning will happen by itself. This approach is in part a reaction against the widespread misunderstanding of the nature of instruction and its consequent abuse. As we have seen, when teachers view instruction as producing learning rather than guiding it, they are likely to upset the learner and interfere with his progress.

We discussed learning through *instruction* in detail in Chapter 5. Instructions provide learners with clues about where to go (consequences), when to go (antecedents), and how to get there (behaviours). These verbal signposts help learners to create experiences from which they can learn, and to evaluate the outcomes of their experiments when the 'natural value' of the outcome is not evident. 'Try doing it this way' means: if you do it this way as an experiment, the value of so doing will become clear to you. Instructions need to be given clearly, simply, and one at a time. Giving too many instructions at a time or too quickly confuses and upsets a learner. If you are simultaneously trying to alter your grip, keep your eye on the ball, lift the club more slowly, keep your left arm straight, and keep your head down, your swing will suffer and so will you.

Being a *demonstrator* is a useful way of transmitting good clues, but the same pit-falls exist as for instruction. Showing someone how to do it is preferable to telling them, because there is less risk of them getting it wrong or getting stuck in the process of turning words back into deeds. But it is still, to the learner, only a suggestion that he has to digest, assimilate and make his own. To show someone how to do something is neither a necessary nor a sufficient condition for their being able to do it. Nadia Comaneci didn't learn to do somersaults just by watching.

Each of these methods of teaching has its place in a programme of skill-learning, but any one used to excess is likely to be counter-productive. First there might be a little bit of instruction about what the learner will be able to do. Then a demonstration of a simple action like mounting the horse or using the vice; some practice at doing it, together with a bit of training and pointing ('Well done, Terry. That's it. Did you see what happened when. . . ?'). Then some time to just play and flounder. Then another chat. And so on. It is probably impossible to prescribe, for a particular skill, a precise rate and sequence for shifting techniques, though the order in which component skills have to be learnt may be pretty clear. The incommunicable art of the teacher is to sense what is right, and to be prepared to change when necessary.

Let us now look at ways of facilitating the acquisition of verbal or symbolic knowledge – the *de facto* goal of most school teaching. The main learning strategies, you will recall, are *understanding*, *remembering*, and *deliberating*, and their general aim is to integrate what is new with what is known so that it becomes embedded in the learner's knowledge system. This sort of learning becomes difficult when the old and new 'structures' are not readily compatible, and when the 'energy' (i.e. need to know, interest) is insufficient to make the 'reaction' go. In school the need-to-know is often absent, and integration therefore fails to occur. As Bruner says: 'The will to learn becomes a problem only under specialized circumstances *like those of a school* (my emphasis) where a curriculum is set, students confined and a path fixed. The problem exists not so much in learning itself, but in the fact that what the school imposes often fails to enlist the natural energies that sustain spontaneous learning – curiosity, a desire for competence, aspiration to emulate a model, and a deep sensed commitment to the web of social reciprocity.'[17] We shall have more to say about this in a minute. Here we want to consider what the teacher can do in such circumstances. If the problem is motivation he can try to suggest motivational bridges to the students – aqueducts that will allow energy to flow to the 'right' place. This is called 'motivating'.

Assuming the learner is willing, and that the problem is that the new knowledge doesn't 'click', the teacher can help by suggesting other kinds of bridge, through which the connection can be made. Instead of waiting for the learner to bolt together his own bridge, you can give him one and say, 'Try this'. It is, as always, completely for the learner to decide whether it works for him or not. Because the terrain of his knowledge is different from yours, his mountains and ravines are differently located, a bridge that works for you will not necessarily span *his* gap. If your explanation doesn't work, it does not mean that the learner is wrong or stupid or lazy. It may mean that you haven't been able to locate and help him overcome his blocks and fill in his holes. (If a teacher misunderstands this, then his unwarranted exasperation is almost sure to flip the student from learning into defending mode. To persist in misunderstanding what you and your teacher believe you *ought* to be able to grasp becomes a threat to self-image and self-esteem).

The suggested bridges may be *logical*, *analogical*, or *personal*. A logical bridge is one that 'follows'. 'If you divide all through by X and then substitute X from Equation 2 into Equation 1, I think you'll find that it will come out.' An analogical bridge tries to create a connection between new and old by using existing knowledge where an analogous connection has already been made. A metaphor is a ready-made set of connections, a prefabricated bridge, that can be used as a temporary way of binding two ideas together – so that their own unique links can be discovered. When you understand how verbal knowledge is acquired, then the metaphors of the 'memory molecule' or of 'digestion' can be dropped. Just as with experiential learning, verbal learning proceeds best when you have a rough model to work on and refine.

The other way of making a temporary bond is to use the glue of personal experience – anecdotes and everyday examples. Though the important things to discover are the conceptual relationships inherent in the subject matter, one may need some concrete detail to hang on to while the abstract links are being dug out. Discarding the metaphor and paring away the unnecessary detail after true integration has taken place is an important finishing touch for the teacher who uses metaphor and example. If his students are left taking the analogy for real, he has misled them.

The first job of the teacher of knowledge is, of course, to *inform* – to give students something to understand – though he may delegate this strategy to a book or a film. But his most intricate task is to aid the process of digestion, as we have just seen. If integration will not occur however, perhaps because there is just nothing with which the new knowledge can hook up, he can at least help them to *remember* it by suggesting and encouraging the use of mnemonic strategies. Setting the times tables to a tune, teaching the acronym 'PA MEND V TRAMS' (for the initial letters of the French irregular verbs) or finding any other kind of clothes-lines on which to peg what is to be remembered – such memory aids are legitimate and valuable. There is no virtue in making rote learning more mechanical than it need be. Remembering things that are not integrated is not a training of the mind but an abuse of it. Even such arbitrary pairings as a face and a name are best associated via a meaningful association, however tortuous it has to be.

The final teaching strategy in this category is *questioning* – a favourite with school teachers. In its minor and more common form it is designed to elicit information that learners are presumed to have. The value of this for the learner is the practice it gives her in retrieving what she knows, but this value is small if the context of practice is different from the context in which recall is eventually going to matter – like an examination hall. If this retrieval context is not known, or if it is known to be variable, then the learner will only be helped if the question-and-answer practice also takes a variety of forms. Repetitive drill is useful only if the form of the drill matches the form of the important test.

The more interesting type of question requires reasoning: it is one to which the learner has the ingredients of an answer but not the answer itself. In order to answer, the learner has to build bridges, and the more bridges she creates, the more tightly but flexibly interwoven her knowledge becomes. Instead of a few big isolated bridges, she is forced to create a Venice, full of by-ways, short cuts and secret passages. The more Venetian her knowledge, the more she can extract from it and more she can do with it.

Is it better to question in this way than to explain? Is 'guided discovery learning' better than 'expository learning?'[18] The answer is, it doesn't matter, so long as what is exposited is *appropriated* by the learner. If she really 'builds it in', rather than just 'tacks it on', then it has the same value as what is discovered. The problem is that for this appropriation to occur more is required than teacher-talk. Integration of what is heard is as much an activity of the learner as is working it out for herself.

All the forms of learning we have talked about so far in this section involve the search for a skill that works or knowledge that fits. As we saw in Chapters 5 and 6, however, learning often involves giving up one's preconceptions before one can be open to the discovery of something better. In the spheres of intellectual, scientific, and artistic endeavour, this giving up appears as the essence of *creativity*. In the personal, interpersonal and emotional domains, it is referred to as *growth, insight*, or *liberation*. The core problem, that of dropping a belief and opening oneself freshly to the facts and the experience of the matter, is the same in both cases. What help can teacher as *liberator* be?

First, here more than anywhere, she can help the learner feel safe, for giving up beliefs, and the disillusionment which may ensue, is a risky and a scary affair. But given that the climate is right, what can the teacher provide in the way of help?

To be creative you have to dare to be different. You have to entertain and play with ideas that seem to your reason silly and illogical, and to your social self, unconventional or heretical. Both, as we know, are potentially dangerous. We are courting craziness on the one hand and rejection on the other. Nonetheless, you need to trust your judgement, when others may be trying to undermine it, that the conventional and logical answers just do not work. And you need to be able to give up trying to 'figure it out' and yet remain receptive to images and promptings that bubble up from deeper, less conscious levels of problem-solving. A teacher can help a learner to be more creative at all these potential sticking points. A teacher who does not see that creativity involves self-trust, leisure, play, imagination, receptivity, and nonsense, will increase the stickiness. (For an expansion of these points, refer back to Section 5.6).

By her attitude, a teacher can help the learner to feel that if a problem is important to her, it *is* important, and to evaluate for herself whether a putative solution works or not. Mostly we are schooled to expect teachers to tell us what is a good solution, and this dependent attitude is inimical to creativity. If Einstein, Wittgenstein, or Gertrude Stein had been inhibited by their teachers, physics, philosophy, and literature would have been the poorer. The best a teacher can do in response to a learner's struggles is to try to understand them, for by so doing she acts as a mirror in which both problem and solution can be seen more clearly. A teacher should also communicate that a failure *of* reason may be due to failure *in* reason, and not to lack of intelligence or effort.

The facilitator of creativity can teach two sorts of deliberate techniques –

those for *generating* ideas, and those for *receiving* ideas. The former include fantasy, dreaming, and brainstorming: activities where logic and 'reasonableness' are intentionally set aside, and images and ideas encouraged to emerge through the use of games.[19] In particular the evaluation of ideas – what Poincaré called 'verification' – is separated from the process of 'illumination', because it often turns out that ideas are rejected prematurely, and that a big shovelful of flint and dirt may well contain a few diamonds. A survey of creative people revealed that more than 90 per cent of them made use of hunches, images and intuitions, first accumulating them, and then sorting them out.[20]

Hand in hand with this throwing up of ideas goes the process that Carl Rogers calls 'toying' with them – a mental play in which their interconnections are explored. Again without evaluation, they are woven together in a leisurely way so that latent connections and relationships reveal themselves, unrestrained for the moment by the need to be 'right'. The teacher can encourage such play if he sees its value, not least by providing the space and time. In his book *Laws of Form* the mathematician George Spencer Brown says: 'To arrive at the simplest truth, as Newton knew and practised, requires years of contemplation. Not activity. Not reasoning. Not calculating. Not busy behaviour of any kind. Not reading. Not talking. Not making an effort. Not thinking. Simply *bearing in mind* what it is that one needs to know. And yet those with the courage to tread this path to real discovery are not only offered practically no guidance on how to do so, they are actively discouraged, and have to set about it in secret, pretending meanwhile to be diligently engaged in the frantic diversions and to conform with the deadening personal opinions which are being continually thrust upon them.'[21] Newton's discoveries were big ones, and so they took him years. Smaller ones may bubble up correspondingly quicker. Creative ideas are like fish: you will not catch them with a hue and cry, nor by jumping into the pond wearing big boots.

Aldous Huxley sums up the nature of creativity, and the appropriate attitude of a teacher towards it:

> Wise passiveness, followed in due course by wise hard work is the condition of creativity. We do not fabricate our best ideas: they 'occur to us', they 'come into our heads'. Colloquial speech reminds us that, unless we give our subliminal mind a chance, we shall get nowhere. And it is by allowing ourselves at frequent intervals to be wisely passive that we can most effectively help the subliminal mind do its work. . . . Wise passiveness is an art which can be cultivated and should be taught on every educational level from the most elementary to the most advanced. . . .[22]

Huxley is talking about meditation, of course, and he goes on to point out that 'wise passiveness', 'receptivity', 'openness to experience', call it what you will, has a pervasive influence on the quality of life, as well as on the quality of problem solving:

> Any method which promises to make life seem more enjoyable, and the common places of everyday experience more interesting should be welcomed as a major contribution to culture and morality. . . . But most of the products of our educational system prefer Westerns and alcohol.

Despite exaggerated claims and over-zealous attacks, meditation facilitates and clarifies both thought and feeling, and I, like Huxley, find it a great pity that schools neglect to provide instruction in this gentle art. It is, I suppose, because the practical techniques are often bound up with religious beliefs and dogma which are irrelevant to their psychological value and function. And the language of religion arouses antipathy and suspicion in the minds of educators who are committed, personally and professionally, to reason, intellect, and will. Teacher-as-liberator needs to see that 'work' and 'play' are different *kinds* of learning, and he needs to appreciate the place and the utility of the playful kind.

9.4 Being a School Teacher

A school teacher can be an orchestrator, a demonstrator, a trainer, a tutor, an instructor, a challenger, and a listener. But he also finds himself in a context that creates additional demands and restrictions that may even be in opposition to his work as a teacher. In many ways he is required to do violence to the ever-changing kaleidoscope of needs, wants, interests, receptivities, and hostilities – his own included – that constitute a class-room. Regardless of how everybody feels, if it's Thursday, Lesson One, then we are going to do 'Measuring the Specific Heat of an Unknown Metal'. Whatever kind of a creature the teacher pulls out of his hat, the audience is expected to cheer, and to want to know how the trick works. And his job is often to try to ensure that all his plants grow at the same rate and blossom at the same time. The fact that even his top O-level class is 'mixed ability' is a nuisance, to be either fought or ignored. He, like his students, is taught to associate lack of success with personal failing, so that he cannot accept the 'natural wastage' of motivation, or the 'thinning out' of ability, without feeling that he, 'the system', or Nature, is at fault in some way. While a driving instructor or a cricket coach sees the drying up of talent or interest as quite natural, the school teacher's efforts are over-shadowed by a pall of censure. He is likely to subscribe to the widespread belief that if a student fails, someone or something is to blame – and he is one of the prime suspects. So, unwilling to indict himself, he will be busy pointing the finger elsewhere: at the students, the syllabus, the examining boards, the head teacher, the governors, the government, the decline in moral fibre, or the parents. Somewhere in this tangle of self-vindication, learning and its facilitation get forgotten. Because it is the only suspect that can be changed without fighting back (the decline in morality, while mute, is agreed to be unstoppable), the *syllabus* gets endlessly tinkered with in the vain hope that the introduction of Health Education, Community Education, Black Studies, or Motorcycle Maintenance will sort things out. This has as much sense as trying to get the car going by painting it a brighter colour.

Many people become school teachers because they enjoy communicating their own interests to others, they like the power, and the conditions seem attractive. But what they find, all too often, is that many of their students remain unimpressed, the power becomes an interminable power-struggle, and the salary and the holidays cease, after a while, to be sufficient compensation. Their original goals denied, they either leave the profession or seek the substitute satisfactions of promotion and self-righteousness. A successful lesson can be redefined as one in which nothing went too badly wrong. Or, as people are finding increasingly at the present time, they can recapture their initial enjoyment in teaching by transferring to the primary level. There the palates are not yet jaded and finicky.

Independent schools, containing a much higher proportion of students who are interested in academic matters and/or who want to do well in public examinations, offer the same attractions.

If she remains in the average secondary school, yet refuses to shield herself with cynicism, the teacher's only remaining option may be to magnify the bright spots. Moments of genuine concern, affection, enthusiasm, or insight light up a long, dull term. I have not yet met a teacher who did not have a small store of such precious memories from her days as pupil as well as teacher. Student teachers are regularly amazed and deeply moved by receiving a farewell card or small present from an apparently hostile class. And a pupil may be disproportionately grateful for a teacher's thoughtfulness in bringing her an interesting magazine article. Such incidents stand out, deriving their brightness from the surrounding dark and their value from their rarity. For some teachers these gleams of gratitude or

talent suffice. For others they do not. Starved of appreciation and acknowledgement they throw in the towel.

Some teachers may be enthusiastic or powerful enough to avoid the
constant battle of 'control'. The twin tools of the 'good' school teacher are
the ability to create pictures of nice, juicy carrots, and a good sharp stick.
They can overcome reluctance and avoid trouble by 'making it interesting'
and 'having good discipline' – a judicious and flexible mixture of seduction
and coercion. Student teachers are taught to produce pretty diagrams and
warned 'not to become too friendly', and both are useful. It is only when
we stand back a little that we see that these ploys are required not by
teaching *per se*, but by the enforced teaching of people who have not chosen
to learn.

Other teachers, though, do not learn to dominate a class by entertainment
or intimidation, and for them the issue of 'control' is a constant, nagging
threat. 'Easy' classes are a chance to relax before joining battle, yet again,
with those that are 'difficult'. Whether the difficulty is theirs alone, or is
experienced by other staff as well, teaching such classes is no fun. The only
solutions are to find ways of rendering the recurrent experience tolerable,
perhaps by fixing the time-table, perhaps by finding someone to blame. Or
to leave. If a teacher cannot or will not adopt the preliminary roles of circus
clown or riot policeman, she may never create the opportunity of fulfilling
her role of teacher.

Moreover, in addition to being inhibited from doing the job she wants to
do, a school teacher finds herself burdened with extra tasks that are part of
the job but unrelated to her idea of teaching and learning. She has to do
dinner duty, playground duty, and bus duty. She is inveigled into looking
after the staff-room coffee fund. She is given student teachers to look after,
whose problems remind her uncomfortably of her own. And she is required
to take onto her own shoulders the total and onerous responsibility of
assessment – reading homework, setting and marking tests, entering pupils
for exams, and writing reports. Little of this is of direct relevance to the
pupils' learning.

Much could, in a climate of goodwill, be performed with more profit by
the learner herself. 'How are you doing?', 'What do *you* think you did
wrong?', are in other, safer teaching relationships more common and more
effective forms of evaluation that are not just diagnostic but are in themselves remedial. Yet in school the sense of partnership, of mutual goals and
mutual trust between teacher and learner is often missing. When it is, the
teacher has to do all the assessment herself lest the learner 'cheat' or lie. The

work generated by this lack of trust takes up a considerable amount of time and money.

So much for teaching *per se*. In the last few sections we shall look at what school is like from the learner's point of view.

9.5 Disappointment with School

Schools (by which I mean here predominantly secondary schools) see themselves as creating educated, employable, harmonious adults. Their existence presupposes first that children will not grow into such adults without help; and secondly that the kind of help they provide is constructive. There is no evidence for or against the first assumption. Too few children grow up without adult 'help' for us to be able to tell whether it is necessary. Certainly adult *models* are essential, but the value of deliberate attempts to influence development is not proven. However, the second assumption – that schools are doing what is necessary and sufficient to achieve their goal – is obviously false.

An increasing number of young people leave school angry, illiterate, and with little sense of integrity and responsibility. They like neither themselves nor other people very much. Defence, often aggressive, is always the priority. So they are not very good at a lot of things, and dare not get better. In what ways is school confusing and failing its clients? What happens, typically between the ages of eleven and thirteen, to turn the bright and willing kittens of the First Year into the slow, cantankerous bisons of the Third?

What happens is that they lose their trust. Many of them wake up to the facts that the goal of school is unobtainable; that even if they could get it, they don't want it; and that even if they wanted it, the means are inappropriate to the end.[23] The declared goal of schooling is to give people *qualifications* and *qualities*. The former goal is clear, and it is equally clear by the Third Year whether a pupil is in the race or not. In these egalitarian days, when the word élite is a dirty one, children are encouraged to believe that school is the great leveller, and that, with sufficient effort, anyone can win. The disillusionment, when it comes at thirteen or so, is therefore all the greater. To discover that you are in fact a loser in a game that you were told you could win makes you feel bad about yourself and resentful towards those who have deceived you.

But a loser might still hope that he will gain such *qualities* as 'education' and 'learning', that he will become a 'whole person', a 'citizen' or whatever other theoretical attributes the school includes in its prospectus. Yet when he tries to find out what these desirable qualities consist of, they either fade away like Scotch mist, or they turn out to be things that he is not so sure he wants or needs after all. He can see that basic skills like reading, writing, and arithmetic are valuable – though, for reasons we shall examine in the next section, he may even reject those. But if the qualities that he can pin down are politeness, neatness, punctuality, and the ability to appreciate Bach and Dickens, then he may reject them because they are often alien to his own personality and culture.

In the present (1984) climate, it is equally reasonable for a young person who could manage to pass three O-levels, or five CSEs, not to bother, because he sees that such qualifications will not lessen the risk of his unemployment.

Another confusion that school creates in some of its clients is a developing and legitimate doubt about the means to the end. If one wants an O-level in French, then some kind of French lesson is probably a good idea. But if a young person has dropped out of the qualification race, of what relevance are French constructions to his search for the qualities of a good grown-up? Or the names of the parts of a kidney bean? Or improper fractions? Or base eight number systems? Or Boyle's Law? If they are 'training of the mind' what precisely are they training? And could it not be better trained by dwelling on things that the learner needs or wants to know? If the knowledge is worthwhile in its own right, why does it not then *feel* worthwhile? If I have to learn it because I might visit France or decide later that I need Maths O-level, how is that people manage perfectly well on their holidays – and I'm more likely to go to Spain anyway? And can't I learn things when I need to? Do I have to be prepared for any eventuality? And if so, why not force me to learn Chinese and how to build a nuclear shelter and deliver babies?

We have said that a teacher may well insist on a learner achieving sub-goals that must be mastered on the way to a major goal of the learner's own choosing. That is sometimes inevitable. But in school the major goal is often obscure, alien or unattainable and the minor goals seem to form, to increasing numbers of teachers and pupils, not stepping stones, but just a heap of broken bricks. They do not lead anywhere and they are no good for building.

9.6 **Disruptive and Stupid Children: A Diagnosis**

For many pupils, school does work. It meets their needs, feeds their interests, and creates opportunities. For others, school holds out rewards that they know they will not get, and do not even want. It provides not challenges but threats, offers punishments that are not so much painful as humiliating; demands the development of a thick skin, studied indifference, and other forms of self-protection. In addition it constitutes a monumental irrelevance to the pressing facts of life, present and future. Like a slave population, the only thing to be gained is the satisfaction and prestige of sabotaging the system, and the only thing to be preserved is the privacy of its own culture.

How to disrupt the system? By refusing or failing to do what you are told to do – what 'they' want you to do. And if what they want you to do in school is learn, you win by refusing to learn even those things that are useful to you. Thus some children short-change themselves, sacrificing learning opportunities in order to upset the teacher and win the respect of their friends. They arrive at the ludicrous position in which learning anything means losing face. To try with success may meet with laughter from other Bad Boys or Girls and even with sarcastic remarks from the teacher. To try and fail means being laughed at by everyone. The only possible solutions are the roles of the Bully or the Smart-Alec or the Dumbo. It is unfortunate and ironic that this sort of Third Division success is only made possible by teachers who see themselves as responsible for getting their pupils to learn. The substantial minority of school children who have chosen to win by losing will not see that they are losing until they stop winning. The only way for a teacher to help them is to stop them winning, and he cannot do that by beating them. He can only remove the prize, and the prize is his own upset and frustration at their failure. As soon as he sees that he is not responsible because he cannot *make* anybody learn, and never has, he can blow the whistle and say 'OK, you win. I give up trying to make you learn. I don't care what you do; please just let the rest of us get on with what we want to do. We won't bother you: you don't bother us. All right?' It will take some days for the taste of this victory to turn to ashes as the players realize what it has been costing them. At this point the fog disperses, and they will be able to see whether there is really anything of value in these lessons or not. Sometimes they will see that there is, and they will then start playing, if not in the First, at least in the Second Division. Then they will begin to learn again.[24]

Teachers who see this feel less threatened by the pupils, more under-standing of them, and at the same time more angry with an institution that makes such a shoddy game possible and encourages it. There must be something wrong, they will think, with an environment in which some children can only preserve their self-respect by being mean and stupid. And this attitude only comes about when such behaviours and attitudes are seen not as character defects, but as ploys: defences that have a purpose and a value to the actor, however bad his performance seems to be.

9.7 School as a Place to Be

School consists of much more than teachers talking. It is a building and it is a society. What sort of an environment is it for a learner? Is it pretty? Is it stimulating? Is it safe?

The physical environment of an ordinary school offers little of interest to explore. Children spend most of their time in class-rooms or in the play-ground. Class-rooms are usually not very stimulating places – decorated with a few posters, perhaps, or bits and pieces of 'work' stuck up on the walls.[25] The lack of opportunities to explore *freely* in school can be gauged from the children's delight in a science lab, in such teasing and complex bits of the world as water taps and gas taps. Their behaviour is reminiscent of the subjects in the old 'sensory deprivation' experiment, who, kept locked up in a bare room, would listen over and over again to a tape of out-of-date stock market reports. And the 'playground', a bare concrete field, with, perhaps, coloured lines on the ground, offers much less scope for experiment than the area of the same name in the local park. Looked at simply as places to be, most schools are neither interesting nor attractive.

It is not surprising then, that for most children school is an opportunity for *social* exploration. If school was not compulsory many children would still turn up to see their friends. A comprehensive school is a very rich and varied interpersonal playground. And as in any closed institution, like a prison or barracks, the relationships in school are intense and of paramount importance. School is the principal place where people experiment with and consolidate the kind of adult they will become. And they do so often with a rather limited experience of what 'adult' means: more limited certainly than in cultures where children do not spend so much time in school. The adults they see most of, who provide them with their role-models, are their parents, their teachers, and people on the TV, politicians, sportsmen and women, actors and rock stars. The only adults they regularly see at work are bus conductors, people serving in shops and cafés and teachers. And many of their attempts to assimilate and emulate these models are conducted in the playground and on the bus home.

The dominant social ambiance within which these trials are carried out is a 'masculine' one, and this is as true of girls' schools as of mixed and boys' schools. The social style that is most successful in school is a tough one. Bravado and a show of fearlessness are admired. Tears, tenderness, open displays of anxiety and need are conspicuous by their rarity and usually arouse hostility and contempt in those, staff and pupils alike, not brave enough to acknowledge their own softness. It is so important to appear not to be hurt that thoughtless cruelty abounds. Students 'take the mickey' out of a new teacher for something to do. Occasionally, when a teacher shows real distress at their constant needling, the children are horrified and ashamed of their casual jibes. Teachers too, get used to dishing out criticism and dispensing, half playfully, barbed comments: and they are not allowed to see how deeply wounding some of their little 'jokes' have been. Most people can remember, still with some pain, experiences from schooldays of being humiliated, wrongly punished, or disbelieved – experiences that the perpetrator probably forgot the next day. School is a place of attack and defence, and only rarely, or within a small group of friends, of openness and trust. Most of the time, for both teachers and pupils, it does not feel safe. Because of the constant risk of exposure, whether in the class-room, staff-room, playground, or sportsground, risks of most kinds are not to be taken. As all significant learning involves risk, schools are not good places for learning. Most children receive a much better education in defensiveness and pretence at school than they do in learning. Ivan Illich once defined an institution as an organization whose method of working was designed to frustrate its declared aim, and said that school was a prime example.[26] This is why. Schools are bad places for learning because they are not safe.

School is the primary cultural transmitter of the myth that one has to be competent, consistent, cool, and in control. Emotion is not wanted, and because all important learning is an emotional business, only trivial or defiant learning is permitted. While adolescents are rightly preoccupied with the mysteries of sex and love, school responds with two or three lessons on reproductive anatomy (often of the rabbit) and the symptoms of VD. Even this amazing topic can be sanitized so that we will talk about anything except our own delicate experience.

The medium of school also transmits false messages about the nature of learning. This dissemination of disinformation is called the 'hidden curriculum'. The way school works presupposes that learning is *painless*; that it is limited by *ability*; that achievement within this limit is determined by *effort*; that learning requires *teaching* and that what is not taught will not be valuable; that information from informal sources is less accurate and less valuable than school knowledge; that most learning is learning *about* things; that *other people know best* what you need to learn; that how you *feel* about learning is irrelevant; that what you learn is independent of *how* and *why* it is acquired; that reward and punishment (extrinsic motivation) produce the same *kind* of learning as interest and enjoyment (intrinsic motivation); that learning is *hard work*; that once 'acquired', a *skill* is potentially available for use in any relevant circumstance, and that whether you then use it is partly a matter of *intelligence*; that *personal experience* of an idea should not affect the way you reason with it; that being able to *repeat* something has a close relationship to having understood it; that changing subjects at arbitrary times does not damage the quality of your learning; and that the dinner ladies contribute less to your understanding of the world than the Head of Science.

9.8 School as a Place to Learn

As a place to learn *intellectual knowledge* and skills, school works well for some children, tolerably for others, and very badly for those we have just discussed. It would work very much better for all if it were safer. As a place to learn the *physical know-how* of sportsfield or workshop it could be worse, though the atmosphere of high personal risk is here compounded by the manifestly low regard in which these skills are officially held. But those creative types of learning that require peace, passivity, and patience, and where the risks would be great wherever they were pursued are unsupported and often actually damaged by the context of school. That this is so is undeniable. The only possible plea in mitigation is that the cost, though high, is worth it. Perhaps the intellectual and social 'pros' outweigh the intuitive and personal 'cons'. However, people are increasingly arguing that the limitations that school imposes on the many in order to obtain advancement for the few are unnecessary and intolerable – and I agree.[27]

One of the functions of this book and its synoptic view of human learning in all its forms has been to show the extent to which schools do those things that they ought not to do, and leave undone those things that ought to be done. They help to build barriers to learning that limit a person's mobility in later life. And they ignore learning situations and learning strategies that are important. 'On entering school our children must adapt to the various demands of classroom efficiency. They are taught to behave "normally", to think rationally and objectively, to relate verbally, and to control rather than cultivate their feelings. They may graduate as good citizens, well educated in the cognitive disciplines, well prepared to function as competents in society, but be strikingly unaware of themselves and others.'[28]

Even within the intellectual sphere, the necessity for *time* and *play* are almost totally ignored, thereby creating learners who can only handle the routine. 'Despite the fact that the greatest advances in man's understanding of reality are made by intuitive leaps of the imagination, and only subsequently verified in rational terms, our education system continues to operate on the assumption that training of the *intellect* is developing man's highest potential.'[29] And: 'The constant activity enforced by many educators does not give young people the leisure which is an essential prerequisite for intellectual or artistic creation.'[30]

The best service that an adult can render a child is to help him to learn how to learn, to develop a powerful set of learning amplifiers, and a learning attitude to life. In traditional cultures, where things move slowly, this is not necessary. When life runs on well-established tracks there is no need to know how to fell trees, build bridges and lay roads. But in the age of Future Shock, the *kali yuga*, as the Hindus call it, when knowledge and values are hotly disputed and rapidly changing, people must be equipped to find their own way. In a society such as our own, more than any other, people need to be Good Learners. To insist that they spend ten years in school is to insist that they be blindfolded and shackled before they reenter, as adults, the human race for knowledge and competence, insight and sensitivity, wisdom and peace. No wonder that few of us get very far. Nor that, when 'Time' is eventually called, we are inclined to leave in a bad humour and with bad grace, frustrated and unfinished.

> Do not go gentle into that good night
> Rage, rage against the dying of the light

This book has thrown up a number of criteria for the facilitation of learning – for the identification of a good learning environment. It has raised a number of questions that we can ask, for example, of a school:

Are pupils encouraged to discuss what matters to them?

Are they encouraged to evaluate their own solutions?

Are they encouraged to experiment with who they are?

Are they encouraged to collaborate?

Are they allowed to be vague and hazy: to tolerate ambiguity and confusion?

Are they encouraged to give up?

Are they taught that play is valuable?

Are their powers of mental play – fantasy, imagination, imagery – expanded?

Are they given time?

Are they taught techniques of relaxation and meditation?

Are they encouraged to be unconventional?

Are they shown how to look inside themselves for answers and the capacity to answer?

Are they listened to attentively?

Are they told how valuable it is to make mistakes?

Are they encouraged to test and question what they and others have taken for granted?

Are they taught how to understand things?

Are they taught how to remember things?

Are they shown models of resourcefulness and flexibility?

Are they helped with the feelings that a learner has?

Are they, in short, helped to become good learners?

I rather suspect, as the reader may have guessed, that there may be some room for improvement.

NOTES

Chapter 1

1. From 'Avatars of the Tortoise'. In *Labyrinths* (Penguin, Harmondsworth, 1970).
2. *The Psychology of Personal Constructs*, vol. 1 and 2 (Norton, New York 1955). The first few chapters of this are reprinted as *A Theory of Personality* (Norton, New York, 1963). Kelly's views have been expounded most notably by Don Bannister and Fay Fransella, *Inquiring Man*, 2nd edn (Penguin, Harmondsworth, 1980).
3. An introduction to the philosophical way of going about this is provided by G. Parkinson, *The Theory of Meaning* (Oxford University Press, 1968).
4. A recent attempt is by David Bohm, *Wholeness and the Implicate Order* (Routledge & Kegan Paul, London, 1980).
5. The best discussions of the relation between map and territory that I know are by Alan Watts: see, for example, his *Nature, Man and Woman* (Abacus, London, 1976). Paul Watzlawick's *How Real is Real?* (Vintage Books, New York, 1977) is also good, as is an essay called 'Do We Need a Reality?' by Carl Rogers, in *A Way of Being* (Houghton Mifflin, Boston, 1980).
6. This is discussed more fully (but very readably) by Fritjof Capra in *The Tao of Physics* (Wildwood House, London, 1975).
7. Karl Popper, *Conjectures and Refutations* (Routledge & Kegan Paul, London, 1969).
8. Thomas Kuhn, *The Structure of Scientific Revolutions* (University of Chicago Press, 1970).
9. More detail on these traditions can be found in any introductory

psychology text-book, such as E. Hilgard, R. Atkinson, and R. Atkinson, *Introduction to Psychology*, 8th edn (Harcourt Brace Jovanovitch, New York, 1983), or M. Gazzaniga, *Psychology* (Harper & Row, San Francisco, 1980). The most accessible summary of *learning* theories is provided by R. Borger and A. Seaborne, *The Psychology of Learning*, 2nd edn (Penguin, Harmondsworth, 1982).

10. See, for example, their famous debate in *Science*, vol. 124, pp. 1057–1066, 1956.

11. B. F. Skinner, *Verbal Behaviour* (Appleton-Century-Crofts, New York, 1957).

12. For a philosophical defence of this point of view see the excellent book by Michael Polanyi called *Personal Knowledge* (Routledge & Kegan Paul, London, 1958).

13. . . . I am asserting. Theorists such as Richard Gregory, whose introductory book *Eye and Brain* (Weidenfeld & Nicolson, London, 1966) is very good, agree! Others, most notably James Gibson in his *The Senses Considered as Perceptual Systems* (Allen & Unwin, London, 1968) don't. An excellent and fair review of theories of perception, and the relevant neurophysiology, is given by Keith Oatley in *Perceptions and Representations* (Methuen, London, 1978).

14. Erwin Schrödinger, *What is Life? and Mind and Matter* (Cambridge University Press, 1967).

15. Quoted by Schrödinger, ibid.

16. This research, and especially its educational implications, are reviewed by Rosalind Driver in *The Pupil As Scientist?* (Open University Press, Milton Keynes, 1983); and also in a paper of mine called 'Teaching and Acquiring Scientific Knowledge' in T. Keen and M. Pope (Eds), *Kelly in the Classroom: Educational Applications of Personal Construct Psychology* (Cybersystems, Montreal, 1984).

17. Taken from W. W. Sawyer, *Mathematician's Delight* (Penguin, Harmondsworth, 1967).

18. This way of putting it is based on that of Werner Erhard. See, for example, Luke Rhinehart, *The Book of est* (Holt, Rinehart & Winston, New York, 1976).

19. R. D. Laing, *Knots* (Penguin, Harmondsworth, 1971).

20. In Albert Einstein, *Ideas and Opinions* (Souvenir Press, London, 1973).

21. In *My Belief* (Panther, St. Albans, 1979).

22. For further reading on this chapter, I recommend the books by Bannister and Fransella, Alan Watts, and Paul Watzlawick mentioned above, in Notes 2 and 5.

Chapter 2

1. A. H. Maslow, *Toward a Psychology of Being* (Van Nostrand, Princeton, 1962).
2. E. J. Murray, *Motivation and Emotion* (Prentice-Hall, New Jersey, 1964).
3. This is a condensed discussion of one in *Wholly Human* (op. cit.).
4. *My Belief* (op. cit.).
5. See Jack Vernon, *Inside the Black Room* (Penguin, Harmondsworth, 1966).
6. For a general review of theories of motivation, see an introductory text such as Hilgard, Atkinson, and Atkinson (op. cit.).
7. See Steven Rose, *The Conscious Brain* (Weidenfeld & Nicolson, London, 1973).
8. See Bannister and Fransella (op. cit.).
9. J. McV. Hunt, 'Experience and the Development of Motivation' in *Personality Growth and Learning* (Open University, Milton Keynes, 1971).
10. David Macfarland's elegant research (see his *Feedback Mechanisms in Animal Behaviour* Academic, London, 1971) argues strongly for this 'priority' view of motivation in animals.
11. See R. Wollheim, *Freud* (Fontana, London, 1971).
12. Interview with Penelope Mortimer in *The Sunday Times* a few years ago.
13. See, for example, Donald Broadbent, *Behaviour* (Methuen, London, 1964).
14. See John Nicholson, *Habits* (Pan, London, 1978).
15. This is a plausible explanation of the refusal to eat in some cases, but by no means all.
16. For a very good review of 'cognitive' influences on motivation, see H. Heckhausen and B. Weiner, 'The Emergence of a Cognitive Psychology of Motivation, in P. Dodwell (Ed), *New Horizons in Psychology*, vol. 2, 2nd edn (Penguin, Harmondsworth, 1980).
17. In *Beyond Freedom and Dignity* (Jonathan Cape, London, 1972).
18. Neil Postman and Charles Weingartner, *Teaching as a Subversive Activity* (Penguin, Harmondsworth, 1971).
19. The terms 'extrinsic' and 'intrinsic' motivation are widely used in the psychology of education and were popularized by Jerome Bruner in *Towards a Theory of Instruction* (Belknap Press, Cambridge, Mass, 1967).

20. Ibid.
21. For further reading, I recommend R. Borger and A. Seaborne, *The Psychology of Learning*, and Phil Evans, *Motivation* (Methuen, London, 1975).

Chapter 3

1. This image I can trace back to two sources, one technical and one not. The technical one is David Marr's paper 'A Theory for Cerebral Neo-cortex', *Proceedings of the Royal Society, Series B*, vol. 176, 1970, where he uses the notion of 'probabilistic mountains'. The other is Edward de Bono's *The Mechanism of Mind* (Penguin, Harmondsworth, 1971) an excellent and underrated book. My 'dunes' are similar to his 'jelly' model of memory.

2. C. Fillmore, 'The Case for Case'. In E. Bach and R. T. Harms (Eds), *Universals in Linguistic Theory* (Holt, Rinehart & Winston, New York, 1968). This earliest formulation of 'case grammar' has since been much discussed, and forms one of the foundations of so-called 'generative semantics', the dominant perspective in post-Chomskean linguistics.

3. The ABC formulation is now common in more 'cognitive' theories of behaviour. See, for example, C. Thoresen and M. Mahoney, *Behavioural Self-Control* (Holt, Rinehart & Winston, New York, 1974).

4. E. Tolman, *Purposive Behaviour in Animals and Man* (Appleton, New York, 1932).

5. The most accessible books by Skinner are *Beyond Freedom and Dignity* (op. cit.) and *About Behaviourism* (Jonathan Cape, London, 1974).

6. Cognitive psychology, though highly sophisticated, is only just beginning to incorporate, in notions such as 'production systems' this fundamental insight. For a detailed treatment see Alan Allport, 'Patterns and Actions: Cognitive Mechanisms are Content-specific' in Guy Claxton (Ed), *Cognitive Psychology: New Directions* (Routledge & Kegan Paul, London, 1980).

7. W. Labov, 'The Logic of Non-standard English'. In N. Keddie (Ed), *Tinker, Tailor . . . The Myth of Cultural Deprivation* (Penguin, Harmondsworth, 1973).

8. This very useful analogy is due to Skinner.

9. The notion of tuning has also been used recently by Donald Norman in his very readable little book *Learning and Memory* (Freeman, San Francisco, 1982).

10. We shall make the distinction between *consciousness* and *awareness* more clearly and more precisely later on.

11. This characterization of classical and operant conditioning as reflecting the response to different kinds of learning *situation*, rather than two fundamentally different *kinds* of learning, could be disputed, but the arguments are beyond the scope of the present book. See, for example, J. A. Gray, *Elements of a Two-Process Theory of Learning* (Academic, London, 1975).

12. Descriptions of this and operant conditioning will be found in most introductory texts such as Borger and Seaborne (op. cit.).

13. In some more sophisticated experiments the discrimination *is* made harder.

14. We shall come back to this form of teaching later when we deal with instruction, 'shaping through language', in Chapter 5.

15. The title of a book by James Herndon (Pitman, London, 1974).

16. D. E. Berlyne, *Conflict, Arousal and Curiosity* (McGraw-Hill, New York, 1960).

17. See D. Kahneman, *Attention and Effort* (Prentice-Hall, Englewood Cliffs, 1973).

18. William James, *The Principles of Psychology* (Holt, New York, 1890).

19. See E. V. S. Westmacott and R. J. Cameron, *Behaviour Can Change* (Globe, Basingstoke, 1981).

20. See Thoresen and Mahoney (op. cit.).

21. In philosophy, for example, P. Hirst and R. S. Peters, *The Logic of Education* (Routledge & Kegan Paul, London, 1970), different definitions of punishment that *do* require 'intention' and 'rule-breaking' are used.

22. G. H. Bower and E. R. Hilgard, *Theories of Learning*, 5th edn (Prentice-Hall, Englewood Cliffs, New Jersey, 1981).

23. 'Learned helplessness' has been investigated by Martin Seligman. See, for example, his *Helplessness: On Depression, Development and Death* (Freeman, San Francisco, 1975).

24. Much research on so-called 'achievement motivation' by researchers like McClelland and Atkinson has investigated this. See, for example, David McClelland, *The Achieving Society* (Van Nostrand, Princeton, 1961).

25. See A. J. Riopelle, *Animal Problem Solving* (Penguin, Harmondsworth, 1967).

26. See, for example, Timothy Gallwey, *The Inner Game of Tennis*

(Jonathan Cape, London, 1975).

27. *Conflict, Arousal and Curiosity* (op. cit.).
28. G. A. Miller, E. Galanter and K. Pribram, *Plans and the Structure of Behaviour* (Holt, Rinehart & Winston, New York, 1960).
29. See, for example, the popularizing book by Robert Ardrey, *The Territorial Imperative* (Collins, London, 1967).
30. An introduction to this area of interpersonal perception and attribution is provided by Don Hamachek, *Encounters with Others* (Holt, Rinehart & Winston, New York, 1982).
31. Sheldon Kopp, *An End to Innocence* (Bantam, New York, 1981).
32. J. Bruner, J. Goodnow, and G. Austin, *A Study of Thinking* (Wiley, New York, 1956).
33. Op. cit.
34. See the earlier discussion of 'learned helplessness' and 'depression'. These are long-term states of which despair is a more transient variety.
35. R. Pirsig, *Zen and the Art of Motor-Cycle Maintenance* (Bodley Head, London, 1974).
36. For further reading I recommend B. F. Skinner's *About Behaviourism* (op. cit.), John Nicholson's *Habits* (op. cit.) and Edward de Bono's *The Mechanism of Mind* (op. cit.).

Chapter 4

1. For a review of these studies, see Watzlawick (op. cit.).
2. See J. Katz and J. Fodor, 'The Structure of a Semantic Theory', *Language* vol. 39, pp. 170–210, 1963.
3. Lewis Carroll, *Through the Looking-Glass* (Penguin, Harmondsworth, 1962).
4. W. Heisenberg, *Physics and Philosophy* (Allen & Unwin, London, 1963).
5. Aldous Huxley, *Island* (Chatto & Windus, London, 1962).
6. See Eleanor Rosch, 'Classification of Real-World Objects: Origins and Representations in Cognition'. Reprinted in P. N. Johnson-Laird and P. C. Wason (Eds), *Thinking: Readings in Cognitive Science* (Cambridge) University Press, 1977).
7. See Marvin Minsky, 'Frame-system theory'. In Johnson-Laird and Wason, ibid.
8. Edward de Bono explains this very well in *The Mechanism of Mind* (op. cit.).

9. More technically, I am suggesting that verbal knowledge can be represented as some kind of associative network in the tradition of A. M. Collins and M. R. Quillian (as described in H. Clark and E. Clark's excellent *Psychology and Language*, Harcourt Brace Jovanovitch, New York, 1977). Most of the structural and functional features of this net I shall leave open here.

10. It may help to refer back to Section 3.1 here.

11. See Clark and Clark (op. cit.) for more detailed knowledge to this whole chapter.

12. Lewis Carroll, in *Through the Looking-Glass* (op. cit.).

13. See, for example, N. Postman and C. Weingartner, *Teaching as a Subversive Activity* (op. cit.).

14. For a review of research on 'discovery learning', see the chapter by Wittrock in E. Keislar and L. Schulman (Eds), *Learning by Discovery: A Critical Review* (Rand McNally, Chicago, 1966).

15. The metaphor of learning as eating is basic to Jean Piaget's view of development, which we return to in Chapter 8.

16. David Ausubel, *Educational Psychology: A Cognitive View* (Holt, Rinehart & Winston, New York, 1968).

17. The background to this and the following sections is well reviewed by Clark and Clark (op. cit.) and by J. R. Anderson, *Cognitive Psychology and its Implications* (Freeman, Oxford, 1980).

18. V. I. Pudovkin, *Film Technique* (Newnes, London, 1933).

19. See for an introduction, John Lyons, *Chomsky* (Fontana, London, 1970).

20. D. Dooling and R. Lackman, 'Effects of Comprehension on Retention of Prose', *Journal of Experimental Psychology*, vol. 88, pp. 216–222, 1971.

21. J. Bransford and M. Johnson, 'Contextual Prerequisites for Understanding', *Journal of Verbal Learning and Verbal Behaviour*, vol. 11, pp. 717–726, 1972.

22. This 'total record' hypothesis has been proposed by John Lilly in *The Centre of the Cyclone* (Paladin, London, 1973) and more formally but more tentatively, by E. Tulving in a book edited by John Brown, *Recall and Recognition* (Wiley, London, 1976).

23. This is Tulving's recently reactivated and well-supported proposal (ibid.)

24. Geoff Lowe, Paper to the British Psychological Society, London, 1982.

25. J. R. Anderson and G. H. Bower, *Human Associative Memory* (Winston, Washington, 1973).

26. In E. Tulving and W. Donaldson, *Organisation of Memory* (Academic, New York, 1972).
27. In G. I. Talland and N. Waugh, *The Pathology of Memory* (Academic, New York, 1969).
28. R. C. Anderson and A. Ortony, 'On Putting Apples into Bottles: A Problem in Polysemy', *Cognitive Psychology*, vol. 7, pp. 167–180, 1975.
29. *Chambers Twentieth Century Dictionary* (Chambers, Edinburgh, 1977).
30. H. Ebbinghaus, *Memory: A Contribution to Experimental Psychology* (Teachers' College, New York, 1885).
31. F. C. Bartlett, *Remembering* (Cambridge University Press, 1932).
32. L. S. Prytulak, 'Natural Language Mediation', *Cognitive Psychology*, vol. 2, pp. 1–56, 1971.
33. L. Standing, J. Conezio, and R. Haber, 'Perception and Memory for Pictures', *Psychonomic Science*, vol. 19, pp. 73–74, 1970.
34. Not everyone would agree with this cavalier dismissal of a large body of research – to put it mildly. Most introductory texts give much fuller and more tolerant (and probably more accurate) reviews, and a detailed defence of 'working memory' is provided by Graham Hitch in Guy Claxton (Ed), *Cognitive Psychology: New Directions* (op. cit.).

   For further reading on this chapter I recommend Ulric Neisser, *Cognition and Reality* (W. H. Freeman, San Francisco, 1976) and John Anderson, *Cognitive Psychology and its Implications* (op. cit.).

Chapter 5

1. Two good supplementary books for this chapter, one a classic, the other up to date, are: M. Wertheimer, *Productive Thinking* (Harper & Row, New York, 1959); and J. St. B. T. Evans, *The Psychology of Deductive Reasoning* (Routledge & Kegan Paul, 1982).
2. This example comes from T. Bever, 'The Cognitive Basis for Linguistic Structures', in J. R. Hayes (Ed), *Cognition and the Development of Language* (Wiley, New York, 1970).
3. This and the 'four card problem' shown in Figure 5.4 are described more fully in P. Wason and P. Johnson-Laird, *Psychology of Reasoning* (Batsford, London, 1972), and by Evans (op. cit.). The 'Licensing Law' experiment is by R. Griggs and J. Cox, *British Journal of Psychology*, vol. 73, pp. 407–420, 1982.
4. Evans, ibid.
5. A. Flew, *Thinking about Thinking* (Fontana, London, 1975).

6. L. Vygotsky, *Thought and Language* (Massachusetts Institute of Technology Press, Cambridge, 1962).

7. A. R. Luria, 'The Directive Function of Speech in Development and Dissolution: Part 1, Development'. Reprinted in R. C. Oldfield and J. Marshall (Eds), *Language* (Penguin, Harmondsworth, 1968).

8. The discussion based around this analogy is obviously very relevant to schools and teaching.

9. J. S. Bruner, *The Process of Education* (Harvard University Press, 1960).

10. See Stanley Milgram, *Obedience to Authority* (Harper & Row, New York, 1974) for a review of this research, as well as perhaps the most unsettling example of it.

11. See Section 3.2.

12. Robert Pirsig, *Zen and the Art of Motor-Cycle Maintenance* (op. cit.).

13. Michael Polanyi, *Personal Knowledge* (op. cit.).

14. The heyday of the discovery learning debate, within which 'guided discovery' was an important concept, was the 1960s. One of the best contributions came from M. C. Wittrock (op. cit.).

15. J. S. Bruner, J. J. Goodnow, and G. Austin, *A Study of Thinking* (op. cit.). The first two, more general, chapters are especially well worth reading.

16. We argued for the 'fuzziness' of natural concepts in Chapter 3.

17. P. Winston, 'Learning to Identify Toy Block Structures'. In P. N. Johnson-Laird and P. C. Wason (Eds), *Thinking: Readings in Cognitive Science* (op. cit.).

18. J. Needham, *Science and Civilisation in China*, vol. 5, Part 2 (Cambridge University Press, 1974).

19. C. R. Rogers, *On Becoming a Person* (Houghton Mifflin, Boston, 1961), chap. 19.

20. For a much broader selection of views on creativity, see P. E. Vernon, *Creativity* (Penguin, Harmondsworth, 1970).

21. Arthur Koestler, *The Act of Creation* (Hutchinson, London, 1964).

22. Richard Jones, *Fantasy and Feeling in Education* (Harper & Row, New York, 1968).

23. For example, *Practical Thinking* (Penguin, Harmondsworth, 1979).

24. Quoted in P. Vernon (op. cit.).

25. Albert Einstein, *Ideas and Opinions* (op. cit.).

26. . . . or the scientist's.

27. Gregory Bateson, *Steps to an Ecology of Mind* (Ballantyne, New York, 1972).

28. The problems involved in measuring 'creativity' are insuperable, and have been tackled most famously by J. W. Getzels and P. W. Jackson, *Creativity and Intelligence* (Wiley, New York, 1962).

29. For further reading I recommend Johnson-Laird and Wason's *Thinking*, and Vernon's *Creativity*, both referenced above.

Chapter 6

1. Goodwin Watson, 'Psychoanalysis and the Future of Education', *Teacher's College Record*, vol. 58, pp. 241–247, 1957.

2. The 'DMZ' was coined by Fritz Perls (see his *In and Out the Garbage Pail*, Bantam, Toronto, 1972). A similar idea is George Gurdjieff's 'the zone of the buffers' (see *Beelzebub's Tales to his Grandson*, Routledge & Kegan Paul, London, 1950).

3. The notions of 'identity' and 'identification' are difficult but important. For further discussions see: Ken Wilber, *No Boundary* (Shambhala, Boulder, Colorado, 1979); Esther Harding, *The I and the Not-I* (Coventure, London, 1977); and Don Hamachek, *Encounters with the Self* (Holt, Rinehart & Winston, New York, 1978).

4. B. Dohrenwend and B. Dohrenwend, *Stressful Life Events: Their Nature and Effects* (Wiley, New York, 1974).

5. This resistance has been referred to by George Kelly (op. cit.) as 'pre-emptive construing'. It has also been discussed most fully in the literature on 'attitude change'. See, for example, N. Warren and M. Jahoda, *Attitudes* (Penguin, Harmondsworth, 1973).

6. See, for example, A. Blumberg and R. Golembiewski, *Learning and Change in Groups* (Penguin, Harmondsworth, 1976); W. R. Bion, *Experiences in Groups* (Tavistock, London, 1961); and, more technically, M. Lieberman, I. Yalom and M. Miles, *Encounter Groups: First Facts* (Basic Books, New York, 1973) and Peter Smith, *Group Processes and Personal Change* (Harper & Row, London, 1980).

7. The classic here is R. D. Laing's *The Divided Self* (Penguin, Harmondsworth, 1965).

8. David Bohm, *Wholeness and the Implicate Order* (op. cit.). Though he is not a psychologist it is interesting to notice how clearly Bohm sees the way in which beliefs are not just cerebral but become perceptual and 'actual' as well.

9. Sheldon Kopp, *Mirror, Mask and Shadow* (Methuen, New York, 1980).

10. Douglas Adams, *The Hitch-hiker's Guide to the Galaxy* (Pan, London, 1979).
11. C. B. Cox and Rhodes Boyson, *Black Paper, 1975* (J. M. Dent, London, 1975).
12. Most notably, Jean-Jacques Rousseau in *Emile* (Dent, London, 1966), and more recently John Holt in *Escape from Childhood* (Penguin, Harmondsworth, 1975) and George Dennison in *Lives of Children* (Penguin, Harmondsworth, 1972).
13. Abraham Maslow, 'Some Educational Implications of Humanistic Psychologies', *Harvard Educational Review*, vol. 38, pp. 685–696, 1968.
14. Don Bannister and Fay Fransella (op. cit.).
15. Albert Einstein (op. cit.).
16. E. Schrödinger (op. cit.).
17. See, for example, W. Rahula, *What the Buddha Taught* (Gordon Fraser, Bedford, 1967).
18. Other discussions of this 'anatomy' can be found in John Rowan, *Ordinary Ecstasy* (Routledge & Kegan Paul, London, 1976); and in J. M. M. Mair, 'The Community of Self', in Don Bannister (Ed), *New Perspectives in Personal Construct Theory* (Academic, London, 1977).
19. Ludwig Wittgenstein, *Tractatus Logico – Philosophicus* (Routledge & Kegan Paul, London, 1961).
20. Alexis de Tocqueville, quoted in *The Faber Book of Aphorisms* selected by W. H. Auden and L. Kronenbourg (Faber & Faber, London, 1964).
21. Though I assert this, it is debatable. Certainly there are those, like Hans Eysenck (e.g. *The Biological Basis of Personality*, C. C. Thomas, Springfield, Illinois, 1969) who take a more 'biological' view of introversion and extraversion.
22. It is often said that 'we achieve only 10 per cent of our potential', though there is no good evidence for this or any other figure. Nonetheless, accounts such as those of Dennison (op. cit.) show irrefutably that many people – children and adults – do 'under-achieve' quite dramatically.
23. The cooker analogy comes from Edward de Bono, *Teaching Thinking* (Temple Smith, London, 1976).
24. William Labov, *The Logic of Non-Standard English* (op. cit.).
25. This explanation has been suggested by Michael Eysenck, *Attention and Arousal* (Springer-Verlag, Berlin, 1982).

26. This 'parable' is told during the *est* training.
27. For further reading I recommend Hamachek, *Encounters with the Self*, and Esther Harding, *The I and the Not-I*, both referenced above.

Chapter 7

1. Different views of the Unconscious are discussed in a very good paper by Erich Fromm called 'Psychoanalysis and Zen Buddhism' in a book edited by E. Fromm, D. T. Suzuki and R. de Martino, *Zen Buddhism and Psychoanalysis* (Souvenir Press, London, 1974).
2. A somewhat similar catalogue is given by Don Hamachek in *Encounters with the Self* (op. cit.). Freudian defences are covered by Richard Wollheim, *Freud* (op. cit.) amongst many others.
3. Isobel Menzies' study *The Functioning of Social Systems as a Defence Against Anxiety* (Tavistock Institute, London, 1970) is a telling analysis of how a nurse's training is structured so that anxiety is avoided or denied.
4. The most famous discussions of bodily defences are by Wilhelm Reich (e.g. C. Rycroft, *Reich*, Fontana, London, 1971) and Alexander Lowen (e.g. *Bioenergetics*, Penguin, Harmondsworth, 1976).
5. Paul Holman, *Introduction to Psychosomatics* (Biodynamic Psychology Publications, London, 1979).
6. A good introduction to the effects of all these drugs is provided by R. M. Julien, *A Primer of Drug Action*, 3rd edn (W. H. Freeman, San Francisco, 1981).
7. See, for example, Sheldon Kopp, *If You Meet the Buddha on the Road, Kill Him* (Sheldon Press, London, 1974).
8. Bryan Magee, *Facing Death* (Kimber, London, 1977).
9. Due, I think, to Albert Ellis, founder of Rational-Emotive Therapy.
10. The 'games' of Berne's 'transactional analysis' all revolve around this manipulativeness. The best introduction, I think, is Thomas Harris' *I'm O.K. – You're O.K.* (Pan, London, 1973).
11. Henri Charriére, *Papillon* (Panther, London, 1970).
12. Ken Wilber's *No Boundary* (op. cit.) contains a very good discussion of projection.
13. In *Mother Night* (Jonathan Cape, London, 1968).
14. What follows is of necessity a simplified and partial view of what is a very delicate, complex, and controversial field.
15. See Section 2.4.

16. Carl Rogers, *On Becoming a Person* (op. cit.).
17. This most elegant summary of our position comes from Bhagwan Shree Rajneesh, *The Book of the Secrets*, vol. 1 (Thames & Hudson, London, 1976).
18. Khalil Gibran, *The Prophet* (Heinemann, London, 1926).
19. Hermann Hesse, *My Belief* (op. cit.).
20. This is called 'The Serenity Prayer' and plays a key role in the work of Alcoholics Anonymous and its sister organization Al-Anon. See *One Day at a Time*, published by Al-Anon (New York, 1978).
21. Karfried Graf von Dürckheim, *The Way of Transformation*, (Unwin, London, 1980).
22. This simple set of 'equations' was taught to me by Denny Yuson (Swami Anand Veeresh).
23. Carl Rogers, *On Becoming a Person* (op. cit.).
24. Karl von Dürckheim, *The Way of Transformation* (op. cit.).
25. The quotations from Jung are from his *Collected Works* (Routledge & Kegan Paul, London, 1953–71).
26. Abraham Maslow, *Toward a Psychology of Being* (op. cit.).
27. Carl Rogers, *On Becoming a Person* (op. cit.).
28. Rogers, ibid.
29. Carl Rogers, *A Way of Being* (Houghton Mifflin, Boston, 1981).
30. Playful and cathartic methods are evocatively described by Ma Satya Bharti in *The Ultimate Risk* (Wildwood House, London, 1980).
31. See Daniel Goleman, *The Varieties of the Meditative Experience* (Rider, London, 1978).
32. Carl Rogers, *On Becoming a Person* (op. cit.).
33. Abraham Maslow, *Toward a Psychology of Being* (op. cit.).
34. For further reading I recommend Carl Rogers, *A Way of Being*, and C. Hall and G. Lindzey, *Theories of Personality*, 3rd edn (Wiley, New York, 1978).

Chapter 8

1. Kurt Vonnegut, Jr., *Deadeye Dick* (Jonathan Cape, London, 1983).
2. Piaget's work is discussed in practically every text-book. A good one that covers much of the research background to this chapter is *Child Development and Personality*, edited by P. Mussen, J. Conger, and J. Kagan, 5th edn (Harper & Row, New York, 1979).
3. For a basic grounding in developmental neuropsychology see Steven

Rose, *The Conscious Brain* (op. cit.).

4. The research evidence for this position is reviewed by Hirsch and Jakobson, in M. Gazzaniga and C. Blakemore (Eds), *Handbook of Psychobiology* (Academic, New York, 1975).

5. See E. Evarts, 'Unit Activity in Sleep and Wakefulness', in G. Quarton et. al. (Eds), *The Neurosciences*, vol. 1 (Rockefeller University Press, New York, 1967).

6. Donald Hebb, *The Organisation of Behaviour* (Wiley, New York, 1949).

7. This formulation is adapted from Werner Erhard, who defines 'the mind' as 'a linear arrangement of multi-sensory total records of successive moments of "now" '.

8. This is a crude summary of Hebb's seminal theory of 'cell assemblies' (see *The Organisation of Behaviour*, op. cit.).

9. This proposal is useful and metaphorical. I have no idea whether the 'real' nervous system solves the problem of emphasizing *relevance* in this way.

10. Research on newborn and very young babies is well reviewed by Tom Bower, *A Primer of Infant Development* (Freeman, San Francisco, 1977).

11. See George Butterworth, *Infancy and Epistemology* (Harvester, Brighton, 1981).

12. See Section 3.8.

13. I shall recap briefly on some of the descriptions of learning strategies in the earlier chapters, and add some speculations about how (and possibly when) they themselves are learnt.

14. It has recently been suggested that infants as young as a few weeks old already possess the ability to imitate facial gestures like sticking their tongues out, but that the ability may become dormant for months, reappearing when the child is about a year old. See Andy Meltzoff, in G. Butterworth, *Infancy and Epistemology* (op. cit.).

15. A. Bandura and R. Walters, *Social Learning and Personality Development* (Holt, Rinehart & Winston, New York, 1963).

16. This paragraph contains the skeleton of what could be fleshed out into a powerful, interesting and, to my mind, plausible theory. But I know of no direct evidence for the link between the on-duty/off-duty and the rough tuner/fine tuner distinctions.

17. At least people are agreeing that the case for a special purpose 'language acquisition device' is very much weaker than had been thought. See

Peter and Jill de Villiers, *Early Language* (Open Books, London, 1979) for discussion of this issue and a review of language development research in general.

18. Mike Scaife of the University of Sussex has done some very nice work on this. See J. Churcher and M. Scaife, 'How Infants See the Point', in G. Butterworth and P. Light, *Social Cognition* (Harvester, Brighton, 1982).

19. For the full enormity of what has to be learnt, refer back to Chapter 4, and to Herb and Eve Clark's book *Psychology and Language* (op. cit.).

20. How the relationship between 'language' and 'thought' develops in the child was the subject of a classical antithesis between Vygotsky, (*Thought and Language*, op. cit.) and Piaget (e.g. *Language and Thought of the Child*, Routledge & Kegan Paul, London, 1926).

21. Paul Harris, 'Transitive Inferences by Four-year-old Children'. Paper presented at the *Society for Research in Child Development* conference, Denver, Colarado, 1975.

22. Margaret Donaldson, *Children's Minds* (Fontana, London, 1978).

23. For a review of cross-cultural development, see M. Cole and S. Scribner, *Culture and Thought: A Psychological Introduction* (Wiley, New York, 1974).

24. Paul Harris' chapter in M. Gruneberg and P. Sykes, *Aspects of Memory* (Methuen, London, 1978).

25. See H. R. Schaffer, *The Growth of Sociability* (Penguin, Harmondsworth, 1971).

26. The process whereby an Identity, a Self-image, are created is discussed in more detail in my *Wholly Human* (op. cit.) and by Gordon Allport in his *Pattern and Growth in Personality* (Holt, Rinehart & Winston, New York, 1961).

27. For further reading I recommend Margaret Donaldson's *Children's Minds* (op. cit.) and Peter and Jill de Villiers' *Early Language* (op. cit.).

Chapter 9

1. *Teaching as a Subversive Activity* is the title of a well-known radical education book by Neil Postman and Charles Weingartner (see Chapter 2, note 18).

2. There are particular learning strategies, like *remembering* and *repeating* that we looked at in Chapter 4, where the amount of integration that results is minimal. But these are special purpose strategies, to be used

not from preference but in those circumstances where integration is blocked. They are models not of learning in general, but of one specialized, limited, nonpreferred *kind* of learning. If the teacher wishes to optimize learning, he should always seek to avoid the circumstances in which these 'brute force and ignorance' methods are necessary. In schools often the very opposite seems to be happening.

3. This is, I think, an exact quotation of the opening sentence of a respectable Ed. Psych. text-book that I looked at five or six years ago. Unfortunately I forget the author.

4. There is some nice research by M. Lepper and D. Greene and others, on what is called 'the undermining effect' (see *The Hidden Costs of Reward*, Lawrence Erlbaum, Hillsdale, New Jersey, 1978). In many circumstances (though not all) when a person is externally rewarded for doing something that they have previously done spontaneously, the action becomes tied to the reward, and the apparent 'intrinsic motivation' is undermined. An explanation for this was suggested in Section 2.7.

5. Even, as we saw in Chapter 7, to the point of psychosis.

6. This point is well made by John Holt in *Teach Your Own* (Lighthouse, Brightlingsea, Essex, 1981).

7. This concern has been most influentially expressed in educational psychology by R. M. Gagné in *The Conditions of Learning*, 3rd edn (Holt, Rinehart & Winston, New York, 1977), where he develops an elaborate but psychologically dated hierarchy of learning processes.

8. See, for example, Michael Shayer and Philip Adey, *Towards a Science of Science Teaching* (Heinemann Educational, London, 1981).

9. From an article entitled 'Learning Objectives? Yes!' in T. Roberts (Ed), *Four Psychologies Applied to Education* (Schenkman, Cambridge, Mass., 1975).

10. See Chapter 5, note 9.

11. For observational but compelling evidence of this, see especially the early books by John Holt, such as *The Underachieving School, How Children Learn*, and *How Children Fail* (Penguin, Harmondsworth, 1971, 1972, and 1973 respectively), and others like *Lives of Children*, by George Dennison (op. cit.), or Jonathan Kozol's *Death at an Early Age* (Bantam, New York, 1968).

12. Albert Einstein, *Ideas and Opinions* (op. cit.).

13. See Tom Sharpe's book *Wilt* (Pan, London, 1978) for advice on how to accomplish the latter.

14. This list is a condensation of a discussion in Postman and Weingartner (op. cit.). We noted briefly other views of good learners in Section 7.10.

15. See Section 5.5.

16. Timothy Gallwey, *The Inner Game of Tennis* (op. cit.).

17. Jerome Bruner, *Towards a Theory of Instruction* (op. cit.).

18. See David Ausubel (op. cit.).

19. The most popular exponent of such methods is Edward de Bono – see, for example, his *Practical Thinking* (op. cit.).

20. Anne Roe, *The Making of a Scientist* (Dodd Mead, New York, 1952).

21. G. Spencer Brown, *Laws of Form* (Allen & Unwin, London, 1969).

22. Aldous Huxley, 'Education on the Non-verbal Level', *Daedalus*, vol. 91, pp. 279–293, 1962.

23. This and other arguments in this section are provided and supported by David Hargreaves, *The Challenge for the Comprehensive School* (Routledge & Kegan Paul, London, 1982).

24. While this sounds almost too good to be true, those who have tried it with persistence and commitment find that it works. In addition to those by George Dennison and Jonathan Kozol (op. cit.) accounts have been provided by James Herndon in *The Way It Spozed To Be* (op. cit.), and Herbert Kohl in *36 Children* (Penguin, Harmondsworth, 1973).

25. Remember I am talking from my experience of the average *Secondary* school.

26. Ivan Illich, *Deschooling Society* (Penguin, Harmondsworth, 1973).

27. See Illich (ibid.); Paul Goodman, *Compulsory Miseducation* (Penguin, Harmondsworth, 1971); Everett Reimer, *School is Dead* (Penguin, Harmondsworth, 1971); and others.

28. Michael Murphy, 'Education for Transcendence', *Journal of Transpersonal Psychology*, vol. 1, pp. 21–32, 1969.

29. Frances Clark, 'Fantasy and Imagination', in T. B. Roberts (Ed), *Four Psychologies Applied to Education* (op. cit.).

30. Edith Weisskopf, 'Some Comments Concerning the Role of Education in the "Creation of Creation" ', *Journal of Educational Psychology*, vol. 42, pp. 185–189, 1951.

BIBLIOGRAPHY

Adams, D. (1979) *The Hitch-hiker's Guide to the Galaxy* London, Pan.

Al-Anon. (1978) *One Day at a Time* New York, Al-Anon.

Allport, D. A. (1980) Patterns and actions: cognitive mechanisms are content-specific. In G. L. Claxton (Ed), *Cognitive Psychology: New Directions* London, Routledge & Kegan Paul.

Allport, G. (1961) *Pattern and Growth in Personality* New York, Holt, Rinehart & Winston.

Anderson, J. R. (1980) *Cognitive Psychology and its Implications* San Francisco, W. H. Freeman.

Anderson, J. R. and Bower, G. H. (1973) *Human Associative Memory* Washington, Winston.

Anderson, R. C. and Ortony, A. (1975) On putting apples into bottles: a problem in polysemy. *Cognitive Psychology*, Vol 7, pp. 167–180.

Ardrey, R. (1967) *The Territorial Imperative* London, Collins.

Ausubel, B. (1968) *Educational Psychology: A Cognitive View* New York, Holt, Rinehart & Winston.

Bandura, A. and Walters, R. (1963) *Social Learning and Personality Development* New York, Holt, Rinehart & Winston.

Bannister, D. and Fransella, F. (1980) *Inquiring Man* 2nd Edition. Harmondsworth, Penguin.

Bartlett, F. C. (1932) *Remembering* Cambridge, Cambridge University Press.

Bateson, G. (1972) *Steps to an Ecology of Mind* New York, Ballantyne.

Berlyne, D. (1960) *Conflict, Arousal and Curiosity* New York, McGraw-Hill.

Bever, T. (1970) The cognitive basis for linguistic structures. In J. R. Hayes (Ed), *Cognition and the Development of Language* New York, Wiley.

Bharti, Ma Satya (1980) *The Ultimate Risk* London, Wildwood House.

Bion, W. R. (1961) *Experiences in Groups* London, Tavistock.

Blumberg, A. and Golembiewski, R. T. (1976) *Learning and Change in Groups* Harmondsworth, Penguin.

Bohm, D. (1980) *Wholeness and the Implicate Order* London, Routledge & Kegan Paul.

Borger, R. and Seaborne, A. (1982) *The Psychology of Learning* 2nd Edition. Harmondsworth, Penguin.

Borges, J. L. (1970) *Labyrinths* Harmondsworth, Penguin.

Bower, G. H. and Hilgard, E. R. (1981) *Theories of Learning* 5th Edition. New Jersey, Prentice Hall, Englewood Cliffs.

Bower, T. (1977) *A Primer of Infant Development* San Francisco, W. H. Freeman.

Bransford, J. and Johnson, M. (1972) Contextual prerequisites for understanding. *Journal of Verbal Learning and Verbal Behaviour* Vol 11, pp. 717–726.

Broadbent, D. E. (1964) *Behaviour* London, Methuen.

Brown, G. D. (1969) *The Laws of Form* London, Allen & Unwin.

Bruner, J. S. (1960) *The Process of Education* Harvard University Press.

Bruner, J. S. (1967) *Towards a Theory of Instruction* Cambridge, Mass., Belknap Press.

Bruner, J. S., Goodnow, J. J. and Austin, G. A. (1956) *A Study of Thinking* New York, Wiley.

Butterworth, G. (1981) *Infancy and Epistemology* Brighton, Harvester Press.

Capra, F. (1975) *The Tao of Physics* London, Wildwood House.

Carroll, L. (1962) *Through the Looking-Glass* Harmondsworth, Penguin.

Chambers Twentieth Century Dictionary (1977) Edinburgh, Chambers.

Charriére, H. (1970) *Papillon* London, Panther.

Churcher, J. and Scaife, M. (1982) How infants see the point. In G. Butterworth and P. Light (Eds), *Social Cognition* Brighton, Harvester Press.

Clark, F. (1975) Fantasy and imagination. In T. Roberts (Ed), *Four Psychologies Applied to Education* Cambridge, Mass., Schenkman.

Clark, H. and Clark, E. (1977) *Psychology and Language* New York, Harcourt Brace Jovanovitch.

Claxton, G. L. (1981) *Wholly Human: Western and Eastern Visions of the Self and Its Perfection* London, Routledge & Kegan Paul.

Claxton, G. L. (1984) Teaching and acquiring scientific knowledge. In T. Keen and M. Pope (Eds), *Kelly in the Classroom: Educational Applications of Personal Construct Psychology* Montreal, Cybersystems.

Cole, M. and Scribner, S. (1974) *Culture and Thought: A Psychological Introduction* New York, Wiley.

Cox, C. B. and Boyson, R. (1975) *Black Paper, 1975* London, J. M. Dent.

de Bono, E. (1971) *The Mechanism of Mind* Harmondsworth, Penguin.

de Bono, E. (1976) *Teaching Thinking* London, Temple Smith.

de Bono, E. (1979) *Practical Thinking* Harmondsworth, Penguin.

Dennison, G. (1972) *The Lives of Children* Harmondsworth, Penguin.

de Villiers, P. and de Villiers, J. (1979) *Early Language* London, Open Books.

Dohrenwend, B. and Dohrenwend, B. (1974) *Stressful Life Events: Their Nature and Effects* New York, Wiley.

Donaldson, M. (1978) *Children's Minds* London, Fontana.

Dooling, D. and Lackman, R. (1971) Effects of comprehension on retention of prose. *Journal of Experimental Psychology* Vol 88, pp. 216–222.

Driver, R. (1983) *The Pupil as Scientist?* Milton Keynes, The Open University Press.

Durckheim, K. (1980) *The Way of Transformation* London, Unwin.

Ebbinghaus, H. (1885) *Memory: A Contribution to Experimental Psychology* New York, Teachers' College.

Einstein, A. (1973) *Ideas and Opinions* London, Souvenir Press.

Evans, J. St. B. T. (1982) *The Psychology of Deductive Reasoning* London, Routledge & Kegan Paul.

Evans, P. (1975) *Motivation* London, Methuen.

Evarts, E. (1967) Unit activity in sleep and wakefulness. In G. Quarton et. al. (Eds), *The Neurosciences, Vol I*. New York, Rockefeller University Press.

Eysenck, H. (1969) *The Biological Basis of Personality* Illinois, C. C. Thomas, Springfield.

Eysenck, M. (1982) *Attention and Arousal* Berlin, Springer-Verlag.

Fillmore, C. (1969) The case for case. In E. Bach and R. T. Harms (Eds), *Universals in Linguistic Theory* New York, Holt, Rinehart & Winston.

Flew, A. (1975) *Thinking about Thinking* London, Fontana

Fromm, E. (1974) Psychoanalysis and zen buddhism. In E. Fromm, D. T. Suzuki and R. de Martino, *Zen Buddhism and Psychoanalysis* London, Souvenir Press.

Gagné, R. M. (1975) Learning objectives? Yes! In T. Roberts (Ed), *Four Psychologies Applied to Education* Cambridge, Mass., Schenkman.

Gagné, R. M. (1977) *The Conditions of Learning* 3rd Edition. New York, Holt, Rinehart & Winston.

Gallwey, T. (1975) *The Inner Game of Tennis* London, Jonathan Cape.

Gazzaniga, M. (1980) *Psychology* San Francisco, Harper & Row.

Gazzaniga, M. and Blakemore, C. (1975) *Handbook of Psychobiology* New York, Academic Press.

Getzels, J. W. and Jackson, P. W. (1962) *Creativity and Intelligence* New York, Wiley.

Gibran, K. (1926) *The Prophet* London, Heinemann.

Gibson, J. J. (1968) *The Senses Considered as Perceptual Systems* London, Allen & Unwin.

Goleman, D. (1978) *The Varieties of the Meditative Experience* London, Rider.

Goodman, P. (1971) *Compulsory Miseducation* Harmondsworth, Penguin.

Gray, J. A. (1975) *Elements of a Two-Process Theory of Learning* London, Academic Press.

Gregory, R. L. (1966) *Eye and Brain* London, Weidenfeld & Nicolson.

Griggs, R. and Cox, J. (1982) The elusive thematic-materials effects in Wason's selection task. *British Journal of Psychology* Vol 73, pp. 407–420.

Gurdjieff, G. (1950) *Beelzebub's Tales to his Grandson* London, Routledge & Kegan Paul.

Hall, C. and Lindzey, G. (1978) *Theories of Personality* 3rd Edition. New York, Wiley.

Hamachek, D. (1978) *Encounters with the Self* New York, Holt, Rinehart & Winston.

Hamachek, D. (1982) *Encounters with Others* New York, Holt, Rinehart & Winston.

Harding, E. (1977) *The I and the Not-I* London, Coventure.

Hargreaves, D. H. (1982) *The Challenge for the Comprehensive School* London, Routledge & Kegan Paul.

Harris, P. L. (1975) *Transitive inferences by four-year-old children*. Paper delivered to the *Society for Research in Child Development* Denver, Colorado.

Harris, P. L. (1978) Developmental aspects of children's memory. In M. Gruneberg and P. Morris (Eds), *Aspects of Memory* London, Methuen.

Harris, T. (1973) *I'm O.K. – You're O.K.* London, Pan.

Hebb, D. O. (1949) *The Organisation of Behaviour* New York, Wiley.

Heckhausen, H. and Weiner, B. (1980) The emergence of a cognitive psychology of motivation. In P. Dodwell (Ed), *New Horizons in Psychology, Vol II* 2nd Edition, Harmondsworth, Penguin.

Heisenberg, W. (1963) *Physics and Philosophy* London, Allen & Unwin.

Herndon, J. (1974) *The Way It Spozed To Be* London, Pitman.

Hesse, H. (1979) *My Belief* St. Albans, Panther.

Hilgard, E. R., Atkinson, R. and Atkinson, R. (1983) *Introduction to Psychology* 8th Edition, New York, Harcourt Brace Jovanovitch.

Hirst, P. and Peters, R. (1970) *The Logic of Education* London, Routledge & Kegan Paul.

Hitch, G. (1980) Developing the concept of working memory. In G. L. Claxton (Ed), *Cognitive Psychology: New Directions* London, Routledge & Kegan Paul.

Holman, J. (1979) *Introduction to Psychosomatics* London, Biodynamic Psychology Publications.

Holt, J. (1971) *The Underachieving School* Harmondsworth, Penguin.

Holt, J. (1972) *How Children Learn* Harmondsworth, Penguin.

Holt, J. (1973) *How Children Fail* Harmondsworth, Penguin.

Holt, J. (1975) *Escape from Childhood* Harmondsworth, Penguin.

Holt, J. (1981) *Teach Your Own* Brightlingsea, Essex, Lighthouse.

Hunt, J. McV. (1971) Experience and the development of motivation. In *Personality Growth and Learning* Milton Keynes, Open University.

Huxley, A. (1962) Education on the non-verbal level *Daedalus* Vol 91, pp. 279–293.

Huxley, A. (1962) *Island* London, Chatto & Windus.

Illich, I. (1973) *Deschooling Society* Harmondsworth, Penguin.

James, W. (1890) *The Principles of Psychology* New York, Holt.

Jones, R. (1968) *Fantasy and Feeling in Education* New York, Harper & Row.

Julien, R. M. (1981) *A Primer of Drug Action* 3rd Edition. San Francisco, W. H. Freeman.

Jung, C. G. (1971) *Collected Works, 1953–1971* London, Routledge & Kegan Paul.

Kahneman, D. (1973) *Attention and Effort* Englewood Cliffs, New Jersey, Prentice-Hall.

Katz, J. J. and Fodor, J. A. (1963) The structure of a semantic theory, *Language*, Vol 39, pp. 170–210.

Kelly, G. (1955) *The Psychology of Personal Constructs* Vols I and II, New York, Norton.

Kelly, G. (1963) *A Theory of Personality* New York, Norton.

Koestler, A. (1964) *The Act of Creation* London, Hutchinson.

Kohl, J. (1973) *36 Children* Harmondsworth, Penguin.

Kopp, S. (1974) *If You Meet The Buddha on the Road, Kill Him* London, Sheldon Press.

Kopp, S. (1980) *Mirror, Mask and Shadow* New York, Methuen.

Kopp, S. (1981) *An End to Innocence* New York, Bantam.

Kozol, J. (1968) *Death at an Early Age* New York, Bantam.

Kuhn, T. (1970) *The Structure of Scientific Revolutions* Chicago, University of Chicago Press.

Labov, W. (1973) The logic of non-standard English. In N. Keddie (Ed), *Tinker, Tailor . . . The Myth of Cultural Deprivation* Harmondsworth, Penguin.

Laing, R. (1965) *The Divided Self* Harmondsworth, Penguin.

Laing, R. (1971) *Knots* Harmondsworth, Penguin.

Lepper, M. and Greene, D. (1978) *The Hidden Costs of Reward*, Hillsdale, New Jersey, Lawrence Erlbaum.

Lieberman, M., Yalom, I. and Miles, M. (1973) *Encounter Groups: First Facts* New York, Basic Books.

Lilly, J. (1973) *The Centre of the Cyclone* London, Paladin.

Lowen, A. (1976) *Bioenergetics* Harmondsworth, Penguin.

Luria, A. R. (1968) The directive function of speech in development and dissolution: Part I. Reprinted in R. C. Oldfield and J. Marshall (Eds), *Language* Harmondsworth, Penguin.

Lyons, J. (1970) *Chomsky* London, Fontana.

Macfarland, D. (1971) *Feedback Mechanisms in Animal Behaviour* London, Academic Press.

Magee, B. (1977) *Facing Death* London, Kimber.

Mair, J. M. (1977) The community of self. In D. Bannister (Ed), *New Perspectives in Personal Construct Theory* London, Academic Press.

Marr, D. (1970) A theory for cerebral neo-cortex. *Proceedings of the Royal Society, Series B* Vol 176, pp. 161–234.

Maslow, A. H. (1962) *Toward a Psychology of Being* Princeton, Van Nostrand.

Maslow, A. H. (1968) Some educational implications of humanistic psychologies. *Harvard Educational Review* Vol 38, pp. 685–696.

McClelland, D. (1961) *The Achieving Society* Princeton, Van Nostrand.

Meltzoff, A. (1981) Imitation, inter-modal co-ordination and representation in early infancy. In G. Butterworth (Ed), *Infancy and Epistemology* Brighton, Harvester Press.

Menzies, I. (1970) *The Functioning of Social Systems as a Defence Against Anxiety* London, Tavistock Institute.

Milgram, S. (1974) *Obedience to Authority* New York, Harper & Row.

Miller, G. A., Galanter, E. and Pribram, K. (1960) *Plans and the Structure of Behaviour* New York, Holt, Rinehart & Winston.

Minsky, M. (1977) Frame-system theory. In P. C. Wason and P. N. Johnson-Laird (Eds), *Thinking: Readings in Cognitive Science* Cambridge, Cambridge University Press.

Murphy, M. (1969) Education for transcendence. *Journal of Transpersonal Psychology* Vol 1, pp. 21–32.

Murray, E. J. (1964) *Motivation and Emotion* New Jersey, Prentice-Hall.

Mussen, P., Conger, J. J. and Kagan, J. (1979) *Child Development and Personality* 5th Edition. New York, Harper & Row.

Needham, J. (1974) *Science and Civilisation in China*, Vol 5, Part 2, Cambridge, Cambridge University Press.

Neisser, U. (1976) *Cognition and Reality* San Francisco, W. H. Freeman.

Nicholson, J. (1978) *Habits* London, Pan.

Norman, D. A. (1982) *Learning and Memory* San Francisco, W. H. Freeman.

Oatley, K. (1978) *Perceptions and Representations* London, Methuen.

Parkinson, G. (1968) *The Theory of Meaning* Oxford, Oxford University Press.

Perls, F. (1972) *In and Out the Garbage Pail* Toronto, Bantam.

Piaget, J. (1926) *Language and Thought of the Child* London, Routledge & Kegan Paul.

Pirsig, R. (1974) *Zen and the Art of Motor-Cycle Maintenance* London, Bodley Head.

Polanyi, M. (1958) *Personal Knowledge* London, Routledge & Kegan Paul.

Popper, K. (1969) *Conjectures and Refutations* London, Routledge & Kegan Paul.

Postman, N. and Weingartner, C. (1971) *Teaching as a Subversive Activity* Harmondsworth, Penguin.

Prytulak, L. S. (1971) Natural language mediation. *Cognitive Psychology*, Vol 2, pp. 1–56.

Pudovkin, V. I. (1933) *Film Technique* London, Newnes.

Rahula, W. (1967) *What the Buddha Taught* Bedford, Gordon Fraser.

Rajneesh, Bhagwan Shree (1976) *The Book of the Secrets, Vol I* London, Thames & Hudson.

Reimer, E. *School is Dead* Harmondsworth, Penguin.

Rhinehart, L. (1976) *The Book of est* New York, Holt, Rinehart & Winston.

Riopelle, A. J. (1967) *Animal Problem Solving* Harmondsworth, Penguin.

Roe, A. (1952) *The Making of a Scientist* New York, Dodd Mead.

Rogers, C. R. (1961) *On Becoming a Person* Boston, Houghton Mifflin.

Rogers, C. R. (1980) *A Way of Being* Boston, Houghton Mifflin.

Rosch, E. (1977) Classification of real-world objects in P. C. Wason and P. N. Johnson-Laird (Eds), *Thinking: Readings in Cognitive Science*. Cambridge, Cambridge University Press.

Rose, S. (1973) *The Conscious Brain* London, Weidenfeld & Nicolson.

Rousseau, J. (1966) *Emile* London, Dent.

Rowan, J. (1976) *Ordinary Ecstasy* London, Routledge & Kegan Paul.

Rycroft, C. (1971) *Reich* London, Fontana.

Sawyer, W. W. (1967) *Mathematician's Delight* Harmondsworth, Penguin.

Schaffer, H. R. (1971) *The Growth of Sociability* Harmondsworth, Penguin.

Schrödinger, E. (1967) *What is Life? and Mind and Matter* Cambridge, Cambridge University Press.

Seligman, M. P. (1975) *Helplessness: On Depression, Development and Death* San Francisco, W. H. Freeman.

Sharpe, T. (1978) *Wilt* London, Pan.

Shayer, M. and Adey, P. (1981) *Towards a Science of Science Teaching* London, Heinemann Educational.

Skinner, B. F. (1957) *Verbal Behaviour* New York, Appleton-Century-Crofts.

Skinner, B. F. (1972) *Beyond Freedom and Dignity* London, Jonathan Cape.

Skinner, B. F. (1974) *About Behaviourism* London, Jonathan Cape.

Skinner, B. F. and Rogers, C. R. (1956) Some issues concerning the control of human behaviour. *Science* Vol 124, pp. 1057–1066.

Smith, P. (1980) *Group Processes and Personal Change* London, Harper & Row.

Standing, L., Conezio, J. and Haber, R. (1970) Perception and memory for pictures. *Psychonomic Science* Vol 19, pp. 73–74.

Talland, G. and Waugh, N. C. (1969) *The Pathology of Memory* New York, Academic Press.

Thoresen, C. and Mahoney, M. (1974) *Behavioural Self-Control* New York, Holt, Rinehart & Winston.

Tolman, E. (1932) *Purposive Behaviour in Animals and Man* New York, Appleton.

Tulving, E. (1976) Euphoric processes in free recall. In J. Brown (Ed), *Recall and Recognition* London, Wiley.

Tulving, E. and Donaldson, W. (1972) *Organisation of Memory* London, Academic Press.

Vernon, J. (1966) *Inside the Black Room* Harmondsworth, Penguin.

Vernon, P. E. (1970) *Creativity* Harmondsworth, Penguin.

Vonnegut, K. (1968) *Mother Night* London, Jonathan Cape.

Vonnegut, K. (1983) *Deadeye Dick* London, Jonathan Cape.

Vygotsky, L. (1962) *Thought and Language* Cambridge, Mass., Massachussets Institute of Technology Press.

Warren, N. and Jahoda, M. (1973) *Attitudes* Harmondsworth, Penguin.

Wason, P. C. and Johnson-Laird, P. N. (1972) *Psychology of Reasoning* London, Batsford.

Watson, G. (1957) Psychoanalysis and the future of education. *Teachers' College Record* Vol 8, pp. 241–247.

Watts, A. W. (1976) *Nature, Man and Woman* London, Abacus.

Watzlawick, P. (1977) *How Real is Real?* New York, Vintage Books.

Weisskopf, E. (1951) Some comments concerning the role of education in the 'creation of creation'. *Journal of Educational Psychology* Vol 42, pp. 185–189.

Wertheimer, M. (1959) *Productive Thinking* New York, Harper & Row.

Westmacott, E. V. S. and Cameron, R. J. (1981) *Behaviour Can Change* Basingstoke, Globe.

Wilber, K. (1979) *No Boundary* Boulder, Colorado, Shambhala.

Winston, P. (1977) Learning to identify toy block structures. In P. N. Johnson-Laird and P. C. Wason (Eds), *Thinking: Readings in Cognitive Science* Cambridge, Cambridge University Press.

Wittgenstein, L. (1961) *Tractatus Logico-Philosophicus* London, Routledge & Kegan Paul.

Wittrock, M. C. (1966) The learning by discovery hypothesis. In E. Keislar and L. Schulman (Eds), *Learning by Discovery: A Critical Review* Chicago, Rand McNally.

Wollheim, R. (1971) *Freud* London, Fontana.

INDEX OF NAMES

SUBJECT INDEX

ACKNOWLEDGEMENTS

Grateful acknowledgement is made to the following for permission to reprint previously published material.

Oxford University Press for quotations from Keynes, G. (Ed) *Blake: Complete Writings* which appear at the opening of each chapter.

Academic Press Inc. and Professor J. Bransford for the line drawing, here reproduced on page 89, taken from Bransford, J. & Johnson, M. (1972) Contextual Prerequisites for Learning, *Journal of Verbal Learning and Verbal Behavior* Vol II, pp. 717–726.